Lecture Notes in Computer Science 6041

Commenced Publication in 1973
Founding and Former Series Editors:
Gerhard Goos, Juris Hartmanis, and Jan van Leeuwen

W0227624

Marco T. Morazán   Sven-Bodo Scholz (Eds.)

Implementation and Application of Functional Languages

21st International Symposium, IFL 2009
South Orange, NJ, USA, September 23-25, 2009
Revised Selected Papers

 Springer

Volume Editors

Marco T. Morazán
Seton Hall University, Department of Mathematics and Computer Science
400 South Orange Avenue, South Orange, NJ 07079, USA
E-mail: morazanm@shu.edu

Sven-Bodo Scholz
University of Hertfordshire, School of Computer Science
College Lane, Hatfield, Herts AL10 9AB, UK
E-mail: S.Scholz@herts.ac.uk

Library of Congress Control Number: 2010936304

CR Subject Classification (1998): F.3, D.3, D.2, F.4.1, D.1, D.2.4

LNCS Sublibrary: SL 1 – Theoretical Computer Science and General Issues

ISSN   0302-9743
ISBN-10   3-642-16477-3 Springer Berlin Heidelberg New York
ISBN-13   978-3-642-16477-4 Springer Berlin Heidelberg New York

springer.com

© Springer-Verlag Berlin Heidelberg 2010
Printed in Germany

Typesetting: Camera-ready by author, data conversion by Scientific Publishing Services, Chennai, India
Printed on acid-free paper   06/3180

Preface

This volume contains the selected peer-reviewed revised articles that were presented at the 21st International Symposium on Implementation and Application of Functional Languages (IFL 2009). IFL 2009 was held September 23–25, 2009 at Seton Hall University in South Orange, NJ, USA. This version of the IFL symposium marked a milestone by being the first ever to be held in the United States. Our goals are to make IFL a regular event held in the USA and in Europe by alternating the host continent every year and to foster collaborations, interactions, and friendships between researchers and practitioners on both continents and beyond.

The IFL symposia bring together researchers and practitioners that are actively engaged in the implementation and the use of functional and function-based programming languages. Every year IFL provides a venue for the presentation and discussion of new ideas and concepts, of work in progress, and of publication-ripe results. Participants are invited to submit either a draft paper or an extended abstract describing work to be presented at the symposium. These submissions are screened by the Program Committee Chair to make sure they are within the scope of IFL. The submissions accepted for presentation appear in the *draft* proceedings distributed at the symposium. Submissions appearing in the draft proceedings are not peer-reviewed publications. After the symposium, authors are given the opportunity to consider the feedback received from discussions at the symposium and are invited to submit revised, full articles to the formal review process. The revised submissions are reviewed by the Program Committee using prevailing academic standards, and the best submissions are chosen to appear in the formal proceedings. This volume is the result of the work done by the IFL 2009 Program Committee and the contributing authors.

Benjamin C. Pierce, the IFL 2009 guest speaker from the University of Pennsylvania, delivered an engaging talk entitled "How to Build Your Own Bidirectional Programming Language." Pierce focused on the semantics and the implementation of programming languages that not only update their output based on changes in the input, but that also update their input based on changes made to the output. In addition, Pierce discussed several sample applications that are well-suited for bidirectional programming languages, like bidirectional transformations on trees for XML documents, on relational data, and on strings. He enthusiastically engaged questions posed by IFL 2009 participants and we thank him for his contribution to IFL 2009.

Following in the IFL tradition, IFL 2009 provided participants with an opportunity to get to know each other and to talk outside the formal setting of presentations with a social event on the second day of the symposium. Participants traveled to Manhattan to visit the observatory at Rockefeller Center and to walk across the Brooklyn Bridge. After the visit to Manhattan, participants traveled to the symposium's banquet dinner in the Ironbound neighborhood of Newark, NJ where they were treated to a traditional Spanish tapas and dinner feast with a flamenco show.

Shortly before IFL 2009, the programming languages community lost one of its most distinguished members. In June of 2009 Peter J. Landin passed away. At IFL, we dearly felt his passing. IFL has honored Peter since 2003 by awarding each year the Peter J. Landin Award to the best article presented at the symposium. The recipients of the award for IFL 2009 are Vincent St-Amour and Marc Feeley, from the Université de Montréal in Canada, for their contribution entitled *"PICOBIT: A Compact Scheme System for Microcontrollers."*

IFL 2009 was made possible by the generous support provided by Jane Street Capital, Seton Hall University's Office of the Provost, Seton Hall University's College of Arts and Sciences, and Seton Hall University's Department of Mathematics and Computer Science. At Seton Hall, a heart-felt thank you for their extraordinary efforts to make IFL 2009 a success is extended to Associate Provost Kirk Rawn, Dean Joseph R. Marbach, Dean Susan Kilduff, Joan Guetti, Lysa D. Martinelli, and Thomas A. McGee. We are equally grateful to Yaron Minsky from Jane Street Capital. A debt of gratitude for addressing every need that came up during the symposium is owed to Rositsa Abrasheva, Florian Buchbegger, and Barbara Mucha. We thank all the members of the Program Committee for their advice, time, and thoughtful reviews and all the members of the organizing committee for their logistical support without which this volume would have never have become a reality. We are very grateful to Daniel P. Friedman from the University of Indiana for selflessly assisting with the editing of the articles appearing in this volume. Finally, we thank the authors for submitting their articles and trusting that we would do our best to positively showcase their work.

In closing, we trust that the readers of this volume will find its contents engaging hopefully inspiring them to start or continue their work on the implementation and the use of functional languages. Make sure to join us at a future version of IFL!

April 2010   Marco T. Morazán
                                                                                                                                      Sven-Bodo Scholz

Organization

Program Committee

Peter Achten	University of Nijmegen, The Netherlands
Jost Berthold	University of Copenhagen, Denmark
Andrew Butterfield	University of Dublin, Ireland
Robby Findler	Northwestern University, USA
Kathleen Fisher	AT&T Research, USA
Cormac Flanagan	UCSC, USA
Matthew Flatt	University of Utah, USA
Matthew Fluet	Rochester Institute of Tech., USA
Daniel Friedman	Indiana University, USA
Andy Gill	University of Kansas, USA
Clemens Grelck	University of Amsterdam, The Netherlands
Jurriaan Hage	Utrecht University, The Netherlands
Ralf Hinze	Oxford University, UK
Paul Hudak	Yale University, USA
John Hughes	Chalmers University, Sweden
Patricia Johann	University of Strathclyde, UK
Yukiyoshi Kameyama	University of Tsukuba, Japan
Marco T. Morazán (Chair)	Seton Hall University, USA
Rex Page	University of Oklahoma, USA
Fernando Rubio	Universidad Complutense, Spain
Sven-Bodo Scholz	University of Hertfordshire, UK
Manuel Serrano	INRIA Sophia-Antipolis, France
Chung-chieh Shan	Rutgers University, USA
David Walker	Princeton University, USA
Viktória Zsók	Eötvös Loránd University, Hungary

Additional Reviewers

Emil Axelsson	Tamás Kozsik	Wouter Swierstra
Duncan Coutts	Koji Nakazawa	Máté Tejfel
Conal Elliott	Michal Palka	Kai Trojahner
Giang Hoang	Frank Penczek	Varmo Vene
Hideya Iwasaki	Zoltán Porkoláb	Janis Voigtländer
Casey Klein	Nick Smallbone	Timothy Zwiebel
Edward Kmett	James Swaine	

Local Organizing Committee

Rositsa Abrasheva	Seton Hall University
Lori Brown	Seton Hall University
Florian Buchbegger	Johannes Kepler Universität
Paul Fisher	Seton Hall University
Joan Guetti	Seton Hall University
Marco T. Morazán (Chair)	Seton Hall University
Kirk Rawn	Seton Hall University
Žanna Slaveniece	AXA Equitable
Michael Soupios	Seton Hall University

Sponsoring Institutions

Jane Street Capital, New York, USA
Office of the Provost, Seton Hall University, USA
College of Arts and Sciences, Seton Hall University, USA
Department of Computer Science, Seton Hall University, USA

Table of Contents

PICOBIT: A Compact Scheme System for Microcontrollers

Vincent St-Amour and Marc Feeley

Université de Montréal
{stamourv,feeley}@iro.umontreal.ca

Abstract. Due to their tight memory constraints, small microcontroller based embedded systems have traditionally been implemented using low-level languages. This paper shows that the Scheme programming language can also be used for such applications, with less than 7 kB of total memory. We present PICOBIT, a very compact implementation of Scheme suitable for memory constrained embedded systems. To achieve a compact system we have tackled the space issue in three ways: the design of a Scheme compiler generating compact bytecode, a small virtual machine, and an optimizing C compiler suited to the compilation of the virtual machine.

1   Introduction

Applications for embedded systems vary greatly in their computational needs. Whereas some modern cell phones, GPS receivers, and video game consoles contain CPUs, memory and peripherals that are comparable to desktop computers, there is at the other extreme embedded systems with very limited resources. We are interested in applications with complex behavior and low speed requirements such as smart cards, remote sensors, RFID, and intelligent toys and appliances. These devices have relatively simple, slow, power efficient processors and only a few kilobytes of memory integrated with peripherals on an inexpensive single chip microcontroller.

Due to the extreme memory constraints such applications are traditionally implemented using low-level languages, typically C and assembler, which give programmers total control and responsibility over memory management at the expense of software development ease and speed. The overall objective of our work is to show that a high-level mostly functional garbage collected language is a viable option in this context. In this paper we explain the design of the PICOBIT system, a very compact implementation of the Scheme programming language which targets these applications. We discuss three variants of the system, which represent different trade-offs and levels of featurefullness. The most compact variant allows Scheme programs to run on microcontrollers with less than 6 kB of ROM and 1 kB of RAM. The system is being used in two notable contexts. It is the firmware of the "PICOBOARD2", a small mobile robot programmable in Scheme which is used to teach introductory computer science at the Université

M.T. Morazán and S.-B. Scholz (Eds.): IFL 2009, LNCS 6041, pp. 1–17, 2010.
© Springer-Verlag Berlin Heidelberg 2010

de Montréal. It is also used to implement the S^3 network protocol stack [1], which implements a basic stack for embedded systems supporting TCP, UDP, ARP, etc.

2   Related Work

Virtual machine-based approaches have been used in the past to run high-level languages in embedded environments. Invariably space savings are achieved by implementing a subset of an existing high-level language. For example, the Java language has been adapted for embedded applications and the most compact version is the Java Card Platform virtual machine [2]. To reduce the memory requirements some important features of Java have been removed, notably garbage collection and the 32 bit integer type (int) are optional, and the 64 bit integer type (long) and threads do not exist. Therefore the programming style is lower-level than with full Java. Moreover smart cards which run Java typically have an order of magnitude more memory than our target platforms.

Due to its small size Scheme has been a popular language to implement in memory constrained settings. Many of the compact systems are based on interpreters and were designed for workstation class platforms. Some of the most compact are based on a compiler generating compact bytecode for a virtual machine. In particular the BIT [3] and PICBIT [4] Scheme systems implement most of the R4RS [5] and target small embedded systems having less than 8 kB of RAM and less than 64 kB of ROM. PICOBIT is a descendent of BIT and PICBIT whose requirements are more modest.

3   Overview

The PICOBIT Scheme system has three parts: the PICOBIT Scheme compiler, the PICOBIT virtual machine, and the SIXPIC C compiler. The PICOBIT Scheme compiler runs on the host development system, which is typically a workstation, and compiles from Scheme to a custom bytecode designed for compactness. The Scheme compiler is itself written in Scheme, though it is not self-hosting.

The PICOBIT VM runs on any platform for which there is a C compiler. Currently, we target the popular Microchip PIC18 family of microcontrollers which are cheap single-chip microcontrollers. The VM executes the bytecode produced by the PICOBIT Scheme compiler. The VM is written in C for portability reasons, since most microcontroller platforms already have C compilers targeting them. Therefore, the PICOBIT virtual machine can be compiled for any microcontroller which has a C compiler, making PICOBIT a highly portable platform.

Finally, we have developed the SIXPIC C compiler, a C compiler which was designed specifically to compile virtual machines. We studied the patterns present in typical virtual machines (and the PICOBIT virtual machine in particular) to

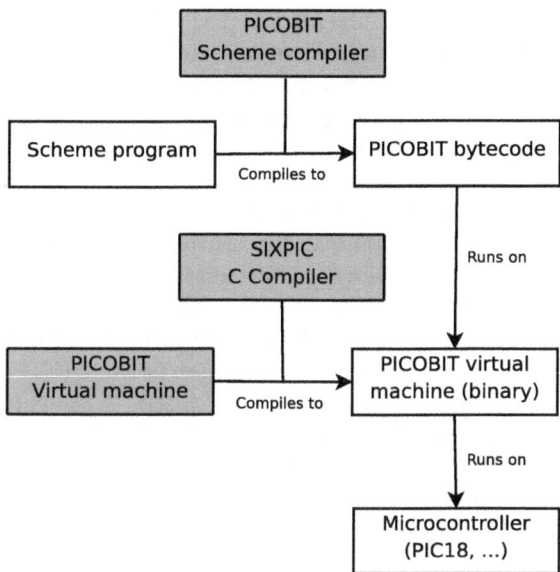

Fig. 1. Workflow of the PICOBIT Scheme system

add specialized optimizations and omit certain features of the C language in order to reduce the size of the generated code for virtual machines. This compiler is typically used to compile the PICOBIT virtual machine.

4 General Approach

Because of the code size limitations of our target environment, our approach was designed with the primary goal of generating compact code. Performance of the generated code was a secondary concern, and has not been addressed at length.

The bytecode the PICOBIT Scheme compiler generates is higher level than raw machine code. The bytecode necessary to accomplish a task is typically more compact than the corresponding machine code. Therefore, the use of interpreted bytecode can lead to savings in a program's code size over the use of machine code. We must keep in mind that the virtual machine needed to execute this bytecode also takes space. However, since the size of the virtual machine is independent of the size of the programs it executes, it is a fixed cost that is amortized over the cost of all the executed programs. We therefore postulate that once applications reach a certain size, the combined sizes of the application's bytecode and of the virtual machine would be smaller than the size of the machine code resulting from the native compilation of the application.

Another key point of our approach is that we control every step of the execution process. By controlling both the Scheme compiler and the virtual machine, we can adapt the bytecode representation to better fit the needs of our applications.

Controlling both the virtual machine and the C compiler which compiles it means that we can specialize the C compiler to use domain-specific optimizations: optimizations that are especially interesting when compiling virtual machines or optimizations that are possible thanks to properties of virtual machines, and would not be valid for all programs.

Finally, the use of a virtual machine also increases the portability of our system. Since the PICOBIT virtual machine is written in a highly portable subset of C, porting it to different architectures is easy. So far, PICOBIT has been ported to the PIC18, MSP430, i386, amd64 and PowerPC architectures, and compiles successfully using the SIXPIC, MCC18, Hi-Tech C, mspgcc, and gcc C compilers. Of course, this portability argument does not yet extend to our SIXPIC C compiler, which currently only supports the PIC18 architecture.

Several versions of the PICOBIT Scheme system exist, catering to different application types and sizes. The full version of PICOBIT supports all the features described in this article, and is suitable for large applications dealing with a large amount of data. A somewhat smaller version of PICOBIT removes support for unbounded precision integers in return for a smaller virtual machine size. Finally, a minimalist version of PICOBIT also exists, called PICOBIT Light, which removes support for unbounded precision integers and byte vectors, is limited to 16 global variables and 128 memory objects, but is much more compact than the full version (5.2 kB versus 15.6 kB). This version is appropriate when building simpler applications that only deal with small amounts of data at the same time. For example, a temperature sensor that sends reports via UDP using the S^3 network stack.

5   Supported Scheme Dialect

Unlike most programming platforms targeting embedded systems, PICOBIT supports a large number of high-level programming language features. It supports a broad subset of the R5RS [6] Scheme standard including macros, automatic memory management, lists, closures and higher-order procedures, first-class continuations and unbounded precision integers as well as some extensions such as byte vectors and lightweight threads.

Other features were consciously excluded due to their lack of usefulness in an embedded context, for instance floating-point, rational and complex numbers, string to symbol conversion (and vice versa), S-expression input, file I/O, `eval`. Omitting these features leads to a smaller, and thus more compact implementation.

5.1   Built-in Data Structures

Being a member of the LISP family of languages, the Scheme language makes heavy use of lists. Therefore, PICOBIT offers built-in support for lists and implements many common list operations. These lists are heterogeneous lists, and can thus be used to implement most other data structures easily.

This flexibility opens possibilities regarding which classes of applications can reasonably be implemented in embedded systems. Indeed, some applications which have been deemed too complex for small embedded systems would be straightforward to implement using advanced data structures, reducing the need for more sophisticated hardware where microcontrollers could suffice.

In addition to lists, PICOBIT offers support for byte vectors, which are equivalent to fixed-width byte arrays, and heterogenous vectors, which are represented as lists. Byte vectors being more efficient than lists for many tasks common on embedded systems (mostly thanks to their $O(1)$ random access), byte vector support is especially interesting on our target platforms. The implementation of byte vectors in the VM is explored in detail in section 7.7.

Finally, PICOBIT also offers limited support for strings.

5.2 First-Class Continuations

First-class continuations are one of Scheme's key features, and accounts for a large part of the language's flexibility. They are usually considered difficult, or costly, to implement, which has led some Scheme implementations to omit them.

Since first-class continuations can be used to implement useful control structures that cannot easily be implemented using traditional embedded development techniques (such as multithreading), we chose to implement them in PICOBIT. To illustrate this, the PICOBIT standard library includes a compact continuation-based multithreading system, implemented in 30 lines of Scheme which compile down to 141 bytes of bytecode. Writing such a multithreading system in C and including it in the virtual machine would have likely resulted in a larger code size. In addition, the same first-class continuation primitives used here could be used to implement backtracking or early exits without any changes to the virtual machine.

6 The PICOBIT Scheme Compiler

The PICOBIT Scheme compiler is a specialized optimizing Scheme compiler which generates bytecode. This bytecode can then be executed using the PICOBIT virtual machine. In order to produce highly compact bytecode, some specialized optimizations have been added to the compiler. Most of these optimizations are made possible by the extensive use of whole program analysis throughout the compiler. When compiling a program, PICOBIT appends it to its standard library and compiles the result. By compiling applications and the standard library as a single program, all the whole-program analyses done in the compiler also apply to the standard library, which leads to more optimization opportunities.

In addition to using selected optimizations to achieve low code sizes, we have designed a custom instruction set, shared by the PICOBIT Scheme compiler and the PICOBIT virtual machine.

6.1 Optimizations

Keeping in mind that the goal of the PICOBIT Scheme system is to produce compact code, the optimizations implemented in the PICOBIT Scheme compiler were chosen mostly for their effect on the resulting code size.

In order to minimize the number of allocations done at runtime, a mutability analysis is done over the whole program at compile-time. Variables that are never mutated are not allocated in memory at runtime, reducing the program's memory footprint and eliminating some variable bookkeeping code, reducing the application code size. For this mutability analysis to be valid, the compiler must analyze the whole program at the same time, which makes PICOBIT's single-program compilation process interesting.

The PICOBIT Scheme compiler also does branch tensioning. Whenever a branch instruction points to another branch instruction, the destination of the first is changed to that of the second, and so on in case of longer branch series. While this optimization is reasonably useful in most compilers, combining it with single-program compilation opens up new possibilities. When using separate compilation, inter-module branches cannot be tensioned, since the nature of such a branch's destination is unknown. However, when using single-program compilation, all destinations are known at compile-time, and what would have been inter-module branches can be tensioned like any other branches, which leads to more optimization opportunities. Tail-called functions that are only called once are thus inlined to completely eliminate a branch instruction.

Finally, a treeshaker [7] was added to the PICOBIT Scheme compiler in order to remove any code that is not actually used in the program from the resulting bytecode. A depth-first search is done on the application (and the standard library) to determine which procedures are reachable from the top level. Only these procedures then end up being compiled to bytecode. The rest are simply ignored.

The use of whole-program compilation combined with a treeshaker has an obvious advantage over the use of separate compilation and linking. When using separate compilation, each compilation unit has to be compiled in its entirety, as it is impossible to know before linking which of its procedures will actually be used. With our approach, however, we can exclude unreachable code from the final binary at compile-time, without having to do link-time optimization.

This treeshaker makes it possible to have a well-furnished standard library and still generate compact output, since any unused library procedures will not be present in the resulting bytecode. In our case, the PICOBIT standard library compiles down to 2064 bytes of bytecode, which can be rather large compared to the size of some programs. A PICOBIT program that does not use strings will not include the string functions of the standard library, and will therefore save 508 bytes.

6.2   The PICOBIT Bytecode

Since our goal is to compile applications to small amounts of bytecode, much of the design of the bytecode was geared towards representing common idioms as compactly as possible.

The PICOBIT virtual machine is a stack-based virtual machine. Therefore, pushing values on the data stack is a common operation for the vast majority of the programs it runs. As such, effort was put towards representing pushing instructions in a compact way. This was achieved by having pushing instructions of

000xxxxx			Push constant x
001xxxxx			Push stack element $\#x$
0100xxxx			Push global $\#x$
0101xxxx			Set global $\#x$ to TOS
0110xxxx			Call closure at TOS with x arguments
0111xxxx			Jump to closure at TOS with x arguments
1000xxxx			Jump to entry point at address $pc + x$
1001xxxx			Go to address $pc + x$ if TOS is false
1010xxxx	xxxxxxxx		Push constant x
10110000	xxxxxxxx	xxxxxxxx	Call procedure at address x
10110001	xxxxxxxx	xxxxxxxx	Jump to entry point at address x
10110010	xxxxxxxx	xxxxxxxx	Go to address x
10110011	xxxxxxxx	xxxxxxxx	Go to address x if TOS is false
10110100	xxxxxxxx	xxxxxxxx	Build a closure with entry point x
10110101	xxxxxxxx		Call procedure at address $pc + x - 128$
10110110	xxxxxxxx		Jump to entry point at address $pc + x - 128$
10110111	xxxxxxxx		Go to address $pc + x - 128$
10111000	xxxxxxxx		Go to address $pc + x - 128$ if TOS is false
10111001	xxxxxxxx		Build a closure with entry point $pc + x - 128$
10111110	xxxxxxxx		Push global $\#x$
10111111	xxxxxxxx		Set global $\#x$ to TOS
11xxxxxx			Primitives (+, return, get-cont, ...)

Fig. 2. The PICOBIT instruction set and its bytecode encoding

different lengths, as shown in figure 2. When operands are short enough (typically 4 or 5 bits), short instructions can be used, leading to savings in code size.

To make the most of these short instructions, the shortest value encodings are assigned to frequently used values, as explained in section 7.4. In addition, global variable encodings are assigned in decreasing order of frequency of use, so that the most frequently used global variables are assigned the shortest encodings, and can therefore be used with the short instructions.

In addition to short pushing instructions, PICOBIT also supports short relative addressing instructions. In some frequently occurring cases, such as a goto-if-false whose destination is no more than 15 bytecodes away, instructions fit in a single byte, rather than the three bytes of an absolute addressing instruction. To make the most of these instructions, we use trace scheduling to position the destination code as close to the instructions that reference this destination.

7   The PICOBIT Virtual Machine

The PICOBIT virtual machine is the part of the PICOBIT system that resides on the target microcontroller and interprets the bytecode generated by the PI-COBIT Scheme compiler. As such, care was taken to build the virtual machine to be as compact as possible, which means that algorithms and data structures are kept simple throughout the virtual machine. That being said, the PICOBIT virtual machine is a full-featured virtual machine which includes a garbage collector, an implementation of unbounded precision integers and support for data structures.

7.1   Environment Representation

The PICOBIT virtual machine being a stack-based virtual machine, environments are represented as stacks. These stacks are themselves represented as PICOBIT lists made of cons cells, allocated in the heap. When looking up a variable in an environment, it is therefore necessary to know its depth in the stack at the current execution point, which can be determined statically.

7.2   Automatic Memory Management

The PICOBIT virtual machine includes a mark-and-sweep garbage collector. Due to the limited amount of memory available on our target systems, a mark-and-sweep garbage collector is especially interesting as the whole heap can be in use at the same time. By comparison, copying garbage collectors can only use half of the available memory at a given time, thereby cutting the heap size in half and limiting the data size of the applications that can be run on a given chip. Another advantage of a mark-and-sweep garbage collector is that the necessary algorithms are simple, which leads to a compact garbage collector.

The Deutsche-Schorr-Waite algorithm [8] is used in the marking phase, and it really shines in an embedded context. Since this algorithm does not need to use a stack to traverse a tree, no memory needs to be allocated for such a stack. Reserving a portion of the heap for such a stack would be an unattractive option, considering the low amount of available memory to begin with. The use of the Deutsche-Schorr-Waite algorithm therefore allows us to use a larger portion of the microcontroller's memory for our heap, enabling more complex applications to be run using PICOBIT.

7.3   Address Space Layout

The distinction between RAM and ROM is important in embedded systems, especially for single-chip microcontrollers. Since there is usually more ROM than RAM available, it is interesting to move as much data as possible to ROM, to leave as much room in RAM as possible for mutable data. Literal values and variables that are never mutated (and whose value is known at compile-time) are stored in ROM whereas mutable variables and temporaries are stored in RAM. Therefore, objects manipulated by the PICOBIT virtual machine can be located either in ROM or in RAM.

To reference these objects, the full version of PICOBIT uses 13-bit encodings, whereas the Light version uses 8-bit encodings. Using shorter encodings obviously reduces the number of objects that can be referenced, as shown in figure 3, but since 8-bit encodings can be manipulated using 8-bit rather than 16-bit machine operations, their use leads to a more compact virtual machine on 8-bit microcontrollers.

Encoding	PICOBIT	PICOBIT Light
0	#f	
1	#t	
2	' ()	
3 – 44	-1 – 40	
45 – 127	41 – 123	ROM values
128 – 255	124 – 251	Heap values
256 – 259	252 – 255	
260 – 511	ROM values	N/A
512 – 4095	Heap values	
4096 – 8191	Byte vector space	

Fig. 3. Object encoding in PICOBIT and PICOBIT Light

In order for objects to contain references to objects stored both in ROM and in RAM, it was necessary to partition PICOBIT's address space. For instance, a pair (whose internal layout is discussed in section 7.4) could have its car stored in ROM and its cdr stored in RAM, in the heap. To reflect this address space partition, the object reference determines whether it points towards a ROM object or a RAM object.

References can denote ROM and RAM objects, and also preallocated constants that occupy no memory. As shown in figure 3, references with a value from 0 to 259 (0 to 44 for PICOBIT Light) refer to immediate values. Preallocating commonly used values reduces the amount of memory, both ROM and RAM, required to store values. Many common operations, in particular arithmetic on small numbers, can therefore be done without allocating any memory. Furthermore, since special short instructions (see section 6.2) exist to handle references with small values, the use of these frequently occurring preallocated constants can help reduce the size of application bytecode.

Finally, the fourth zone of PICOBIT's address space is used for byte vectors. The use of this zone will be detailed in section 7.7.

To simplify, and therefore reduce the size of, the virtual machine, RAM and ROM objects have the same layout, which only depends on their type, not on their location. Further details about these layouts are found in section 7.4.

7.4   Object Representation

The PICOBIT virtual machine being designed for dynamic languages, it is necessary to encode objects stored in memory along with their type and garbage collection information.

First of all, all objects are 32 bits wide, whether they are stored in ROM, along with the program, or in RAM, in the heap. We can therefore consider the heap as a simple array of objects, and short indices can be used to refer to objects instead of longer pointers, which leads to a compact object representation. Having a single object size also simplifies garbage collection. Instead of having to figure out where objects begin and end, the sweeping phase of the garbage collector

PICOBIT

	0		8	16	24	31
Integer	00	G C	to next cell		low 16 bits	
Closure	01	G C	entry point		to environment	
Pair	1	G C	car	000	cdr	
Symbol	10	G C	0000000000000	001	0000000000000	
String	10	G C	to char list	010	0000000000000	
U8vector	10	G C	length	011	to contents	
Continuation	1	G C	to parent	100	to closure	

PICOBIT Light

	0		8	16	24	31
Integer	G C	0000000	value			
Closure	G C	01	entry hi	to environment	00000000	entry lo
Pair	G C	000010	car	cdr	00000000	
Symbol	G C	0000011	0000000000000000000000000			
String	G C	0000101	to char list	0000000000000000		
Continuation	G C	1	entry hi	to environment	to parent	entry lo

Fig. 4. Object encodings in PICOBIT and PICOBIT Light

only has to iterate on the array representing the heap. In addition, since the garbage collection flags are located in the same place for objects of all types, it is not necessary to know the exact type of an object when sweeping it.

In addition to being all the same size, PICOBIT objects all follow the same general structure, as shown in figure 4. These similarities reduce the number of virtual machine primitives needed to access the data contained in objects, as the same primitives can be used on most data types. Once again, needing fewer data access primitives helps keep the PICOBIT virtual machine's size small.

7.5   Unbounded Precision Integers

A feature that sets PICOBIT apart from most other embedded programming environments is the availability of unbounded precision integers. Traditionally, embedded programming environments on 8-bit microcontrollers offer support for numeric values up to 32 bits wide. However, larger values are needed in some embedded applications. For instance, the S^3 network stack, which runs on top of the PICOBIT system, uses 48 bit integers to store MAC addresses. Large integral values are also necessary for some cryptographic calculations, for instance the SHA family of cryptographic hashing functions, which need values up to 512 bits wide.

Embedded applications also often need to keep track of time, sometimes with a high degree of precision (when controlling machinery, for example). If an application keeps track of time at the microsecond level using a 32-bit value, a wraparound will occur every hour or so. To handle such wraparounds, complex logic might have to be included in the application, leading to an ad-hoc bignum implementation.

The support for large integers in embedded systems can also create opportunities to do processing that would traditionally be done on host systems or specialized hardware directly on microcontrollers, therefore reducing latency and bandwidth needs, and increasing the autonomy of such embedded systems.

As can be seen in figure 4, unbounded precision integers are encoded in PICOBIT as linked lists of 16 bit values. At the end of each list is either the integer 0 or -1, to represent the sign. 0, -1 and other small integers have dedicated encodings and do not need to be represented as linked lists. The use of this "little-endian" representation simplifies the bignum algorithms in particular for numbers of different lengths.

On versions of PICOBIT which do not support unbounded precision integers (including PICOBIT Light), integers are limited to 24 bits, and encoded directly in the object.

7.6   First-Class Continuations

Many Scheme systems implement first-class continuations by copying the stack into the heap with each call to `call/cc`, which can cause an important overhead both in terms of speed and in terms of space.

PICOBIT avoids this overhead by avoiding the use of a call stack, and directly allocating each continuation in the heap like any other object. Manipulating continuations is therefore as simple and efficient as manipulating any other object. In effect, this representation gives us first-class continuations for free. Thus, operations on continuations are implemented as simple virtual machine instructions. Being allocated in the heap, discarded continuations are garbage collected, regardless of how they have been used.

As shown in figure 4, continuations are represented as a chain of continuation objects, each containing a reference to its parent continuation and a reference to a closure object. The closure object contains the entry point of the function associated to the continuation and the enclosed environment.

This representation of continuations is very compact, with two objects (the continuation object and the closure object) per frame. When using the multithreading system included in the PICOBIT standard library, each thread only causes an overhead of one continuation frame, or 8 bytes. Applications with several threads, such as systems monitoring multiple sources of input, can thus be implemented with a very low memory footprint.

7.7   Byte Vectors

Unlike other PICOBIT objects, byte vectors do not necessarily occupy four bytes. In order to guarantee fast random access, byte vectors have to be allocated as a single contiguous space of the appropriate size. To preserve the advantages brought by having all objects of the same size in the heap, we allocate byte vectors in a different section of memory. As such, references with values over 4095 point to objects within this zone, which we call the byte vector space.

Like the heap, the byte vector space is allocated by increments of four bytes. However, unlike with the heap, contiguous segments of any length (bounded by the size of the byte vector space) can be allocated in the byte vector space. A simple first-fit allocation algorithm is used to decide where to allocate each byte vector.

In addition to the byte vector contents which are located in the byte vector space, byte vectors are also composed of a header, containing the length of the byte vector and a pointer to the start of the contents (as seen in figure 4). These headers are stored in the heap, and as such are four bytes wide and follow the same general layout as any heap object.

PICOBIT Light does not offer support for byte vectors, which removes the need for a separate byte vector space, and simplifies several algorithms of the virtual machine, leading to a more compact VM.

8   The SIXPIC C Compiler

When using the PICOBIT Scheme system, the total size of the software running on the target system is the sum of the size of the PICOBIT virtual machine and of the application programs, and our goal is to minimize that total size. As we have seen earlier, the PICOBIT Scheme compiler was designed to generate compact application bytecode. The size of the virtual machine remains, and in some cases it can account for an important part of the whole system. While the PICOBIT virtual machine can be compiled with any C compiler, some savings in code size can be achieved by using a specialized C compiler to compile it. The SIXPIC C compiler is one such compiler.

The SIXPIC C compiler was designed to generate compact code, especially when compiling virtual machines. This was done by analyzing the code of typical virtual machines (including the PICOBIT virtual machine) to find and then optimize common patterns. This analysis also showed us which features of the C language were seldom used for virtual machines, and could therefore be omitted from SIXPIC. In addition to reducing the complexity of the compiler, some of these omissions also opened possibilities for optimization which would not have been valid otherwise.

8.1   Restrictions

Even though virtual machines are complex pieces of software, they do not make use of every single feature of the C language. Therefore, while designing SIXPIC, some features could be left out and some others were restricted to the subset actually used by most virtual machines.

The first notable omission is support for floating point numbers. Since the PICOBIT Scheme system does not support them, and that most microcontrollers do not support floating point operations, this omission is pretty straightforward.

Since virtual machines typically manage their data structures at the bit level (especially in embedded systems), ordinary C structs are not generally useful in the context of virtual machines.

A more controversial restriction would be that SIXPIC does not support recursive (or mutually-recursive) functions. At first glance, this might appear restrictive. However, since typical virtual machines consist mostly of a `switch` statement in a loop, recursion is not needed. This omission is what makes our specialized calling convention possible.

8.2   Calling Convention

To support recursive functions, a call stack is usually needed. Most modern workstation architectures provide hardware support for such stacks, which makes the compiler's job easier. However, most microcontroller architectures do not offer such support, which means that the compiler would need to build a software stack in memory in order to support recursive functions. The creation and use of such a stack increases the complexity, and therefore the size, of the generated code. By giving up support for recursive functions, no such stack is needed anymore and it becomes possible to use a calling convention which passes function arguments in pre-determined registers. This approach is taken by the leading embedded C compilers, such as Microchip's Hi-Tech C® compiler.

With the SIXPIC C compiler, we take this approach further. Since we do not support recursive functions, every variable (be it a local variable, a global variable, or a function parameter) can be allocated at a static location. We then use whole-program analysis to determine which variables interfere with each other and use the results to do register allocation for the whole program all at once.

Since the location of each variable is known at compile-time, we can avoid moving values to and from the registers needed by the calling convention. Instead, we use a specialized calling convention where the caller moves the arguments directly in the registers where the callee's local variables reside, as shown in figure 5.

8.3   Optimizations

As with the PICOBIT Scheme compiler, the optimizations present in the SIXPIC C compiler were chosen for their impact in reducing the size of the resulting code.

First of all, our register allocation algorithm does register coalescing. Since the SIXPIC C compiler does whole-program register allocation, register coalescing can be used more broadly. Instead of being limited to coalescing virtual registers inside each function, as would be the case with intra-procedural register allocation, global register allocation makes it possible to coalesce registers being used in two different functions. With our specialized calling convention (see subsection 8.2), such opportunities occur enough to be worthwhile. We measured that

C code	Stack-based	Register-based	Specialized

`byte f (byte x) {`
`  return x + 3;`
`}`
`byte y = 3;`
`f(y);`
`...`
	`...`
	`  push $y`
	`  call $f`
	`...`
	`f: pop $x`
	`...`
		`...`
		`  move $y A`
		`  call $f`
		`...`
		`f: move A $x`
		`...`
			`...`
			`  move $y $x`
			`  call $f`
			`...`
			`f:`
			`...`

Bytes of PIC18 machine code:	20	12	8

Fig. 5. Comparison between a stack-based calling convention, a register-based calling convention and our specialized calling convention

the use of register coalescing reduces the size of the generated code by around 4.5%, mostly by eliminating move instructions between coalesced registers. Out of the 2420 byte cells found in the PICOBIT virtual machine, 1453 end up being coalesced. After register allocation, only 324 bytes of RAM are necessary for the VM's variables, excluding the heap.

By looking for patterns in the code of several virtual machines, we noticed that the `switch/case` construct was extensively used, especially for instruction decoding. PICOBIT is no exception. We also noticed that most of the `switch/case` statements used in virtual machines respected several other properties, including the absence of `default` labels and the presence of mostly contiguous label numbers. We therefore worked on an implementation of `switch/case` that would generate compact code, especially when the above properties hold. After trying several implementations, we settled on a branch table-based approach which, despite the absence of computed branches on the PIC18 architecture, generates compact code in the cases that interest us.

Like the PICOBIT Scheme compiler, SIXPIC does trace scheduling. The benefits explained in section 6.1 also apply to SIXPIC, since it also does single-program compilation. When compiling the PICOBIT virtual machine, 519 jumps are shortened thanks to trace scheduling and 228 are eliminated altogether, which saves 6.3% of the virtual machine size.

Instead of providing an external set of hardware access routines with which applications can be linked, these routines are defined in terms of the compiler's abstract assembly language. When compiling a program, SIXPIC joins these routine's control flow graphs to the program's, and uses the resulting graph for the rest of the compilation process. Therefore, all the whole-program optimizations described above are run on these routines at the same time, resulting in a greater optimization potential.

Finally, the SIXPIC C compiler uses, like the PICOBIT Scheme compiler, a treeshaker to remove any unused code from the generated executable, reducing its size. As is the case with the Scheme compiler, SIXPIC appends its standard library to application programs, then compiles only the reachable parts. Once again, the use of this treeshaker helps SIXPIC achieve low application code sizes by excluding unused code in the application (or in the standard library).

9   Experimental Results

9.1   Bytecode-Based Approach

As we anticipated, a bytecode-based approach to embedded application development leads to compact application sizes.

In figure 6, we show examples of programs used with the PICOBOARD2 robot, and the amount of bytecode required for each. As we can see, all these programs, even relatively sophisticated ones like a web server, can be represented compactly using bytecode. These small code sizes were obtained despite PICOBIT having a large (2064 bytes) standard library, thanks to the treeshaker, which removes unused parts of the library from the final bytecode.

We have also compared the S^3 TCP/IP stack, which is used with the PICO-BIT Scheme system, to Adam Dunkels's uIP [9] stack, which is written in C and is compiled natively to machine code. Both stacks implement a similar set of features and share most design decisions. They can be therefore considered roughly equivalent for our comparison's purposes.

When compiling S^3 with the PICOBIT Scheme compiler, we obtain 3.1 kB of bytecode whereas when we compile the uIP stack using Microchip's MCC18 compiler, we obtain a 10.0 kB binary. Thus compiling to bytecode resulted in the application being about three times as compact.

Since the bytecode is useless without the PICOBIT virtual machine to interpret it, we have to include the size of the virtual machine to get realistic figures. When comparing the size of the whole systems (see figure 7), the natively compiled uIP is about twice as compact as the combination of S^3 and of the PICOBIT virtual machine.

However, the size of the virtual machine is a fixed cost which is independent of the size of the application it interprets. Therefore, the cost of the virtual machine is amortized over all the applications it executes.

Program	Code size (B)
Flashing led	9
Follow the light	101
Remote control	106
Hello	355
Light sensors	374
Multi-threaded presence counter	599
Web server	1033

Fig. 6. Example PICOBOARD2 programs

Stack	Code size (kB)	VM size (kB)	Total size (kB)
S^3	3.1	15.6	18.7
uIP	10.0	-	10.0

Fig. 7. Comparison between the S^3 and uIP embedded network stacks

Version	SIXPIC	MCC18	Hi-Tech C
Full PICOBIT	17.5 kB	24.8 kB	15.6 kB
Without bignums	13.0 kB	17.0 kB	11.6 kB
PICOBIT Light	7.2 kB	8.0 kB	5.2 kB

Fig. 8. Size comparison between the different versions of the PICOBIT VM compiled with various C compilers

Since TCP/IP stacks are complex applications, we believe that the compactness of bytecode versus machine code that we have observed when compiling S^3 would hold when compiling other complex applications. We therefore expect that for sufficiently large applications, our bytecode-based approach would lead to smaller system sizes than a native compilation-based one. Due to their smaller size, we expect that the restricted versions of PICOBIT will fare even better in this regard.

Keeping in mind that our motivation was to execute larger programs on smaller chips, the fact that our bytecode-based approach will likely behave better than native compilation for sufficiently large programs is promising.

9.2   Specialized C Compiler

Another key element of our approach towards embedded development is the use of a specialized C compiler optimized towards virtual machines. So far, this approach looks promising, but a sufficiently optimizing general-purpose C compiler can still generate more compact code than our specialized SIXPIC C compiler, as is shown in figure 8.

Thanks to its domain-specific optimizations, SIXPIC outperforms Microchip's MCC18 general-purpose C compiler by about 42% when compiling the PICOBIT virtual machine. However the more mature Microchip's Hi-Tech C compiler generates code that is 12% more compact than SIXPIC's, likely due to its broader range of general-purpose optimizations. We expect that adding more domain-specific optimizations to the SIXPIC C compiler will allow it to close the gap.

10   Future Work

While some work has already been done towards making the PICOBIT bytecode compact, it has mostly consisted in observing the generated code and finding more compact encodings by hand. An interesting, and more rigorous, approach would be to use Huffman encoding on the bytecode to further reduce its size. Such an approach has been successful [10] for several virtual machines, and could lead to reductions in application code size.

Some work also remains to be done on the SIXPIC C compiler to handle in a more compact fashion some common virtual machine idioms. So far, work has been done to leverage several interesting properties of virtual machines, most notably their lack of recursive functions, but some observed virtual machine patterns are not yet properly exploited by SIXPIC.

Finally, as previously mentioned, the instruction set and data types of the PICOBIT virtual machine, even though they were chosen and designed with the Scheme language in mind, are general enough to support other dynamic languages, such as Python or Perl. The Factor language also comes to mind, as a dynamically-typed garbage-collected stack-based language could integrate well with the stack-based PICOBIT virtual machine.

11   Conclusion

We have presented an implementation of the Scheme programming language which is suitable for programming small microcontrollers. The system supports several high-level constructs not usually available in microcontroller development tools, including garbage collection, higher-order procedures, first-class continuations, threads, and unbounded precision integers. Our approach tackles the space issue in three ways: the design of a Scheme compiler generating compact bytecode, a small virtual machine, and an optimizing C compiler suited to the compilation of the virtual machine. Although there are still avenues for improvement that we will pursue in our future work, our results show that a fairly featurefull Scheme system can run on platforms with only a few kilobytes of memory. For instance, it allows a basic network protocol stack (S^3) to run on a microcontroller with less than 19 kB of ROM.

References

[1] St-Amour, V., Bouchard, L., Feeley, M.: Small Scheme Stack: a Scheme TCP/IP stack targeting small embedded applications. In: Proceedings of the 2008 Workshop on Scheme and Functional Programming, pp. 11–18 (2008)
[2] Sun Microsystems, Inc.: Java card 3.0.1 platform specification (2009)
[3] Dube, D.: BIT: A very compact Scheme system for embedded applications. In: Proceedings of the Workshop on Scheme and Functional Programming, pp. 35–43 (2000)
[4] Feeley, M., Dube, D.: PICBIT: A Scheme system for the PIC microcontroller. In: Proceedings of the Fourth Workshop on Scheme and Functional Programming, pp. 7–15 (2003)
[5] Clinger, W., Rees, J.: The Revised[4] Report on the algorithmic language Scheme (1991)
[6] Kelsey, R., Clinger, W., Rees, J.: The Revised[5] Report on the algorithmic language Scheme. Higher-Order and Symbolic Computation 11(1) (1998)
[7] Semantic Microsystems: MacScheme + Toolsmith, a LISP for the future (1987)
[8] Schorr, H., Waite, W.M.: An efficient machine-independent procedure for garbage collection in various list structures. Commun. ACM 10(8), 501–506 (1967)
[9] Dunkels, A.: Full TCP/IP for 8-bit architectures. In: MobiSys 2003: Proceedings of the 1st international conference on Mobile systems, applications and services, pp. 85–98 (2003)
[10] Latendresse, M., Feeley, M.: Generation of fast interpreters for Huffman compressed bytecode. In: IVME 2003: Proceedings of the 2003 workshop on Interpreters, virtual machines and emulators, pp. 32–40 (2003)

Introducing Kansas Lava

Andy Gill, Tristan Bull, Garrin Kimmell,
Erik Perrins, Ed Komp, and Brett Werling

Information Technology and Telecommunication Center
Department of Electrical Engineering and Computer Science
The University of Kansas
2335 Irving Hill Road
Lawrence, KS 66045
{andygill,tbull,kimmell,esp,komp,bwerling}@ittc.ku.edu

Abstract. Kansas Lava is a domain specific language for hardware description. Though there have been a number of previous implementations of Lava, we have found the design space rich, with unexplored choices. We use a direct (Chalmers style) specification of circuits, and make significant use of Haskell overloading of standard classes, leading to concise circuit descriptions. Kansas Lava supports both simulation (inside GHCi), and execution via VHDL, by having a dual shallow and deep embedding inside our `Signal` type. We also have a lightweight sized-type mechanism, allowing for MATLAB style matrix based specifications to be directly expressed in Kansas Lava.

1 Introduction

In the Computer Systems Design Lab (CSDL) at KU we build systems in hardware and software. We are also avid users of Haskell. Lava [1], an Embedded Domain Specific Language (EDSL) for expressing hardware level concerns, is a natural way for a CSDL member to think about constructing and expressing our systems. In this paper, we introduce our version of Lava, called Kansas Lava, and describe how we use modern functional language techniques including applicative functors and type functions to improve the overall expressiveness of our hardware simulation and synthesis toolkit, and work towards a unified development story of specification to implementation.

Lava is the name given for a family of Haskell hosted Embedded DSLs for expressing (typically) gate-level hardware descriptions. In general, Lava is a *design pattern* for EDSL construction, when trying to capture hardware concerns. This section provides an overview of the well-known Lava design pattern, and in the next section we introduce our variant of Lava.

The central idea in Lava is that, under the correct conditions, we can observe a function as a circuit. Consider this half adder description.

```
halfAdder :: (Bit,Bit) -> (Bit,Bit)
halfAdder (a,b) = (carry,sum)
  where carry = and2 (a,b)
        sum   = xor2 (a,b)
```

M.T. Morazán and S.-B. Scholz (Eds.): IFL 2009, LNCS 6041, pp. 18–35, 2010.

Given suitable input, it is possible to execute this function directly.

```
> halfAdder (high,low)
(low,high)
```

We can extract the truth table for the `halfAdder` by applying it to all possible inputs.

```
> [ (b1,b2,halfAdder b1 b2) | b1 <- [low,high], b2 <- [low,high] ]
[ (low,low,(low,low),
  (low,high,(low,high),
  (high,low,(low,high),
  (high,high,(high,low) ]
```

This is classical functional programming. As well as executing this `halfAdder`, in Lava we can also *extract* the internal wiring of the function by applying `halfAdder` to suitability constructed dummy arguments. Consider the following implementation of Lava.

```
data Bit = High | Low | Xor2 Bit Bit | And2 Bit Bit | Var String

and2 (a,b) = And2 a b
xor2 (a,b) = Xor2 a b
high = High
low = Low
```

This is a traditional deep embedding of a domain specific language. In this case, the language is Lava itself. Now, if we apply `halfAdder` with suitably annotated `Vars`, we get a data structure that contains the internal structure of the `halfAdder` function.

```
> halfAdder (Var "a",Var "b")
(And2 (Var "a",Var "b"),Xor2 (Var "a",Var "b"))
```

From structures that represent these wiring diagrams, we can generate structural VHDL that represents the wire routing between established components. In this way, compiling combinational circuits is straightforward, if tedious. Compiling sequential circuits, however, exposes a critical shortcoming with the original Lava design pattern. Specifically, there is no easy way to observe the wiring cycles that exist in sequential circuits. Addressing this issue led to a fork in the design specifics of Lava implementations.

Consider the following circuit for computing the parity of an ongoing signal.

```
-- Parity specification
parity :: Bit -> Bit
parity input = output
  where
    output = xor2 (delay output,input)
```

`parity` is defined as the `xor2` of the current `input` value with the value of `parity` on the previous cycle. The `delay` combinator takes a signal that changes over time, and *delays* the output by one clock cycle.

The earlier trick of using `Var` as a dummy argument inside our deep DSL does not work directly. Assuming we have augmented our deep DSL to include `delay`, applying `parity` to an instance of `Var` gives an infinite result.

```
> parity (Var "x")
Xor2 (Delay (Xor2 (Delay (Xor2 (Delay (...
```

There are two common solutions to the problem of infinite computation resulting from circular definitions. One solution is to use monads (or similar categorical structure) to wrap the result in a way that circularity becomes observable. This is the approach taken by Singh [2]. Using monads has the advantage that it avoids unsafe Haskell constructs and can be expressed in idiomatic Haskell. The disadvantage is that the type of parity changes, as well as the specific form of the specification body, compromising the declarative flavor of the hardware description.

A second solution to reifying specifications like `parity` relies on the fact that the internal definition of `parity` is represented using a cyclic graph structure. With the ability to observe sharing [3,4] we can extract these cycles, though we need to be careful not to lose some equational reasoning options. In practice, observable sharing does not interfere with Haskell's pure idioms, and is arguably more declarative.

Both solutions for resolving cycles result in a netlist structure of gates and wiring. From this netlist, generating VHDL is straightforward. Lava becomes a macro language inside Haskell for writing combinational and sequential circuits. A VHDL synthesizer compiles the generated VHDL to implementations in FPGA or another silicon technology. The Lava concept has been both influential and successful. Lava has been used to build a number of FPGA based hardware solutions [2,5], and has also had tremendous success in helping teach hardware design at both the graduate and undergraduate level [6].

2 Kansas Lava

Kansas Lava is an effort to extend the Lava design pattern with modern functional programing technology. In particular, we attempt to scale up the ideas in Lava to operate on larger circuits and with larger basic components.

- Kansas Lava uses a single `Signal` type for all types of signals. Some versions of Lava use overloading to interpret constructs in either a synthesis or simulation mode. Our experience is that a single concrete type is easier to work with in practice, and we have included the two main interpretations into our `Signal` type. Ultimately this allows a closer fit between our specifications of behavior and synthesizable code. We give an example of this process in section 8.
- Like other Lava implementations before it, Kansas Lava supports both synthesis and simulation. This supports a workflow where first a simulation model is developed, then refined to a synthesizable variant, then further refined to satisfy performance constraints.

– Kansas Lava uses modern Haskell idioms. We define `Signal` as an applicative
  functor [7]. Arithmetic is overloaded over `Signal`, so we can use standard
  arithmetic operators and represent constants. This leads to simpler and more
  Haskell-like circuit specifications.
– Kansas Lava has direct support for including new blocks of existing VHDL
  libraries as new, well typed primitives. This allows Kansas Lava to be used
  as a high-level glue between existing solutions.
– Kansas Lava includes simple type checking over binary representations. What
  might be used as a single polymorphic entity inside Lava will be instantiated to a specific, monomorphically sized implementation in VHDL. This
  type checker is lightweight, as described in section 6.
– Kansas Lava uses an implementation of sized types, built using type functions. This library includes sized 1 and 2 dimensional matrices, along with
  sized signed and unsigned numerical representations. In Haskell, requiring a
  14-bit unsigned value is unusual, but in hardware, we often know and want to
  enforce a specific width and format. We describe our sized type mechanism
  in section 4.

The primary contribution of our work so far is bringing together all the above
elements into a single modern framework. One of our target applications – wireless communication circuits – makes heavy use of matrix operations to express
encoding and decoding mechanisms [8], so we pay careful attention to support
a straightforward encoding of such operations. In particular, the use of type
functions to implement sized types makes matrix operations clear and straightforward. Furthermore, we believe our use of sized types for both ranged values
and indices is novel and useful when specifying hardware.

3   `Signal` for Synthesis and Simulation

Building up small Lava circuits for bit-level operations is a well understood
process. One aspect that is unusual about Kansas Lava is the coupling between
the model and the synthesizable circuit, which both are embedded in the single
`Signal` type. In this section, we introduce the Kansas Lava `Signal` type and
give examples of its use.

A `Signal` is a value that is typically represented by a `signal` in VHDL, and
implemented by a physical vector of wires. A `Signal` of a specific type represents
an infinite sequence of elements of this type. Semantically, we model `Signal` as

$$\texttt{Signal } \alpha = Nat \rightarrow \alpha$$

where Nat is a clock cycle count.

Kansas Lava provides basic primitives that act over types such as `Signal Bool`.
For example, a simple xor over two signals has the type

```
xor2 :: Signal Bool -> Signal Bool -> Signal Bool
```

Literally, `xor2` takes two signals of boolean values, and return a signal of booleans. The half adder from section 1 can be given the descriptive type

```
halfAdder :: (Signal Bool,Signal Bool) -> (Signal Bool, Signal Bool)
```

We denote an infinite stream of boolean values using `low` or `high` for streams of `True` and `False` respectively.

```
low  :: Signal Bool
high :: Signal Bool
```

Many interesting signals can be constructed; for example a multiplexer

```
mux2 :: Signal Bool -> (Signal a, Signal a) -> Signal a
```

where the `mux2` selects between two signals based on a boolean signal argument.

Furthermore, `Signal` is an applicative functor [7]. The applicative functor provides a clean way of expressing computation over time-varying streams of values. For `Signal` the applicative functor operators have the type

```
pure  :: a -> Signal a
(<*>) :: Signal (a -> b) -> Signal a -> Signal b
(<$>) :: (a -> b) -> Signal a -> Signal b
```

We can generate infinite sequences of a single specific value, and we can merge a sequence of functional values with a sequence of arguments using individual applications, giving a sequence of results. This raises the question of how to realize a `Signal` of functional values in hardware.

`Signal` α is a dual representation, combining an infinite sequence of α values with a deep embedding of the structure of computation. With this shared representation, all synthesizable circuits can be simulated directly, but not all circuits can be synthesized.

In Kansas Lava, the distinction between synthesizable and non-synthesizable hinges on the presence of applicative functor constructs. The applicative functor provides a convenient interface for specifying behavior but is unsuitable for synthesizable circuits. This distinction induces the design flow illustrated in figure 1. We start with a Haskell model, then use applicative functors to rebuild the model in a way that understands time, then we factor out the applicative functor, where the remaining circuit is now synthesizable.

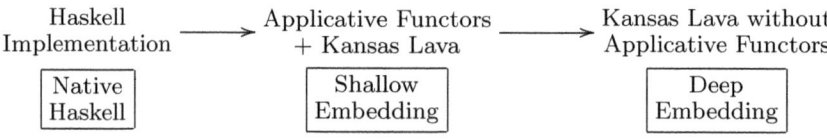

Fig. 1. Kansas Lava Design Flow

4   Sized Types and Sized Matrices

Many specifications of behaviors for error correcting codes are expressed in terms of matrices. In this section, we describe matrices in Kansas Lava, which use a sized type implementation to catch size mismatches statically. The basic type of a matrix is `Matrix ix a`, where `ix` is a type encoding of the *size*, and `a` is the type of elements of the matrix. A vector of boolean values of size 32 has the type `Matrix X32 Bool`. The sized types from `X1` to `X256` are provided, and other larger numbers are straightforward to construct. We consider matrices as a hybrid between lists and tuples. Like tuples, the type completely determines the number of elements that the matrix contains, and like lists every element in the matrix has the same type.

Matrices are created by coercion from a standard list.

```
> :t matrix
matrix :: (Size i) => [a] -> Matrix i a
> matrix [1..4] :: Matrix X4 Int
[ 1, 2, 3, 4 ]
```

When creating a matrix, you must specify the type. We display matrices as list of elements, with traditional spacing between elements. These matrices are functors, so we can `fmap` (functor map) over these matrices.

```
> let m = matrix [1..4] :: Matrix X4 Int
> fmap (*2) m
[ 2, 4, 6, 8 ]
```

Kansas Lava also supports multi-dimensional matrices. As in the case of single dimension matrices, we create them from a *flat* list, with the size determining the partitioning of the input list.

```
> matrix [1..12] :: Matrix (X3,X4) Int
[ 1,  2,  3,  4,
  5,  6,  7,  8,
  9, 10, 11, 12 ]
```

For two dimensional matrices, the show routine renders the matrix as a single list, using layout to denote the partitioning. From this basis, we can build combinators to operate over matrices, performing functions like transpositions, splicing, and joining.

Incorporating matrix sizes allows general functions to be defined. For example, `identity` creates an identity matrix.

```
> :t identity
identity :: (Size x, Num a) => Matrix (x, x) a
> identity :: Matrix (X4,X4) Int
[ 1, 0, 0, 0,
  0, 1, 0, 0,
  0, 0, 1, 0,
  0, 0, 0, 1 ]
```

The type of `identity` states that the result must be a square matrix, and the elements must admit `Num`.

The X_n type has a concrete realization in the form of a natural between 0 and $n-1$. This represents the range of possible valid index values for a specific array. The `ix` type is not just a phantom type [9] to represent size, it also is one of the ways we index into a `Matrix`. Indexing has the type

```
(!) :: (Size ix) => Matrix ix a -> ix -> a
```

Sized types are useful for ensuring consistences between the matrix sizes. For example, the definition of matrix multiply is

```
mm :: (...) => Matrix (x,y) a -> Matrix (y,z) a -> Matrix (x,z) a
mm a b = forAll $ \ (i,j) -> sum [ a ! (i,r) * b ! (r,j) | r <- all ]
```

The type captures exactly the requirement that the number of columns in the first matrix must match the number of rows in the second matrix. The `forAll` function creates a new matrix from a function that takes a matrix index and returns the element at that index.

Sized types allow computation on types. The type of `beside`, which places two matrices side by side is

```
beside (...) => Matrix (x,y1) a -> Matrix (x,y2) a -> Matrix (x,y3) a
```

Ignoring the type constraint for a moment, an example of its use is

```
> let i = identity :: Matrix (X4,X4) Int
*Main> i `beside` i
[ 1, 0, 0, 0, 1, 0, 0, 0,
  0, 1, 0, 0, 0, 1, 0, 0,
  0, 0, 1, 0, 0, 0, 1, 0,
  0, 0, 0, 1, 0, 0, 0, 1 ]
```

So what is the actual type of `beside`, including class constraints? Consider possible ways we may use sizes at compile time.

- We want to know the total size of the result matrix, if we know the sizes of the two arguments.
- Alternatively, we want to be able to infer the type of a specific argument, if we know the size of the other argument and the result.

We provide these capabilities using explicit type functions [10], providing an `ADD` and `SUB` at the type level. These are type *functions* and provide inference in a single direction. For example, the type `ADD X2 X3` maps to `X5`.

For each of the arguments and the result, we provide a single type function that can compute the sized type, given the following type to `beside`.

```
beside
  :: ( Size m, Size left, Size right, Size both
     , ADD left right ~ both
     , SUB both left ~ right
     , SUB both right ~ left
     ) => Matrix (m, left) a -> Matrix (m, right) a -> Matrix (m, both) a
```

In English, this means that m, left, right, and both are all sized types. The result column count both is the sum of the left column count and the right column count. The ~ operator indicates type equality.

Given the ability to represent sizes at the type level, we can use them for both the sizes of matrices as well as the size of numerical representations. Haskell libraries provide a small number of specifically sized signed and unsigned representations, but often in circuits more precise control of sizes is required, such as Int9 (a signed 9-bit integer) or Word34 (an unsigned 34-bit integer). Sized matrices are used to encode arbitrarily sized signed and unsigned numbers.

```
data Signed ix = Signed (Matrix ix Bool)
data Unsigned ix = Unsigned (Matrix ix Bool)
```

In Kansas Lava, we provide instances of Num, Enum, Bits, and other standard classes for both Signed ix and Unsigned ix. The implementation given here is the specification; for efficiency we utilize an underlying encoding of Signed and Unsigned using an Integer. The Signed and Unsigned types provide a standard interface for modular arithmetic in Haskell.

```
> let x = 100 :: Signed X8
> x
100
> x + 1
101
> x * x
16
```

5   Sized Types and Hardware Representations

In Kansas Lava, like many Haskell programs, types reveal a great deal about implementation. Kansas Lava uses a small set of types from which all circuits are constructed. Table 1 gives a list of the basic types used. For these types, we have selected specific VHDL implementations.

- Signal Bool is a boolean that changes over time. In hardware, it is represented by a single wire, either for control or data.

    ```
    i0 : in std_logic
    ```

- Signal (Unsigned ix) is a unsigned number.

    ```
    i0 : in std_logic_vector(ix-1 downto 0);
    ```

- Matrix ix1 (Signal (Unsigned ix2)) is a group of signals, where each signal represents a signed number that changes over time. In addition, we know the number of elements in this group statically.

    ```
    i0,i1,i2,...,iix1 : in std_logic_vector(ix2-1 downto 0);
    ```

Table 1. Types in Kansas Lava

Type	Hardware Representation
Signal α	Clocked value of type α that changes over time
Matrix $\phi\ \alpha$	1 dimensional matrix of α with ϕ elements
Matrix $(\phi_1, \phi_2)\ \alpha$	2 dimensional matrix of α with ϕ_1 column, and ϕ_2 rows.
Signed ϕ	Signed number represented using ϕ bits.
Unsigned ϕ	Unsigned number represented using ϕ bits.
Bool	a boolean; True or False.

– Signal (Matrix ix1 (Unsigned ix2)) is a *single* time-varying value, that represents a group of unsigned numbers. It is represented by a single signal of size MUL ix1 ix2, which is the concatenation of the matrix elements.

```
i0 : in std_logic_vector(ix1 * ix2 - 1 downto 0);
```

In this way, the choice of type at the Lava level is directly reflected into the choice of type at the VHDL level. The user can tune their representation choice to take into account the Haskell level model and the interface required in VHDL.

6   Implementation of Kansas Lava

The implementation of Kansas Lava follows the patterns of its predecessors by using a deep embedding of Signal to represent the circuit shape. We use IO-based observable sharing [4], and make heavy use of overloading. We currently have three back ends: VHDL, schematic, and a debugging output format. All three back ends share the same reification implementation and type inference mechanism for VHDL-level signals.

The Signal type is a tuple of a shallow and deep embedding.

```
data Signal a = Signal (Seq a) (Driver E)
```

The shallow embedding is a Seq, which is an infinite stream with the ability to include unknown values, and includes an optimization for constant streams.

```
data Seq a = (Maybe a) :~ (Seq a)
           | Constant (Maybe a)
```

Seq is an applicative functor, so the standard applicative functor interface can be used to construct shallow embedded behaviors.

A Driver is a data structure that represents a wire, which may be an (named) output from another entity, a global input pad, or a constant integer.

```
data Driver s = Port Var s
              | PathPad [Int]
              | Lit Integer
```

The type E is a wrapper around an Entity, used to simplify reification.

```
data E = E (Entity (Ty Var) E)
```

Entity is the central data type inside our embedding.

```
data Entity ty s = Entity Name [Var] [(Var,Driver s)] [[ty]]
```

An Entity is a globally scoped name representing a specific function, a list of named output ports, a list of input ports with the values that drive them, and finally some type information about the entity. An entity inside Kansas Lava corresponds one-to-one to an entity in VHDL, though we do not choose to implement all our entities this way.

Consider xor2 high (bitNot low), which has two entities xor2 and bitNot. The result Signal becomes a tree of entities.

```
Signal (Constant (Just False))
    (Port "o0" (E (Entity "xor2"
                        ["o0"]
                        [("i0",Lit 1),
                         ("i1",Port "o0" (E (Entity "bitNot"
                                                    ["o0"]
                                                    [(i0,Lit 0)]
                                                    [...])))]

                        [...]))
    )
```

This shallow and deep embedding inside Signal is constructed by having every primitive operator split Signal into shallow and deep components, performing operations on each, then rebuilding a new Signal.

We observe sharing over the E type using the data-reify package. The reify function has the type

```
reify :: E -> IO (Graph (Entity (Ty Var))
```

```
data Graph e = Graph [(Int,e Int)] Int
```

We reuse the Entity type after reification, where Drivers are replaced with node identifiers representing the driving node. This structure is a netlist, and variants of this exist in all the recent variants of Lava. VHDL generation is simply a pass that traverses the netlist graph, mapping each Entity to either a VHDL entity instantiation or an equivalent behavioral expression. Figure 2 in section 7 shows an example fragment of VHDL generated from Lava.

6.1   Type Inference for VHDL Generation

Performing reification allows us to observe cycles in a circuit specification, which is necessary to generate VHDL from the Kansas Lava deep embedding. Unfortunately, the ability to observe the circuit structure doesn't provide sufficient information needed to generate VHDL. This is because the sized type information— from which it is possible to derive VHDL signal widths—is not maintained in the deep embedding.

Kansas Lava sized types ensure that a circuit is *constructed* correctly, but when decomposing the deep embedding of the circuit, this information has been discarded. The representation of an **Entity** maintains all of the input drivers for the **Entity** in a single homogeneous list, which requires the type parameter for **Signals** to be removed. By not maintaining type information in the deep embedding, we gain flexibility and the ability to include externally-defined VHDL entities without having to adapt the deep embedding data structure. On the other hand, throwing away the type information requires us to reconstruct the information to generate VHDL. This reconstruction is performed in parallel with reification. Type reconstruction is performed as an inference step, implemented using equivalence sets of types, where the equivalence is dictated by the Haskell types; a straightforward implementation of substitutions and their unification.

As an example, consider the generation of type equivalences for the polymorphic **mux2** function.

```
mux2 :: Signal Bool -> (Signal a,Signal a) -> Signal a
```

Assuming the inputs are called "cond" (the **Signal Bool**), "a" and "b", and the output is called "r", the inference algorithm infers the following partition. The second element in the outer set indicates that the signals "a", "b" and "c" all inhabit the same type equivalence set.

$$\{ \, \{ \, \text{bit, cond} \, \}, \, \{ \, a, b, r \, \} \, \}$$

Given the equivalence relation for a single entity, the equivalence relation for an entire circuit is constructed by iteratively merging equivalence classes. If the input for one entity is connected to the output of a second entity, the equivalence classes of the input and the output are merged.

This process repeats for each input/output connection. When the inference has completed, each equivalence class should have a single ground (i.e. monomorphic sized) type, which is then assigned as the type to all of the nodes within that equivalence class. If an equivalence class contains *no* ground types, then the circuit is polymorphic, which we report as an error. This can happen if there is an unused loop of signals with no connecting type "edges" to give the loop a type.

7   Representing Addressable Memory

The Kansas Lava **delay** construct is used to create registers. When generating VHDL, Kansas Lava will represent these registers as primitive flip-flop elements. Each delay element will result in a collection of primitive flip-flops of the requisite width. While modern FPGA fabrics are reasonably register-rich, there remains a limit on the number of registers available. Moreover, a register is only capable of storing a single value: to represent addressable memory as registers, it is necessary to construct the address decoding logic as a multiplexer in the Lava design. Furthermore, each element in the address space will consume a number of flip-flops resources equal to the data width stored in the memory. As a consequence, memories with an address space of even moderate size represented in this way can quickly consume the available register resources.

As an alternative to distributed memory implemented using flip-flops, most FPGAs also contain a number of dedicated components which allow that allows the implementation of larger memories without consuming register resources. These memories, termed BRAMs in Xilinx technical documentation, are less plentiful than flip-flops, yet allow for the implementation of a smaller number of larger memory elements.

In addition to the restricted number of dedicated BRAM resources, these elements exhibit a different timing behavior than distributed RAM. For example, BRAM reads take two clock cycles, as compared to the single-cycle read time of registers. The two-cycle latency of BRAMs complicates their use in Lava designs, which—when restricted to using only delays for memory elements—has a purely synchronous stream semantics, with values produced on every clock cycle. The addition of BRAM elements complicates this semantics, due to the introduction of a read latency. While the performance impact of this latency can be minimized, as reads can be pipelined, an engineer using Lava must take extra care to account for read latencies when designing circuits.

7.1 Modeling Memories in Kansas Lava

Kansas Lava models a BRAM as a function mapping a memory operation to a value. A memory operation can either be a read, containing an address, or a write, containing both an address and a value to be written.

```
data MemOp a d = R a | W a d
type Memory a d = Signal (MemOp a d) -> Signal d
```

Kansas Lava implements this memory model in the shallow embedding of Kansas Lava using a Haskell Map for storing memory contents and a queue of values that captures the read latency of BRAMs. The single-step interpretation of a memory operation is shown in the memop definition below.

```
type MemRep a d = (Map a d, [d])
memop :: Ord a => MemRep a d -> MemOp a d -> (MemRep a d,d)
memop (m,ds) (R a) = ((m,vs),v)
  where val = M.lookup a m
        (v,vs) = dequeue (enqueue val ds)
memop (m,ds) (W a d) = ((m',vs),v)
  where m' = M.insert a d m
        (v,vs) = dequeue (enqueue 0 ds)
```

The memop function takes a map (m), a queue of delayed values (ds), and a memory operation. The function returns a new map and queue, along with a value. This single-step memory interpretation can be lifted to a Seq–based interpretation by using an accumulating map over Seqs.

The deep embedding of a BRAM element is implemented as a special `Entity` that takes a single input (the memory operation) and generates a single output. When rendered to VHDL, the memory operation for a BRAM with an address of a bits and with a data value size of d bits will result in an $(a + d + 1)$ bit signal. The least significant bit represents the BRAM write-enable signal, while bits a downto 1 represent the address for both reads and writes, and bits $a + d + 1$ downto $a + 1$ represent the data value for a write. Kansas Lava provides `readMem` and `writeMem` functions which perform the relevant bit packing, as there is currently no way to directly represent Haskell data values in VHDL. These functions are lifted to the `Signal` type, using the Haskell constructors for the shallow embedding and performing bit concatenation for the deep embedding.

The deep embedding of a memory component is rendered to behavioral VHDL, as described by the Xilinx synthesis documentation, rather than directly instantiated. Figure 2 shows a fragment from the VHDL produced for an 8-bit address × 8-bit data BRAM. The type `sig_o_2_ram_type` declares a VHDL array type of the requisite size, used by the BRAM signal `sign_o_2_ram`. The `sig_o_5` assignment represents the packing of a read operation (with zeros for the high data bits and the least-significant write-enable bit). The address signal, `i2`, is exposed as an input port to the enclosing VHDL entity, which is not shown. The signal assignments `sig_o_7`, `sig_o_6`, and `sig_o_4` perform the bit slicing from elements of the memory operation. In the synchronous `synch` process, the bit `sig_o_4` determines if the memory is written or read.

8   A Extended Example of Kansas Lava

We are using Kansas Lava to construct hardware implementations of communication circuits for forward error correction (FEC) codes over wireless fading channels. One component in a (FEC) circuit, an interleaver, performs a reordering of coded bit sequences to mitigate the effects of burst channel noise.

Coded bits within a communication frame are transmitted out-of-order, which allows bit errors due to short noise bursts to be distributed in reasonably even fashion across the frame. This makes it less likely that adjacent coded bits will be corrupted, a condition from which it is challenging to recover the intended bit transmission using our chosen error correction scheme. In the implementation of the interleaver, we use a *permutation* on the order of bits in the sequence to be communicated.

The permutation f is applied in the transmission circuit, and the inverse permutation f^{-1} is applied in the receiving circuit. Permutations are applied on a per-frame basis, the domain (and range) of the permutation function operates over a finite domain. We can model the permutation f as a mapping from logical bit address to transmitted bit address.

Representing such a permutation as a function is a challenge due to the requirement that the permutation appear random. In general, a random permutation cannot be described in more compact form than just enumerating the input to output address mapping. Moreover, the particular properties of the communication channel may impose additional characteristics on the permutation, for

```
signal sig_o_2 : std_logic_vector(7 downto 0);
signal sig_o_7 : std_logic_vector(7 downto 0);
signal sig_o_6 : std_logic_vector(7 downto 0);
signal sig_o_4 : std_logic;
signal sig_o_5 : std_logic_vector(16 downto 0);
type sig_o_2_ram_type is array(0  to 255) of std_logic_vector(7 downto 0);
signal sig_o_2_ram : sig_o_2_ram_type;
begin
  sig_o_5 <= to_unsigned(0,8)&unsigned(i2)&to_unsigned(0,1);
  sig_o_7 <= sig_o_5(16 downto 9);
  sig_o_6 <= sig_o_5(8 downto 1);
  sig_o_4 <= sig_o_5(0);
  synch: process (clk,i1,sig_o_4,sig_o_7) is
    begin
      if rising_edge(clk) then
          if sig_o_4='1' then
              sig_o_2_ram(conv_integer(sig_o_6)) <= sig_o_7;
              sig_o_2 <= (others => '0');
          else
              sig_o_2 <= sig_o_2_ram(conv_integer(sig_o_6));
          end if;
      end if;
    end process;
```

Fig. 2. VHDL generated for memory components

example, that adjacent input bits be separated by a minimum distance in the transmitted sequence. These requirements combine to make an algorithmic definition of the permutation difficult, if not impossible.

We have developed a general interleaver circuit that utilizes a BRAM component to implement the permutation, as shown in figure 3. A user describes the permutation as a list of pairs [(Addr,Addr)] mapping input address to output address. The inverse permutation is constructed by reversing the order of the pair elements. The circuit initializes a BRAM with the contents of this mapping. As bits arrive in sequence, a counter provides an input address to the ROM, which will yield the address in the permuted frame where the bit should be positioned.

The input bit is written to a buffer at the generated address. To allow the circuit to continually generate permuted values, the circuit uses a double-buffering technique, where the input bits for one frame are written to a BRAM, while at the same time the permuted input bits for the *previous* frame are read. In this way, the circuit allows permutation phases to be pipelined, with a one-frame latency.

In the circuit schematic, the `toggle` counter will change at every rollover of the address counter. The toggle output is connected to multiplexers in front of each buffer BRAM. In one mux, a high toggle output will select the read operation for the buffer, while a low toggle output will select the write operation. For the other mux, the selection is reversed. Finally, a multiplexer connected to the output ports of the BRAMs will select the output from the buffer that is currently being read, based on the toggle output.

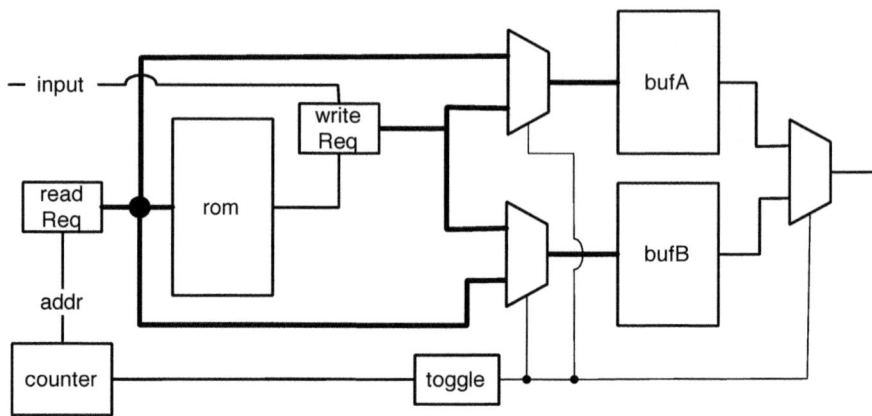

Fig. 3. Permutation Circuit Schematic

```
permute :: (...) =>  [(d, d)] -> Time -> Signal Bool -> Signal Bool
permute permutation clk input = out
  where out = mux2 toggle_z_zz bufA bufB
        addr = counter clk
        permRead = readMem addr

        rom = bram permutation clk permRead

        writeReq = writeMem rom input_zz
        readReq = readMem addr_zz

        muxA = mux2 toggle_z readReq writeReq
        muxB = mux2 toggle_z writeReq readReq

        bufA = bram initBuf clk muxA
        bufB = bram initBuf clk muxB
        initBuf = [(i,False) | i <- [minBound..maxBound]]
        toggle = delay clk high (toggle 'xor2' overflow)
           where overflow = (addr .==. 0)

        addr_zz = delayN 2 clk addr
        input_zz = delayN 2 clk input
        -- the 'toggle' has a built-in 1-cycle delay,
        -- so we only delay 1 cycle
        toggle_z = delayN 1 clk toggle
        toggle_z_zz = delayN 2 clk toggle_z
```

Fig. 4. Permutation Circuit in Lava

Figure 4 shows the description of the permutation circuit in Kansas Lava. The **permutation** parameter defines the mapping from input bit address to output bit position. The **input** parameter is the frame bit input sequence, and the circuit output is the bit sequence of the permuted frame. Within the circuit definition, the **bram** function instantiates a BRAM with the supplied contents. The remainder of the internal signals corresponds to those in the figure.

This Lava definition demonstrates a complication of using memory components. It is necessary to manually add **delay** components to compensate for read latencies. This is indicated in the definitions by a _z suffix to a signal name. The result of the ROM read introduces a 2-cycle latency, so it is necessary to add two delays in the **input** signal to insure that data values line up with write addresses. Similarly, the **toggle** signal is delayed two cycles for the input to the memory read/write operations, and then a further two cycles for the buffer read output, since that too introduces a two-cycle delay.

9 Related Work

The idea of having a program that generates code is an old one, as are the ideas behind Lava itself. The original ideas for Lava can be traced back through work on the Ruby [11] hardware description language and prior to that, μFP [12]. Both of these rely upon the close similarity of circuits and functional languages. Both involve taking input and returning output, and both can represent state (using registers or using streams) as feedback loops. A good summary of the principles behind Lava specifically can be found in [1].

ForSyDe [13] is a system that is close in spirit to Kansas Lava. Like Kansas Lava, ForSyDe is intended to support the modeling of system level concerns, and is also embedded in Haskell. Kansas Lava circuits are clocked circuits, with all **Signal** computations based on a stream-based model of computation. ForSyDe offers support for several additional models of non-terminating computation in addition to clocked synchronous **Signals**. ForSyDe directly supports both a shallow and deep embedding of **Signals**. The two embeddings provided as separate implementations with the same interface, and the ForSyDe programmers can use Haskell import directives to choose which to invoke. Finally, ForSyDe uses type classes (rather than the more recently developed type functions) to implement basic type-level arithmetic to model arbitrary sized wiring patterns. Kansas Lava's use of type functions allows for overloading of sized types and indexing. In particular, in Kansas Lava, the sizes are themselves first class values, and can be used for indexing, giving cleaner and lighter weight matrix specifications.

JHDL [14] is a hardware description language, embedded in Java, which shares many of the same ideas found in Lava. In JHDL, structural circuits are straightforward to express by writing stylized Java programs, and the computational mechanisms provided by Java can be productively used when generating these structural circuits.

There are many other hardware description languages that either use a functional language, or have a functional basis. We refer the reader to the comprehensive comparative review authored by the developers of ForSyDe [15].

10   Conclusions and Future Work

Kansas Lava represents a continuation and expansion on the heritage of Lava. The inclusion of sized types provides a straightforward embedding of a low-level hardware concern within Haskell, leveraging modern facilities provided by Haskell extensions.

Prior Lava work has identified a series of design decisions with associated trade-offs. These include various implementation strategies of shallow vs. deep embedding and of observable sharing. We have endeavored to choose an implementation strategy that leverages these design alternatives in a modular and general manner.

Kansas Lava is an ongoing and actively supported project. As such, we intend to continue to improve and extend the library to include more sophisticated data modeling capabilities. It is clear that developing efficient hardware requires close attention to the performance implications of implementation choices, which are often abstracted away in a functional language. We believe a principled approach to program manipulation [16], using type-based transformations that preserve computational behavior while modifying performance, has the potential to bridge the gap between specification and implementation by allowing an abstract specification to be incrementally refined to suitable implementations.

A further direction of inquiry involves the expression of more sophisticated control patterns in Kansas Lava. For example, the introduction of BRAM into Lava requires an engineer to manually manage deviations from the synchronous stream model of computation. Embedding timing properties within a Lava specification as types may allow the automatic insertion of control logic to compensate for timing incompatibilities. In addition to the case demonstrated by BRAMs, where timing latencies are statically known, this can be expanded to situations where timing properties are dynamic, allowing the inclusion of components such as SDRAM that exhibit non-deterministic timing behavior.

Acknowledgments

We would like to thank the members of CSDL at KU, and the IFL referees for useful and detailed feedback.

References

1. Bjesse, P., Claessen, K., Sheeran, M., Singh, S.: Lava: Hardware design in haskell. In: International Conference on Functional Programming, pp. 174–184 (1998)
2. Singh, S., James-Roxby, P.: Lava and jbits: From hdl to bitstream in seconds. In: FCCM 2001: Proceedings of the the 9th Annual IEEE Symposium on Field-Programmable Custom Computing Machines, Washington, DC, USA, pp. 91–100. IEEE Computer Society, Los Alamitos (2001)
3. Claessen, K., Sands, D.: Observable sharing for functional circuit description. In: Thiagarajan, P.S., Yap, R.H.C. (eds.) ASIAN 1999. LNCS, vol. 1742, p. 62. Springer, Heidelberg (1999)

4. Gill, A.: Type-safe observable sharing in Haskell. In: Proceedings of the 2009 ACM SIGPLAN Haskell Symposium (September 2009)
5. Singh, S.: Designing reconfigurable systems in lava. In: International Conference on VLSI Design, p. 299 (2004)
6. Axelsson, E., Björk, M., Sheeran, M.: Teaching hardware description and verification. In: IEEE International Conference on Multimedia Software Engineering, International Symposium on Microelectronics Systems Education, pp. 119–120 (2005)
7. McBride, C., Patterson, R.: Applicative programing with effects. Journal of Functional Programming 16(6) (2006)
8. Moon, T.K.: Error correction coding: mathematical methods and algorithms. Wiley Interscience, Hoboken (2005)
9. Leijen, D., Meijer, E.: Domain specific embedded compilers. In: 2nd USENIX Conference on Domain Specific Languages (DSL 1999), Austin, Texas, pp. 109–122 (October 1999)
10. Chakravarty, M.M.T., Keller, G., Jones, S.P.: Associated type synonyms. In: ICFP 2005: Proceedings of the Tenth ACM SIGPLAN International Conference on Functional Programming, pp. 241–253. ACM, New York (2005)
11. Jones, G., Sheeran, M.: Circuit design in ruby. In: Staunstrup (ed.) Formal Methods for VLSI Design. Elsevier Science Publications, Amsterdam (1990)
12. Sheeran, M.: mufp, a language for vlsi design. In: LFP 1984: Proceedings of the 1984 ACM Symposium on LISP and functional programming, pp. 104–112. ACM, New York (1984)
13. Sander, I.: System Modeling and Design Refinement in ForSyDe. PhD thesis, Royal Institute of Technology, Stockholm, Sweden (April 2003)
14. Bellows, P., Hutchings, B.: JHDL - an HDL for reconfigurable systems. In: Annual IEEE Symposium on Field-Programmable Custom Computing Machines, p. 175 (1998)
15. Jantsch, A., Sander, I.: Models of computation and languages for embedded system design. IEE Proceedings on Computers and Digital Techniques 152(2), 114–129 (2005); Special issue on Embedded Microelectronic Systems
16. Gill, A., Hutton, G.: The worker/wrapper transformation. Journal of Functional Programming 19(2), 227–251 (2009)

iTasks 2: iTasks for End-users

Bas Lijnse[1,2] and Rinus Plasmeijer[1]

[1] Institute for Computing and Information Sciences (ICIS),
Radboud University Nijmegen, The Netherlands
[2] Faculty of Military Sciences,
Netherlands Defense Academy, Den Helder, The Netherlands
{b.lijnse,rinus}@cs.ru.nl

Abstract. Workflow management systems (WFMSs) are systems that generate, coordinate and monitor tasks performed by human workers in collaboration with automated (information) systems. The iTask system (iTasks) is a WFMS that uses a combinator language embedded in the pure and lazy functional language Clean for the specification of highly *dynamic* workflows. iTask workflow specifications are *declarative* in the sense that they only specify (business) processes and the types of data involved. They abstract from user interface and storage issues, which are handled *generically* by the workflow engine.

Earlier work has focused on the development of the iTask combinator language. The workflow language was implemented as an engine that evaluated task combinator expressions and generated interactive web pages. Although suitable for its original purpose, this architecture has proven to be less so for generating practically usable workflow support systems.

In this paper we present a new implementation of the iTask system that implements the combinator library using a service based architecture that exposes the workflow and a user friendly Ajax client. Because user interface issues are outside the scope of workflow specifications, and cannot be specified explicitly, it is crucial that the generic operationalization of the declarative interaction primitives is of adequate quality. We explain the novel generic libraries we have developed for this purpose.

1 Introduction

Workflow management systems (WFMSs) are systems that generate, coordinate and monitor tasks performed by human workers in collaboration with automated (information) systems. Many contemporary WFMSs suffer from lack of flexibility. This is partially caused by the *static* nature of the languages used for modeling the business processes they coordinate. To address this limitation the iTask system has been developed. This system uses a function combinator library embedded in the pure and lazy functional programming language Clean to model business processes, and allows specification of highly dynamic workflows. The iTask system uses *declarative* specifications of tasks. Task specifications define what has to be done, by whom and when. However, they do not specify

M.T. Morazán and S.-B. Scholz (Eds.): IFL 2009, LNCS 6041, pp. 36–54, 2010.

how tasks are presented to users, how results are entered, or how progress is visualized. These operational details are taken care of fully automatically.

Earlier work [6,9,11,12] has focused primarily on the benefits of the iTask system for programmers. Its goal has been to develop and extend the iTask combinator library to be able to express powerful, yet concise, specifications of arbitrary business processes. For this purpose a prototype implementation of the iTask engine with a minimum level of usability that could be used to simulate workflow scenarios by expert users has been sufficient.

In this paper we present a new implementation of the iTask system that uses a service based architecture to enable a practically applicable interface for end-users. Since user interaction is considered a declarative aspect of the iTask language and outside the scope of a workflow specification, it is *critical* for the usefulness of the iTask system that the generic framework performs adequately in this area. We show how we operationalize workflow specifications in such a way that, for end-users, selecting and working on tasks is no more difficult than the use of an average e-mail client.

The contributions of this paper are the following:

- We present a new implementation of the iTask system. We discuss its new service based architecture and key features, and how it compares to previous implementations.
- We explain the declarative nature of the iTask system. We discuss *what is* specified by iTask expressions, and *what is not*. We show *how* workflow specifications are operationalized by the iTask engine.
- We present a novel generic web interface library in Clean. This library provides *type-driven* Html visualizations of data as well as editable Ajax forms for manipulating data.

The remainder of this paper is organized as follows: First we cover the concept of declarative workflow specification in the iTask system in Section 2. Then an architectural overview of the iTask system is given in Section 3. The generic web-interface library is explained in Section 4. We discuss related work in Section 5 after which final concluding remarks are given in Section 6.

2   Declarative Workflow Specification

The iTask combinator language is designed for declarative specification of workflows. This means that the specifications describe *what* has to be done, not *how*. However, one cannot speak of a language being declarative without specifying at which level of granularity. The level of abstraction of a domain determines whether a specification can be classified as declarative at that level. Since this level is not always immediately clear, especially in workflow languages, we elaborate on it some more in this section.

2.1   When Is a Workflow Specification Declarative?

The iTask system is based on the idea that in workflow support systems, the only differences that really matter between two systems are: 1) The (business) process they support, and 2) The data that is exchanged between actors. Everything else that is needed to build these systems can be generic. The iTask system provides both a specification language to describe the processes and data, as well as a framework that provides the generic foundation that operationalizes them.

In this context, we classify a specification as declarative when everything in it specifies either data or process. Contrary to what is sometimes called declarative workflow, a process can be specified very rigidly but still be considered declarative with respect to this definition. A specification that also specifies issues such as presentation, or storage is considered not declarative in this context. A quick glance at the signature of one of the iTask primitives for interacting with users in Figure 1 illustrates this best. For instance, the `enterInformation` primitive yields a task that asks a user to provide some information. This primitive describes the action that is needed to achieve some goal, but leaves entirely open *how* information is entered.

2.2 The iTask Workflow Language

Above we have already loosely mentioned the iTask specification language, yet we have not explained how it is defined and implemented. The iTask language is a domain specific language embedded in the pure and lazy functional programming language Clean. It is essentially an API of functions and (monadic) function combinators that is used to construct complex functions that when evaluated compute the tasks that have to be done. However, from the point of view of a workflow programmer, the combinator API is just a collection of primitives and operators that are used to define workflows in a syntax that just happens to have a striking resemblance to Clean.

The central concept of iTask workflow specifications is that everything is a task that produces a *typed* result once it is done. Tasks are represented by the abstract Clean type `:: Task a`, where `a` is the type of the result of the task. Although everything is a task, we can still make a distinction between *basic tasks* and *combined tasks*. Basic tasks are the smallest units of work like entering some data in a form, or reading a piece of data from a database. From these basic tasks, larger more complex tasks are constructed using *task combinators*. For example the monadic bind combinator (`>>=`), where the result of the first task is passed to a function that computes the second. By combining tasks sequentially, in parallel or conditionally, tasks of unlimited complexity can be constructed. A short excerpt with common tasks and combinators from the iTask API is shown in Figure 1[1]. The full API consists of many more basic tasks and combinators, like for instance, for interacting with users, generic storage and retrieval, access to meta-data of other workflows and users. Examples of iTask workflow specifications have been given in [9,11].

2.3 Implementation Consequences

As can be seen in the API in Figure 1, workflow specifications in the iTask system define nothing more than data and process. However, a complete executable

---

[1] Context restrictions on overloaded types have been omitted for clarity.

workflow system is generated from just that and nothing else. A major consequence of this design is that this generic foundation that is used to generate a working system from these high level specifications must be of such quality, that there is no need to further hack or tweak the system after generation. When this is not the case the risk exists that clever programmers will find ways to abuse the workflow language to force for example a specific interface layout. This clutters the workflow definitions and makes them no longer declarative.

Of course there are domains where generic solutions are far inferior to specialized instances. Entering a location for example, is easier by putting a marker on a map than by entering coordinates in a form. For these situations the iTask system provides the possibility to define custom domain libraries that contain data types and task primitives along with specializations of the generics. This enables the use of custom code when necessary without cluttering the workflow specifications.

— Basic tasks —

```
// Ask a user to enter information.
enterInformation      :: question   → Task a
// Ask a user to enter information while subject information is shown
enterInformationAbout :: question s → Task a
// Show a message to a user
showMessage           :: message    → Task Void
// Show a message and subject information to a user
showMessageAbout      :: message s → Task Void
// Create a value in the data store
dbCreateItem          ::                    Task a
// Read a value from the data store
dbReadItem            :: !(DBRef a) → Task (Maybe a)
```

— Task combinators —

```
// Lift a value to the task domain
return         :: a                        → Task a
// Bind two tasks sequentially
(>>=)  infixl 1 :: (Task a) (a → Task b)  → Task b
// Assign a task to another user
(@:)   infixr 5 :: UserId    (Task a)      → Task a
// Execute two tasks in parallel
(-&&-) infixr 4 :: (Task a) (Task b)  → Task (a,b)
// Execute two tasks in parallel, finish as soon as one yields a result
(-||-) infixr 3 :: (Task a) (Task a) → Task a
// Execute all tasks in parallel
allTasks       :: ([Task a] → Task [a])
// Execute all tasks in parallel, finish as soon as one yields a result
anyTask        :: ([Task a] → Task a)
```

Fig. 1. A short excerpt from the iTask API

3   The Revised iTask System

As mentioned in Section 1 the original iTask system was used primarily to explore the design of a workflow language based on function combinators. However, experiments with building applications beyond the level of toy examples showed that much hacking and tweaking was necessary to build somewhat usable applications. Examples of such tweaking are: the use of multiple variants of essentially the same task: `chooseTaskWithButtons` and `chooseTaskWithRadios`, or the use of presentation oriented data types such as `HtmlTextArea` instead of just `String`. To be able to generate iTask applications at the level of usability that may be expected from contemporary web-based information and workflow systems, without cluttering the workflow specifications with presentation issues, a major redesign of the iTask engine was necessary.

3.1   Original Architecture

Originally the architecture of the iTask system as presented in [10,9] was that of a simple web application that dynamically generated Html pages. The content of these pages was generated by a program compiled from an iTask workflow specification and a generic base system. This architecture is depicted graphically in the left diagram of Figure 2. Page content generation was performed by application of a workflow definition to an initial state which yielded an output state that accumulated Html code. The abstract type `Task a` of task primitives and combinators was defined as `Task a :== *TSt → (a,*TSt)` which is Clean's notation for a function that takes a unique state of type `TSt` and returns a value of type `a` and new state. Additionally to generating the Html code for the tasks to display on the page, `TSt` also accumulated ad-hoc meta-data about tasks, which was used to generate the navigation components for switching between tasks. When users triggered some event in the generated page, like clicking a button or changing the content of a textbox, the event was sent to the server by reloading the entire page, and used to generate the updated page. This was necessary because each event could potentially cause the workflow to be reduced or the user interface to be different.

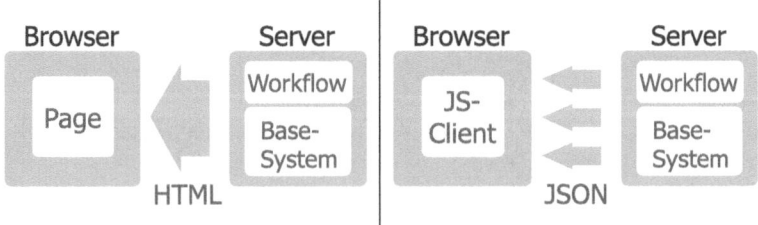

Fig. 2. Architecture old (left) and new (right) iTask system

3.2 Fundamental Problems

The original architecture, though suitable for showing the expressive power of the combinators, suffered from some scalability problems. When used in a more realistic setting, this architecture has a number of fundamental problems.

1. The first issue is one of separation of concerns. The original implementation of the task combinators as functions that both compute the advancement in a workflow *and* the representation of that workflow as a user interface only works for small examples. As soon as you want to define more intricate workflow combinators or put higher demands on the user interface, the implementations of the workflow combinators quickly becomes too complex to manage.

2. Another problem, which is related to the previous issue, is that in the original architecture the only way to interact with iTask workflows was through the web interface. There was no easy means of integrating with other systems. The obvious solution would be to add some flavor of remote procedure calling to the system, but this would then also have to be handled *within* the combinators, making them even more complex.

3. The final issue, which may appear trivial, is the necessity to reload an entire page after each event. This approach is not only costly in terms of network overhead, it also inherently limits the possibilities for building a decent user interface. Essential local state, such as cursor focus, is lost during a page reload which makes filling out a simple form using just the keyboard nearly impossible.

3.3 Improved Architecture

To solve the problems described in the previous section, a drastic redesign of the iTask system was needed. The only way to address them was to re-implement the iTask combinator language on top of a different architecture.

The architecture of the new iTask implementation is a web-service based client-server architecture and is shown in head to head comparion with the old architecture in Figure 2 and illustrated in more detail in Figure 3. The major difference between the old and new architecture is that the new server system does not generate web pages. Instead, it evaluates workflow specifications with stored state of workflow instances to generate data structures called *Task Trees*. These represent the current state of workflows at the task level. These trees contain structural information: how tasks are composed of subtasks, meta-data: for example, which user is assigned to which task, and task content: a definition of work that has to be done. For interactive tasks, the content is a high-level user interface definition that can be automatically generated, which will be explained in Section 4. Task trees can be queried and manipulated by a client program through a set of JSON (JavaScript Object Notation: A lightweight data-interchange format) web services.

The overview shown in Figure 3 illustrates how the various components in the server correspond with components in the client. The workflow specifications are queried directly through the workflow directory service. The authentication service queries the user store. All other services use the task trees as intermediate representation. In the next section, the computation of task trees and the individual services are explained in more detail.

The iTask system provides a default web based Ajax client system, described in Section 3.5, that lets users browse their task list, start new workflow instances and work on multiple tasks concurrently. However, because the service based architecture nicely separates the computation of workflow state from presentation, and communication is based on open web standards, it is also easy to integrate with external systems. For example, we have also built a special purpose client written in Python that monitors a filesystem for new documents and starts a new workflow for processing that simply uses the same services as the standard client.

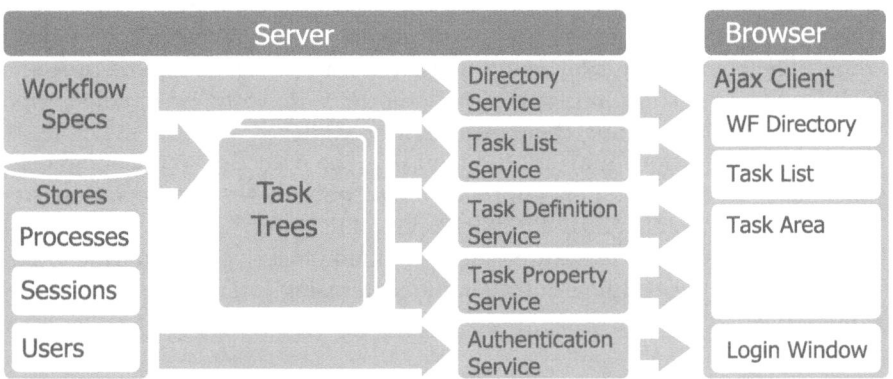

Fig. 3. A detailed architecture overview

3.4   The Server System

The server system manages a database with the state of all active workflow instances (processes) and user and session information. It offers interaction with the workflow instances through JSON webservices. Requests to these services are HTTP requests that use HTTP POST variables to pass arguments. Responses are JSON encoded data structures. The server system is generated by compiling a Clean program that evaluates the startEngine function defined by the iTask base system. This function takes a list of workflow specifications as its argument. The iTask system provides two implementations of the startEngine function. One implements a simple HTTP server, which is useful for development and testing. The other implements the server system as a CGI application for use with third party web server software.

Task Tree Computation. The core task of the server system is to compute and update representations of the current states of executing workflow processes. The central internal representation of the state of a workflow instance that is computed by a combinator expression is a data structure called *Task Tree*. It is a tree structure where the leaves are the atomic tasks that have to be performed, and the nodes are compositions of other tasks. It is the primary interface between the workflow specifications and the rest of the framework and is queried to generate task lists and user interface definitions. Task trees are defined by the following Clean data type:

```
:: TaskTree                                                                    1
 = // A stand-alone unit of work with meta-data                                2
   TTMainTask         TaskInfo TaskProperties  [TaskTree]                      3
   // A task composed of a sequence of tasks                                   4
 | TTSequenceTask    TaskInfo                   [TaskTree]                      5
   // A task composed of a set tasks to be executed in parallel                6
 | TTParallelTask    TaskInfo                   [TaskTree]                      7
   // A task that interacts with a user                                        8
 | TTInteractiveTask TaskInfo (Either TUIDef    [TUIUpdate])                    9
   // A task that monitors an external event source                           10
 | TTMonitorTask     TaskInfo [HtmlTag]                                        11
   // A completed task                                                         12
 | TTFinishedTask    TaskInfo                                                  13
                                                                              14
// Shared node information: task identifiers, labels, debug info etc.          15
:: TaskInfo                                                                    16
// Task meta-data for main tasks, assigned user, priority etc.                 17
:: TaskProperties                                                             18
```

Every function of type Task a generates a (sub) task tree. Combined tasks use their argument tasks to compute the required sub task trees. Because an explanation of task tree generation is impossible without examining the combinators in detail, we will restrict ourselves to a demonstration of their use by means of an example. Let's consider the following simple workflow specification:

```
bugReport :: Task Void                                                         1
bugReport = reportBug >>= fixBug                                               2
where                                                                          3
  reportBug :: Task BugReport                                                  4
  reportBug = enterInformation "Please describe the bug you have found"        5
                                                                               6
  fixBug :: BugReport → Task Void                                              7
  fixBug bug = "bas" @: (showMessageAbout "Please fix the following bug" bug)  8
```

Figure 4 graphically illustrates two task trees that reflect the state of this workflow at two moments during execution. The tree on the left is produced during the execution of the first reportBug task. The bind (>>=) combinator only has a left branch, which is the TTInteractiveTask that contains a user interface definition for the bug report form. The tree on the right is produced during the execution of fixBug. At this point the leftmost branch is reduced to a TTFinishedTask and the @: has been expanded to a subtree consisting of a bind of some getUserByName task, that is finished, and a TTMainTask containing the TTInteractiveTask with the interface definition for showing the bug report.

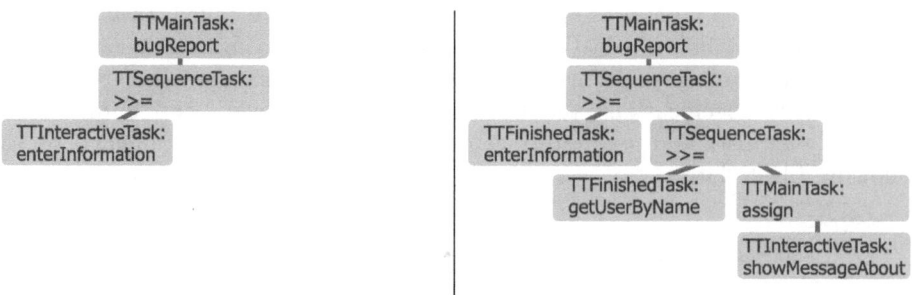

Fig. 4. Task tree during reportBug (left) and fixBug (right)

The Authentication Service. The iTask server maintains a user and role database such that (parts of) workflows can be restricted to users with special roles, and roles may be used to find the right type of worker to do a certain task. The server handles authentication of clients and keeps a database of authenticated time-limited sessions. This service consist of two methods, /handlers/authenticate which accepts a username and password and yields a session key to access the other services, and /handlers/deauthenticate that can be passed a session key to explicitly terminate a session.

The Workflow Directory Service. In order to initiate new workflow instances, the iTask server offers a directory service to browse the available workflow definitions. The server maintains a hierarchical directory of available workflows that are filtered by the roles of a user. The /handlers/new/list method yields the list of possible workflows and subdirectories for any given node in the hierarchy. The /handlers/new/start method starts a new instance of a workflow definition and returns a task identification number for the top level task of that workflow instance.

The Tasklist Service. Users can find out if there is work for them through the tasklist service. The /handlers/work/list method yields a list of all *main tasks* assigned to the current user along with the meta-data of those tasks. This list is an aggregation of all active tasks in all workflow instances the current user is involved in. Because tasks are often subtasks of other tasks, parent/child relation information is also available in the list entries to enable grouping in a client.

The Task Service. To actually get some work done, users will have to be able to work on tasks through some user interface. Because the tasks are highly dynamic, no fixed user interface can be used. Therefore, the iTask system uses a generic library to generate high-level user interface definitions that are interpreted by the client. The /handlers/work/tab method returns a tree structure that represents the current state of a workflow instance. This tree data is used by a client either to render an interface, or to adapt an already rendered interface. When a user updates an interactive control, this method is called with the event passed as an argument. This yields a new tree that represents the updated state of the workflow after this event and possibly events from other users. This process is explained in more detail in Section 4.

The Property Service. To update the meta-data of a workflow instance, for example to reassign tasks to different users or change their priority, the service /handlers/work/property may be used. This service can set any of the meta-data properties of a workflow instance.

3.5 The Client System

Although the iTask system focuses on workflow specification and execution on the server, the average end-user will only interact with this server through a client. While the JSON service API is not limited to one specific client, the iTask system provides a default Javascript client built with the ExtJS framework. ExtJS is a Javascript library that facilitates construction of "desktop like" Ajax applications with multiple windows, different kinds of panels, and other GUI components in a web browser. The iTask client runs in any modern web browser and provides everything a user needs to view and work on tasks. Figure 5 shows a screenshot of the iTask client with multiple tasks opened. The client user interface is divided into three primary areas in a layout that is common in e-mail client applications. This similarity is chosen deliberately to ease the learning of the application. The area on the left of the screen shows a folder hierarchy that accesses the workflow directory service. New workflow instances can be started by clicking the available flows in the folders. The top right area shows a user's *task list*, and the final main area is the lower right *task area*. In this part of the

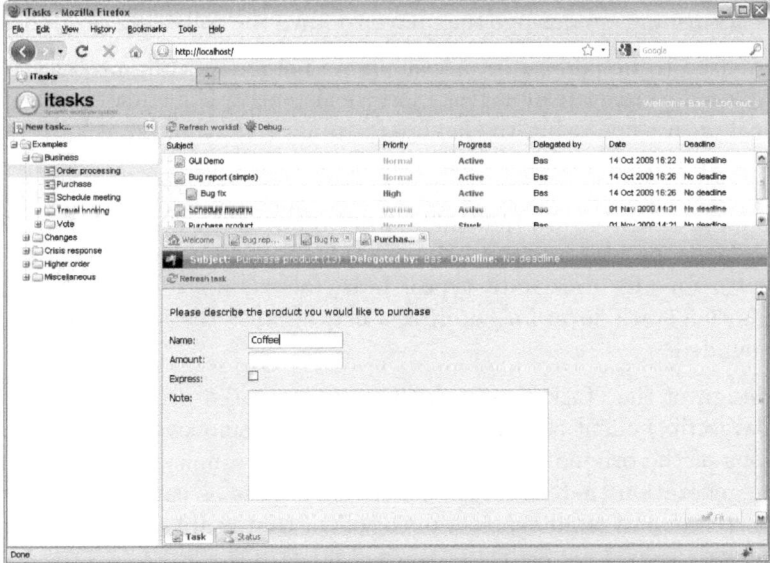

Fig. 5. The iTask client interface

interface area users can work on multiple tasks concurrently in a series of tabs. New tabs are opened by clicking items in the task list.

The most interesting feature of the client application is its ability to dynamically render and update arbitrary user interfaces defined by the server. It constructs the user interfaces required to work on tasks by interpreting a definition it receives from the server. It then monitors all interactive elements in the interface and synchronizes changes to them with the server in the background. The server processes the user input and responds by sending instructions to adapt the user interface when necessary. A big advantage of this design is that the server is kept synchronized with the client. This way the server can provide immediate feedback or dynamically extend an interface without the need for page refreshes. It also means that tasks can be reassigned at any moment without losing any work.

4   Dynamic Generic Web-Interfaces

One of the primary reasons for redesigning the iTask using a different architecture was to improve the user experience for end-users. In this section we show how the new iTask system makes use of the new architecture to operationalize the declaritive user interaction primitives of the specification language.

For basic tasks like `enterInformation` or `displayMessageAbout` to be operationalized, the iTask system needs to be able to generate forms for entering data and visualizations of data to display. Because user interface issues are an aspect that is abstracted from in the iTask specification language, it is *essential* that its implementation is able to generate satisfactory user interfaces. For *any* type that someone defines in a workflow specification, the system needs to be able to generate forms and renderings that have to have the following properties:

- They need to be laid out in a visually and ergonomically pleasing way.
- They need to react responsively and consistently. The cursor should follow a logical path when using the keyboard to navigate through a form and there must never be unexplainable loss or change of focus.
- They must communicate clearly what is optional and what is mandatory. The forms must ensure that mandatory input is entered.
- They must be able to adapt dynamically depending on the choice of constructor for algebraic data types. It is, for example, simply impossible to generate a static form for entering a list, because the number of elements is unbounded.

The redesign of the iTask system with a service based architecture and standalone (Javascript) client as explained in Section 3 removes the implicit usability limitations of the original iTask system. It enables a new approach to dynamic interface generation that uses *type generic functions* as can be defined in Clean [1] on the server and an interpreter in the client that is able to meet the demands stated above.

Figure 6 shows the user interface that is generated for the `BugReport` type used in the `enterInformation` task of the `bugReport` example in Section 3.4:

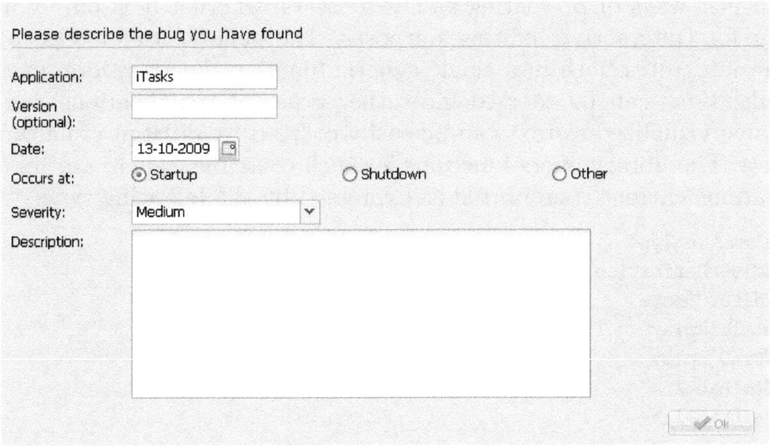

Fig. 6. An automatically generated form

```
:: BugReport =                                                          1
   { application  :: String                                             2
   , version      :: Maybe String                                       3
   , date         :: Date                                               4
   , occursAt     :: BugOccurence                                       5
   , severity     :: BugSeverity                                        6
   , description  :: Note                                               7
   }                                                                    8
:: BugSeverity  = Low | Medium | High | Critical                       9
:: BugOccurence = Startup | Shutdown | Other Note                      10
```

The demands stated above are all applicable to this relatively simple type already. It contains both optional and mandatory parts, it has to adapt dynamically when the Other constructor is chosen and it has a wide variety of input elements that have to be arranged in a pleasing layout. An attentive reader may even spot that different input controls are used to select a constructor in Figure 6 for BugOccurence and BugSeverity. This choice is not specified explicitly, but is decided by a layout heuristic in the interface generation.

4.1 Key Concepts

The iTask system generically provides generic user interfaces through the interplay between two type generic functions. The first one, gVisualize, generates visualizations of values that are rendered by the client. The second one, gUpdate, maps updates in the rendered visualization back to changes in the corresponding values. Before explaining these functions in detail, we first introduce the key concepts underlying their design.

Visualizations. Visualizations in the iTask system are a combination of pretty printing and user interface generation. The idea behind this concept is that they are both just ways of presenting values to users, whether it is purely informational or for (interactive) editing purposes. The generic user interface library therefore integrates both in a single generic function. Furthermore, most types of visualizations can be coerced into other types of visualizations. For example: a value visualized as text can be easily coerced to an Html visualization, or vice versa. The library offers functions for such coercions. There are six types of visualizations currently supported as expressed by the following type:

```
:: VisualizationType                                              1
   = VEditorDefinition                                            2
   | VEditorUpdate                                                3
   | VHtmlDisplay                                                 4
   | VTextDisplay                                                 5
   | VHtmlLabel                                                   6
   | VTextLabel                                                   7
```

And four actual visualizations:

```
:: Visualization                                                  1
   = TextFragment String                                          2
   | HtmlFragment [HtmlTag]                                       3
   | TUIFragment TUIDef                                           4
   | TUIUpdate TUIUpdate                                          5
```

The VHtmlDisplay and VTextDisplay constructors are pretty print visualizations in either plain text or Html. The VHtmlLabel and VTextLabel constructors are summaries of a value in at most one line of text or Html. Labels and display visualizations use the same constructor in the Visualization type. The VEditorDefinition and VEditorUpdate visualizations are explained in the next two subsections.

User Interface Definitions. When a value is to be visualized as an editor, it is represented as a high-level definition of a user interface. These TUIDef definitions are delivered in serialized form to a client as part of a TTInteractiveTask node of a task tree. A client can use this definition as a guideline for rendering an actual user interface. The TUIDef type is defined as follows:

```
:: TUIDef                                                         1
   = TUIButton TUIButton                                          2
   | TUINumberField TUINumberField                                3
   | TUITextField TUITextField                                    4
   | TUITextArea TUITextArea                                      5
   | TUIComboBox TUIComboBox                                      6
   | TUICheckBox TUICheckBox                                      7
   ...                                                            8
   | TUIPanel TUIPanel                                            9
   ...                                                            10
:: TUIButton =                                                    11
   { name         :: String                                       12
   , id           :: String                                       13
   , text         :: String                                       14
   , value        :: String                                       15
```

```
, disabled      :: Bool                                       16
, iconCls       :: String                                     17
}                                                             18
:: TUIPanel =                                                 19
{ layout        :: String                                     20
, items         :: [TUIDef]                                    21
, buttons       :: [TUIDef]                                    22
...                                                          23
}                                                            24
```

Components can be simple controls such as buttons described by the TUIButton
type on line 11, or containers of other components such as the TUIPanel type on
line 19 that contains two containers for components: One for its main content,
and one additional container for action buttons (e.g. "Ok" or "Cancel").

User Interface Updates. To enable dynamic user interfaces that adapt without replacing an entire GUI, we need a representation of incremental updates.
This is a visualization of the difference between two values expressed as a series
of updates to an existing user interface.

```
:: TUIUpdate                                                 1
= TUIAdd TUIId UIDef                                         2
| TUIRemove TUIId                                            3
| TUIReplace TUIId UIDef                                     4
| TUISetValue TUIId String                                   5
| TUISetEnabled TUIId Bool                                   6
:: TUIId :== String                                          7
```

New components can be added, existing ones removed or replaced, values can
be set and components can be disabled or enabled. The TUIId is a string that
uniquely identifies the components in the interface that the operation targets.
The one exception to this rule is the TUIAdd case, where the TUIId references the
component *after* which the new component will have to be placed.

    User interface updates are computed by a local structural comparison while
traversing an old and new data structure simultaneously. This ensures that only
substructures that have changed are being updated.

Data Paths. In order to enable updating of values, it is necessary to
identify substructures of a data structure. A DataPath is a list of integers
(::DataPath :== [Int]) that are indexes within constructors (of arity > 0) when
a data structure is being traversed. Figure 7 show some example DataPaths for
a simple binary tree. DataPaths are a compact, yet robust identification of substructures within a data structure.

Data Masks. When a data structure is edited, it is possible that during this
editing, parts of the structure are temporarily in an "invalid" state. For example
when an element is added to a list: between the structural extension of the list
and the user entering the value of the new element, the list is in a state in which
one of its elements has a value, but that is not entered by the user. To indicate

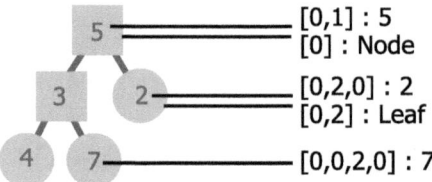

Fig. 7. Data paths for a value of type ::Tree = Node Tree Int Tree | Leaf Int

which parts of a data structure have been accessed by a user we use the DataMask concept. A DataMask is simply a list of all paths that have been accessed by a user (::DataMask :== [DataPath]). This additional information is used to enhance usability by treating components that have not been touched by a user different from those that the user has already touched. For example, validation of only those fields in a form that have already been filled out.

4.2   The Big Picture

With the key concepts explained, we can now sketch the big picture of how user interfaces of interactive tasks are handled. This process consists of three main steps:

1. An initial user interface definition (TUIDef) representing the current value of a data structure and its mask is generated by a generic function on the server. This definition is rendered by the client and event handlers are attached to interactive components to notify value changes.
2. When a user changes an interactive component, an encoding of this change and the data path of the component are sent back to the server and interpreted by another type generic function that updates the data structure and mask to reflect the change.
3. The updated data structure is compared to its previous value and if there is a structural difference, a list of TUIUpdate is computed and sent back to the client. The client interprets these instructions and modifies the interface accordingly.

In the next section we will explain some of the machinery behind those steps. For reasons of brevity we do not go into implementation details, but explain the key data structures and type signatures of key functions instead.

4.3   Low Level Machinery

The core machinery of the library consists of two generic functions: gVisualize and gUpdate. Instances of these functions for concrete types can be automatically derived. Because these functions have been designed favoring pragmatism over elegance, the library exposes them through a set of wrapper functions:

```
//Visualization wrappers (under condition that gVisualize exists for type a)    1
visualizeAsEditor       :: String DataMask a → ([TUIDef],Bool)                  2
                           | gVisualize{|*|} a                                  3
visualizeAsHtmlDisplay :: a → [HtmlTag]                                         4
                           | gVisualize{|*|} a                                  5
determineEditorUpdates :: String DataMask DataMask a a → ([TUIUpdate],Bool)     6
                           | gVisualize{|*|} a                                  7
...                                                                             8
//Update wrappers (under condition that gUpdate exists for type a)             9
updateValueAndMask      :: String String a DataMask *World → (a,DataMask,*World) 10
                           | gUpdate{|*|} a                                     11
...                                                                            12
```

Tasks such as enterInformation use the visualizeAsEditor wrapper to create the
content of a TTInteractiveTask node in the task tree. All interactive components
are given an identifier derived from their data path within the data structure.
This enables the client to send back updates when such a component is updated.
When a client sends an event to the server, the updateValueAndMask wrapper is used
to process the update. Its first two arguments are a string representation of the
data path, and a string representation of the update. The last parameter is the
unique world. Clean uses uniqueness typing to facilitate stateful functions by
threading an abstract World value. The main reason that updates are impure,
is that it enables impure specializations for specific types. For example when
updating a Maybe Date from Nothing to Just, the current date can be set as value.
After updating a value and mask, the determineEditorUpdates wrapper is used to
create task content containing an incremental update for the client GUI.

Although the generic functions are never called directly, and for normal use
only *derived* for types, we conclude this section with a brief overview of their
type signatures and arguments to give an impression of what goes on under the
hood.

```
generic gVisualize a ::                                                         1
  (VisualizationValue a)                                                        2
  (VisualizationValue a)                                                        3
  VSt → ([Visualization], VSt)                                                  4
                                                                                5
:: VisualizationValue a = VValue a DataMask | VBlank                            6
:: VSt =                                                                        7
    { vizType          :: VisualizationType                                     8
    , idPrefix         :: String                                                9
    , label            :: Maybe String                                        10
    , currentPath      :: DataPath                                            11
    , useLabels        :: Bool                                                12
    , onlyBody         :: Bool                                                13
    , optional         :: Bool                                                14
    , valid            :: Bool                                                15
    }                                                                         16
```

The first two arguments are wrapped values of type a with their mask, or an
undefined blank. The last argument that is both input and output of gVisualize

is the visualization state. This state contains all parameters relevant to the
visualization and is used to keep track of global properties. The `optional` field
in the structure is used to mark parts of editor visualizations as optional. A
specialization of `gVisualize` for the `Maybe a` type sets this field to true, and then
produces a visualization of type of `a`. When a visualization of an optional value
that is `Nothing` needed, there is no value of type `a` available. In that case `VBlank`
values are used. The `valid` field of `VSt` is used to validate mandatory fields. It is
updated at each interactive element and set to `False` when a non-optional field
is not masked. This validation is used to disable completion of a task until its
form has been filled out completely.

```
generic gUpdate a        :: a        *USt → (a, *USt)            1
:: *USt =                                                        2
    { mode               :: UpdateMode                           3
    , searchPath          :: DataPath                             4
    , currentPath         :: DataPath                             5
    , update             :: String                               6
    , consPath            :: [ConsPos]                            7
    , mask               :: DataMask                             8
    , world              :: *World                               9
    }                                                            10
:: UpdateMode = UDSearch | UDCreate | UDMask | UDDone            11
```

The `gUpdate` function traverses a data structure recursively and at each point
transforms the value and state according to one of four modes. In `UDSearch` mode,
the `currentPath` path field is compared to the `searchPath` field and `update` is applied
when they are equal. The `mode` is then set to `UDDone` and the `mask` field is updated
to include the value of `currentPath.`. In `UDDone` mode, the function does nothing
and is just an identity function. When a constructor of an algebraic data type is
updated to one that has a non-zero arity, the `gUpdate` function needs to be able
to produce default values for the substructures of the constructor. It uses its
`UDCreate` mode to create these values. In this mode, the `gUpdate` ignores its input
value and returns a default value. The last mode is the `UDMask` mode, which adds
the paths of all substructures to the `mask` as it traverses the data structure. This
is used to compute a complete mask of a data structure.

5 Related Work

The iTask system is a workflow management system, and is therefore comparable
with other WFMSs. However, unlike many contemporary WFMSs (e.g. YAWL,
WebSphere, Staffware, Flower, Bonita), the iTask system does not use a graphical
formalism for the specification of workflows, but uses a compact combinator
language embedded in a general purpose functional language instead.

Although the iTask system is a WFMS, many web applications can be considered workflow support systems in some way or another. Therefore one could also
view the iTask system as a more general framework for (rapid) development of
web applications. This makes it comparable with other web development frameworks found in functional languages like WASH/CGI [14]and HAppS [5] in Haskell,

XCaml in OCaml, or the frameworks available in dynamic scripting languages like Rails [13] in Ruby or Django [2] in Python. While these frameworks aim to simplify the development of any type of web application, the iTask system will only be suitable for applications that can be sensibly organized around tasks.

The final body of work that may be classified as related is not so much related to the iTask system itself but rather to its new generic web visualization library. Other functional web GUI libraries exist like the WUI combinator library in Curry [4], or the iData toolkit [8] in Clean that powered previous iTask implementations. The new iTask visualization library differs from those libraries in that it makes use of an active Ajax client, in this case built with the ExtJS framework [3]. This gives the generated editors more control over the browser than is possible with plain Html forms, hence enabling the generation of more powerful "desktop-like" user interfaces. However, the iTask client is a single application that interprets instructions generated on the server and is not to be confused with client side application frameworks such as Flapjax [7]. Such frameworks could be used as a replacement for ExtJS in alternative iTask clients.

6 Conclusions

In this paper we have presented a new implementation of the iTask system. This new implementation uses a service-based architecture combined with an active client. This approach enables the generation of more user-friendly interfaces for end-users without compromising the declarative nature of the iTask language.

Although seemingly superficial, improved usability is a crucial aspect of the implementation of the iTask workflow language, because the iTask system generates executable systems solely from a workflow specification and *nothing else*. Hence, the generation quality largely determines the usefulness of the language.

A direct consequence of, and a primary motivation for, this work is that it enables case study and pilot research to validate the effectiveness of the function combinator approach to workflow modeling used by the iTask system in scenarios with real end-users. Not surprisingly, such realistic case studies in the context of supporting disaster response operations are planned for the coming years.

More information, examples and downloads of the iTask system can be found at: http://itasks.cs.ru.nl/.

Acknowledgement

The authors would like to thank Jan Martin Jansen and the anonymous reviewers for their insightful comments, and Steffen Michels for exploring some early ideas about combining server-side generic programming with client-side Javascript.

References

1. Alimarine, A., Plasmeijer, R.: A generic programming extension for Clean. In: Arts, T., Mohnen, M. (eds.) IFL 2002. LNCS, vol. 2312, pp. 168–186. Springer, Heidelberg (2002)

2. Django framework, urlhttp://www.djangoproject.com/
3. ExtJS framework, urlhttp://www.extjs.com/
4. Hanus, M.: High-level server side web scripting in Curry. In: Ramakrishnan, I.V. (ed.) PADL 2001. LNCS, vol. 1990, pp. 76–92. Springer, Heidelberg (2001)
5. Jacobson, A.: Haskell application server (2006), urlhttp://happs.org/
6. Koopman, P., Plasmeijer, R., Achten, P.: An executable and testable semantics for iTasks. In: Scholz, S.-B. (ed.) Proceedings of the 20th International Symposium on the Implementation and Application of Functional Languages, IFL 2008. Technical Report, vol. 474, pp. 53–64. Univeristy of Hertfordshire, UK (2008)
7. Meyerovich, L., Guha, A., Baskin, J., Cooper, G., Greenberg, M., Bromfield, A., Krishnamurthi, S.: Flapjax: A programming language for ajax applications. Tech report, CS-09-04, Brown University, Providence, RI (April 2009)
8. Plasmeijer, R., Achten, P.: iData for the world wide web - Programming interconnected web forms. In: Hagiya, M., Wadler, P. (eds.) FLOPS 2006. LNCS, vol. 3945, pp. 242–258. Springer, Heidelberg (2006)
9. Plasmeijer, R., Achten, P., Koopman, P.: iTasks: executable specifications of interactive work flow systems for the web. In: Proceedings of the 12th International Conference on Functional Programming, ICFP 2007, Freiburg, Germany, October 1-3, pp. 141–152. ACM Press, New York (2007)
10. Plasmeijer, R., Achten, P., Koopman, P.: An introduction to iTasks: defining interactive work flows for the web. In: Horváth, Z., Plasmeijer, R., Soós, A., Zsók, V. (eds.) CEFP 2007. LNCS, vol. 5161, pp. 1–40. Springer, Heidelberg (2008)
11. Plasmeijer, R., Achten, P., Koopman, P., Lijnse, B., van Noort, T.: An iTask case study: a conference management system. In: Koopman, P., Plasmeijer, R., Swierstra, D. (eds.) AFP 2008. LNCS, vol. 5832, pp. 306–329. Springer, Heidelberg (2009)
12. Plasmeijer, R., Jansen, J.M., Koopman, P., Achten, P.: Declarative Ajax and client side evaluation of workflows using iTasks. In: Proceedings of the 10th International Conference on Principles and Practice of Declarative Programming, PPDP 2008, Valencia, Spain, July 15-17, pp. 56–66 (2008)
13. Ruby on Rails, urlhttp://rubyonrails.org/
14. Thiemann, P.: WASH/CGI: server-side web scripting with sessions and typed, compositional forms. In: Krishnamurthi, S., Ramakrishnan, C.R. (eds.) PADL 2002. LNCS, vol. 2257, pp. 192–208. Springer, Heidelberg (2002)

ChalkBoard: Mapping Functions to Polygons

Kevin Matlage and Andy Gill

Information Technology and Telecommunication Center
Department of Electrical Engineering and Computer Science
The University of Kansas
2335 Irving Hill Road
Lawrence, KS 66045
{kmatlage,andygill}@ku.edu

Abstract. ChalkBoard is a domain specific language for describing images. The ChalkBoard language is uncompromisingly functional and encourages the use of modern functional idioms. ChalkBoard uses off-the-shelf graphics cards to speed up rendering of functional descriptions. In this paper, we describe the design of the core ChalkBoard language, and the architecture of our static image generation accelerator.

1   Introduction

Options for image generation abound. Functional languages and image generation have been courting for decades. Describing the mathematics of images in functional languages like Haskell [1] is straightforward. Yet there is no clear choice for describing images functionally, and then efficiently rendering them.

There certainly are many image generation choices in Haskell. The popular cairo[2], for example, is an efficient image language, based on imperatively drawing shapes onto a canvas, with a Haskell IO port of the API. We are explicitly interested in exploring purely functional representations of images and want to understand if they can be made efficient.

The ChalkBoard project is an attempt to bridge the gap between the clear specification style of a language with first-class images, and a practical and efficient rendering engine. Though systems like cairo offer the ability to use created images as new components, the hook here is that with the first-class status offered by pure functional languages comes clean abstraction possibilities, and therefore facilitated construction of complex images from many simple and composable parts. This first-class status traditionally comes at a cost—efficiency. Unless the work of computing these images can be offloaded onto efficient execution engines, then the nice abstractions become tremendously expensive. This paper describes a successful attempt to target one such functional image description language to the widely supported OpenGL standard.

Figure 1 gives the basic architecture of ChalkBoard. Our image specification language is an embedded Domain Specific Language (DSL). An embedded DSL is a style of library that can be used to capture and cross-compile DSL code, rather than interpret it directly. In order to do this and allow use of a polygon-based back-end, we have needed to make some interesting compromises, but

M.T. Morazán and S.-B. Scholz (Eds.): IFL 2009, LNCS 6041, pp. 55–71, 2010.

the ChalkBoard language remains pure, has a variant of functors as a control structure, and has first-class images. We compile this language into an imperative intermediate representation that has first-class *buffers*—regular arrays of colors or other entities. This language is then interpreted by macro-expanding each intermediate representation command into a set of OpenGL commands. In this way, we leverage modern graphics cards to do the heavy lifting of the language.

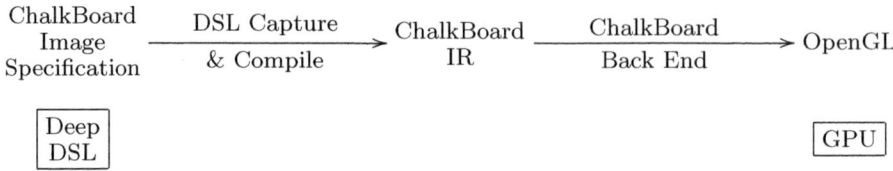

Fig. 1. The ChalkBoard Architecture

Both subsystems of ChalkBoard are written in Haskell, and are compiled using GHC [3]. We have plans for other back ends for ChalkBoard that share the same Intermediate Representation (IR), but in this paper we focus on how we use OpenGL to achieve fast *static* image generation from a purely functional specification. Specifically, this paper makes the following contributions.

- We pursue an efficient functional representation of images. In order to do this, we build a simple image generation DSL, modeled on Elliott's Pan [4], but with an abstract principal data type to facilitate introspection.
- To allow DSL capture, we needed to impose some restrictions on the form of expressions. In particular, we identify challenges with capturing maps over functors and introduce our solution, the observable O, which should be reusable in other DSLs.
- Having captured our DSL, we need a vehicle to experimentally verify our image generation ideas. We describe the design of our ChalkBoard accelerator and give some initial performance results for our ChalkBoard compiler and runtime system that demonstrate that ChalkBoard has sufficient performance to carry out these future experiments.

Our intent with the technology discussed in this paper is that it will be of immediate applicability, as well as serve as a basis for future dynamic image generation and processing tools, all of which will be executing specifications written in functional languages.

2   Functional Image Generation

As a first example of ChalkBoard, consider drawing a partially-transparent red square over a partially-transparent green circle. The image we wish to draw looks like Figure 2.

We can describe the picture in Figure 2 using the following ChalkBoard specification.

Fig. 2. Square over Circle

```
board = unAlpha <$> (sq1 `over` cir1 `over` boardOf (alpha white))    1
  where                                                               2
    cir1 =  move (0.2,0.2)                                            3
         $  choose (withAlpha 0.5 green) (transparent white)          4
        <$> circle                                                    5
    sq1  =  move (-0.2,-0.2)                                          6
         $  choose (withAlpha 0.5 red) (transparent white)            7
        <$> square                                                    8
```

This fragment of code specifies that

- A circle (line 5), colored green with 50% transparency (line 4), is moved slightly up and to the right (line 3).
- A square (line 8), colored red and also with 50% transparency (line 7), is moved slightly down and to the left (line 6).
- Both these shapes are placed on a transparent background (line 4 & 7).
- The red square is placed on top of the green circle, which is on top of a white background (line 1).

In order to understand the specifics of the ChalkBoard language, we need to think about types. In ChalkBoard, the principal type is a `Board`, a two dimensional plane of values. So a color image is a `Board` of color, or RGB. A color image with transparency is `Board` of RGBA. A region (or a plane where a point is either in a region or outside a region) can be denoted using `Board` of `Bool`. Table 1 lists the principal types of `Board`s used in ChalkBoard.

The basic pattern of image creation begins by using regions (`Board Bool`) to describe primitive shapes. ChalkBoard supports unit circles and unit squares, as well as rectangles, triangles, and other polygons. The primitive shapes provided to the ChalkBoard user have the following types:

```
circle    :: Board Bool
square    :: Board Bool
rectangle :: Point -> Point -> Board Bool
triangle  :: Point -> Point -> Point -> Board Bool
polygon   :: [Point] -> Board Bool
```

Table 1. Boards and Type Synonyms in ChalkBoard

`Board RGB`	Color image
`Board RGBA`	Color image with transparency
`Board Bool`	Region
`Board UI`	Grayscale image
`type UI = Float`	Values between 0 and 1
`type R = Float`	Floating point coordinate
`type Point = (R,R)`	2D Coordinate or point

To "paint" a color image, we map color over a region. Typically, this color image would be an image with the areas outside the original region being completely transparent, and the area inside the region having some color. This mapping can be done using the combinator `choose`, and the `<$>` operator.

```
choose (alpha blue) (transparent white) <$> circle
```

We choose alpha blue for inside the region, and transparent white outside the region. The `<$>` operator is a map-like function which lifts a specification of how to act over individual points into a specification of how to translate an entire board. The types of `choose` and `<$>` are

```
choose :: O a -> O a -> O Bool -> O a
(<$>)  :: (O a -> O b) -> Board a -> Board b
```

`choose` is a `bool`-like combinator that we partially apply, and `<$>` is an `fmap`-like combinator. The type `O a` is an *observable* version of `a`. We can consider `O` to have this trivial definition, though `O` is actually an abstract type.

```
data O a = O a    -- working definition; to be refined.
```

We will redefine our `O` type and consider its implementation in section 6.

ChalkBoard provides all point-wise functions and primitives already lifted over `O`. For example, the colors, and functions like `alpha` and `transparent` have the types

```
red                :: O RGB
green              :: O RGB
blue               :: O RGB
alpha              :: O RGB -> O RGBA
transparent        :: O RGB -> O RGBA
```

Our boards of `RGBA`, or images of transparent color, can be combined (overlaid) into new boards of `RGBA`.

```
(choose (alpha blue) (transparent white) <$> circle)
                    `over`
(choose (alpha green) (transparent white) <$> square)
```

The combinator over is used to lay one Board onto another Board.

```
over :: Board a -> Board a -> Board a
```

Also, these boards of RGBA can be (value) transformed into Board RGB, true color images. Again, this translation is done using our map-like operator, <$>, and a point-wise unAlpha.

```
unAlpha <$>
    ((choose (alpha blue) (transparent white) <$> circle)
                      'over'
    (choose (alpha green) (transparent white) <$> square))
```

unAlpha removes the alpha component of RGBA, leaving RGB.

As well as translating point-wise, ChalkBoard supports the basic spatial transformational primitives of scaling, moving and rotating, which work over *any* Board.

```
scale   :: Float          -> Board a -> Board a
scaleXY :: (Float,Float) -> Board a -> Board a
move    :: (Float,Float) -> Board a -> Board a
rotate  :: Float          -> Board a -> Board a
```

This is a significant restriction over the generality provided in Pan, and one we intend to lift in a future version of ChalkBoard.

Finally, we also have a primitive for constructing a (conceptually infinite) Board of a constant value, which has the type

```
boardOf :: O a -> Board a
```

Using these combinators, ChalkBoard constructs images by combining primitives and translating them in both *space* and *representation*, ultimately building a Board RGB. ChalkBoard also supports importing of images as Board RGBA, and other Board creation primitives, for example font support, are planned.

3   ChalkBoard Example: Drawing Lines

Now that we have our fundamental primitives and combinators, we can build more interesting, complex combinators. We can build a box combinator which takes two points and constructs a region box between them.

```
box :: (Point,Point) -> Board Bool
box ((x0,y0),(x1,y1)) = polygon [(x0,y0),(x1,y0),(x1,y1),(x0,y1)]
```

Using this box function, we can build a straight line region builder.

```
straightline :: (Point,Point) -> R -> Board Bool
straightline ((x1,y1),(x2,y2)) width =
          move (x1,y1)
        $ rotate (pi /2 - th)
        $ box ((-width/2,0),(width/2,len))
  where
          (xd,yd)  = (x2 - x1,y2 - y1)
          (len,th) = toPolar (xd,yd)
```

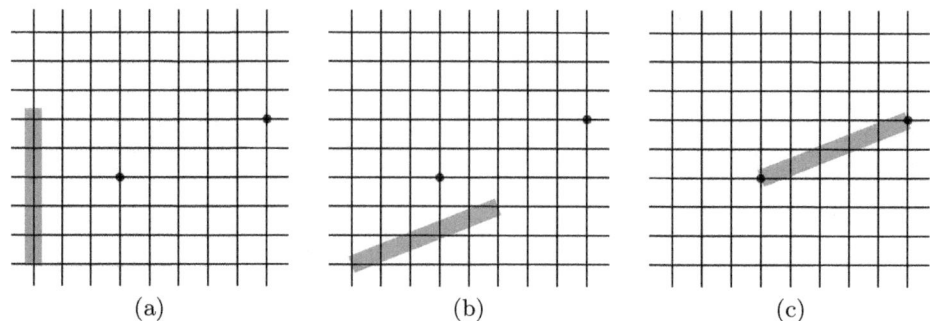

Fig. 3. How `straightline` works

Figure 3 illustrates how `straightline` operates. Assuming the dots are the target start and end points of our straight line, and the bottom left intersection is (0,0), we draw a box of the correct size and width (a), rotate it (b), then move it to the correct location. There are other ways of writing `straightline`, but this is compositionally written.

Now we can draw lines between arbitrary points of arbitrary thicknesses, and we can simulate curved lines using many of these straight segments together. To do this, we have a function, `outerSteps`, which counts a (specified) number of steps between 0 and 1, inclusive.

```
> outerSteps 5
[0.0,0.2,0.4,0.6,0.8,1.0]
```

The result here is a set of 6 values, or the 5 steps of size 0.2 between 0 and 1. Using `outerSteps`, we *sample* a function that encodes the curved line. We draw the curved line by drawing straight lines between the sample points, and filling in any infidelity at the joins between these lines with small dots the size of the width of the lines.

```
functionline :: (UI -> Point) -> R -> Int -> Board Bool
functionline line width steps = stack
                [ straightline (p1,p2) width
                | (p1,p2) <- zip samples (tail samples)
                ] `over` stack
                        -- not the first or last point
                [ dotAt p | p <- tail (init samples) ]
    where
        samples = map line (outerSteps steps)
        dotAt p = move p $ scale width circle
```

Figure 4 gives examples of `functionline` being used on a function with 3, 10, and 50 segments. Figure 4 shows how with a higher number of samples the quality of rendering the curved line improves.

In fact, all these functions are already defined with the ChalkBoard library, but are given here as an illustration of the flavor of ChalkBoard and how it

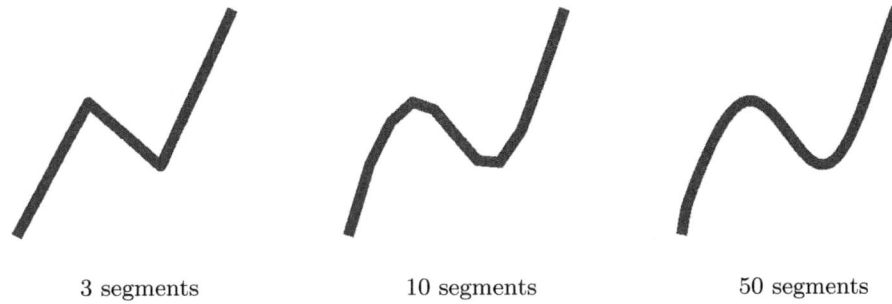

3 segments   10 segments   50 segments

Fig. 4. Examples of `functionline`

compromises between continuous boards, and discrete components on these boards. Collectively, ChalkBoard combinators give a clean and productive environment for scripting images.

4   Considerations with Compiling ChalkBoard

ChalkBoard has a simple semantic model. A `Board` of α is a field of α-values over $\mathcal{R}^2$, where $\mathcal{R}^2$ is a floating point coordinate for two dimensions.

$$\texttt{Board } \alpha = (R, R) \rightarrow \alpha$$

This is exactly the model used in Pan [4], on which the ChalkBoard language is based. Pan uses this semantic model of a function directly to implement a `Board`, but though we too share the same semantic model, we want a different implementation.

- In ChalkBoard, `Board` is *abstract*, specifically to admit the possibility of future representation optimizations. In Pan, the equivalent of `Board` is implemented as an explicit function, directly guided by the semantic model. Our choice of abstraction limits the language to using only the built-in combinators for `Board` transformation. This is a significant restriction, especially when compared to the full expressiveness of `Pan`, and one we intend to revisit in the future.
- ChalkBoard is intended as a system for constructing complex images, consisting of perhaps tens of thousands of individual components. The functional representation precludes this being efficiently rendered, though techniques like the worker/wrapper transformation [5] could be used to translate an explicit function into something like our abstract representation.

Consider the ChalkBoard image in Figure 2. We will use this example to illustrate a number of the challenges with optimizing a chalkboard specification of an image. Figure 2 was generated by first building a `Board Bool` for each of the two basic shapes, using our `<$>` on each board to convert it to a `Board RGBA`, and then using `move` to move these boards to the desired locations. Finally, these two boards are overlaid, using `over`, and the alpha channel is removed for rendering as a color image.

Our plan of attack is to augment the representation of `Board` internally, replace the shape primitives with more complex information about what is being rendered, and attempt to translate our tree of operations into the drawing of polygons. Rendering polygons is something OpenGL does extremely efficiently. We will allow fallback onto the slower pixel sampling if needed. The longer term goal is to allow most user-written ChalkBoard specifications to be compiled efficiently, and tell the user when a board is being rendered using the fallback sampling. Currently, however, the ChalkBoard language discussed in this paper is limited enough that no fallback is ever actually needed.

5   Capturing the Domain Specific Language ChalkBoard

ChalkBoard is a language that describes boards, and these boards are functor-like. The language provides mechanisms for (1) describing the creation of boards, and for creating boards from boards, using (2) spacial transformations and (3) a functor-style `map`. In this section, we will consider how to express all three of these language aspects in a deep embedding of the ChalkBoard language.

Constant boards are captured using a `Constant` constructor, inside `Board`.

```
data Board a where
        Constant :: O a -> Board a
        ...
```

Here we use GADT [6] syntax for `Board` because of the ability to declare constructors that are specialized to monomorphic instances, and we present each of the principal constructions individually.

Primitives shapes, like circles and squares, are regions, or `Board Bool`. They are represented inside the data structure `Board` using a list of points that mark a convex boundary of the region.

So for primitives we have the constructor

```
data Board a where
        Polygon :: (...) -> Board Bool
        ...
```

We can see the use of the monomorphic constructor here.

Representing squares is easy using the four corner points, but what about the points around a circle? There are infinitely many corner points on a circle, that is, there are infinitely many points that match, for example, the equation

$$\sqrt{x^2 + y^2} = 0.5$$

Graphic rendering systems approximate the circle using a small number of corners on a small circle and a larger number of corners on a larger circle. At this point, we appeal to classical functional programming and *defer* the decision about how many points to use to approximate the circle using a function. The type of the `Polygon` constructor is

```
data Board a where
        Polygon :: (Float -> [Point]) -> Board Bool
        ...
```

The `Float` argument is the resolution of the final polygon. Specifically, it is an approximation of how many pixels a line of unit length would affect. We can now give a definition for `square` and `circle`.

```
square :: Board Bool
square = Polygon (const [(-0.5,-0.5),(-0.5,0.5),(0.5,0.5),(0.5,-0.5)])

circle :: Board Bool
circle = Polygon $ \ res ->
    let ptcount = max (ceiling res) 3
    in [ (sin x/2,cos x/2)
       | x <- map (* (pi/(2 * fromIntegral ptcount)))
                (take ptcount [0..])
       ]
```

`sin` and `cos` are used to find the x and y points on a unit circle (after scaling), and the number of points is dictated by the size of the final circle. The point count formula used here generates reasonable images, but remains open to further tuning.

Spacial transformations are also handled using a single `Board` constructor, which combines all the relevant transformations.

```
data Board a where
        Move   :: (Float,Float) -> Board a -> Board a
        Scale  :: (Float,Float) -> Board a -> Board a
        Rotate :: Float          -> Board a -> Board a
        ...

move :: (Float,Float) -> Board a -> Board a
move (x,y) = Move (x,y)

scale :: Float -> Board a -> Board a
scale w = Scale (w,w)

rotate :: Radian -> Board a -> Board a
rotate r = Rotate r
```

Finally, we have our functor map (or `fmap`) like operators. Consider the following attempt at a `fmap` constructor.

```
data Board a where
        Fmap :: forall b . (b -> a) -> Board b -> Board a  -- WRONG
        ...

(<$>) = Fmap
```

This can be used to successfully *typecheck* a ChalkBoard-like language and *construct* a representation of `Board`, but we run into a fatal problem when we try to walk the `Board` tree during compilation. Here `b` can be any type; we have lost the type information about what it was. We can expect an `<$>` over a `Board Bool` to have a completely different operational behavior than an `<$>` over a `Board RGB`! When walking our tree and performing our abstract attribute grammar interpretation, we get stuck.

We address this problem by assuming our pointwise function is a function over our observable type `O`. So we have the corrected

```
data Board a where
        Fmap :: forall b . (O b -> O a) -> Board b -> Board a
        ...

(<$>) = Fmap
```

and we also require our `O` type to hold runtime type information, as described in section 6. It looks like using `O` just postpones the problem, and does not solve it. By forcing pointwise manipulations to be expressed in the `O` language, we can observe what the user intended, without requiring that *every* function be directly promoted into a `Board` equivalent.

We can now construct basic abstract syntax trees for ChalkBoard, using our `Board` data type. For example

<code>scale 2 (choose red green <$> square)</code>

represents the creation of a red square on a green background. It constructs the `Board` tree

<code>Scale (2,2) (Fmap (...) (Polygon (...)))</code>

We can extract the specific polygon points contained inside the `Polygon` constructor when we are compiling for OpenGL because in context we know the size of the target image. The challenge is how do we extract the first argument to `Fmap`? To do so, we use our observable type, `O`.

6   O, the Observable

The data type `O`, which we nickname *the observable*, is the mechanism we use to observe interesting values. The idea is that an observable can simultaneously have a shallowly and deeply embedded interpretation of the same constructed expression. We can use the shallow interpretation to directly extract the value of any `O` expression, and we examine the deep interpretation to observe how a result was constructed. Specifically, the data definition for `O` is

```
data O a = O a E        -- abstract in ChalkBoard API
```

`E` is a syntax tree of possible `O` expressions. By limiting the ways of building `O`, we allow `O` expressions to be built only out of primitives we know how to compile. In ChalkBoard, `E` has the definition

```
data E = E (Expr E)
data Expr e
        = Var Int        | Lit Float        | Choose e e e
        | O_Bool Bool    | O_RGB RGB         | O_RGBA RGBA
        | Alpha UI e     | UnAlpha e
        ...
```

We use implicit recursion inside `Expr` so we can share this functor-style representation of `Expr` between our expression inside O and the internal compiler; see [7] for a detailed description of this design decision.

To illustrate how we build our primitives, the definition of `choose` is

```
choose :: O a -> O a -> O Bool -> O a
choose (O a ea) (O b eb) (O c ec) = O (if c then a else b)
                                      (E $ Choose ea eb ec)
```

We can also build primitive O values using our `Obs` class.

```
class Obs a where
    o :: a -> O a
```

That is, only instances of `Obs` can construct objects of type O a. ChalkBoard uses this to provide a way of taking a value of `Bool`, `RGB`, `RGBA`, or `Float` and lifting it using the o function into the O structure. In many ways, this is a restricted version of `return` for monads, or `pure` for applicative functors [8].

So how do we actually observe a function? By giving a dummy argument and observing the resulting expression. The `Expr` type above contains a `Var` constructor specifically for this purpose. If we take the example

```
choose red green :: O Bool -> O RGB
```

We can pass in the argument 'O ⊥ (Var 0)' to this function, and get the result

```
O ⊥ (E (Choose
          (E (O_RGB (RGB 1 0 0)))
          (E (O_RGB (RGB 0 1 0)))
          (E (Var 0))))
```

where the structure of the `choose` and the arguments are completely explicit. Using this trick, we can observe the function argument to our functor because we require the argument and result type to both be of type O. Ignoring the type change between the function argument to `Fmap` and its tree representation, our earlier example can be parsed into

```
    Scale 2 (Fmap (E (Choose
                      (E (O_RGB (RGB 1 0 0)))
                      (E (O_RGB (RGB 0 1 0)))
                      (E (Var 0))))
                  (Polygon (...))
            )
```

thus allowing compilation.

7   ChalkBoard IR

We use both the inspection of the Board structure itself and the observation of O objects to construct our ChalkBoard abstract syntax tree. From here, compilation is a matter of implementing the attribute grammar interpretation over this tree in a way that leverages OpenGL's polygon pushing abilities. We translate into a ChalkBoard Intermediate Representation (CBIR), then interpret CBIR on the fly into OpenGL commands.

Statement	stmt ::= allocate dest (x,y) back	Allocate Buffer
	| **buffersplat** dest src pointmaps	Splat Texture
	| **colorsplat** dest col points	Splat Color
	| **delete** src	Deallocate
	| **save** src filename	Write to file
	| **exit**	
Background	back ::= col	Background Color
	| Ptr	Pointer to an Image
Color	col ::= RGB	RGB Constant
	| RGBA	RGBA Constant
	dest,src ::= buffer-id	
	pointmap ::= (point,point)	
	pointmaps ::= $pointmap_1$, $pointmap_2$, ..., $pointmap_n$ $n \geq 3$	
	point ::= (u,v)	
	points ::= $point_1$, $point_2$, ..., $point_n$ $n \geq 3$	
	x,y ::= int	
	u,v ::= float	

Fig. 5. ChalkBoard Intermediate Representation

Figure 5 gives the syntax of CBIR. There are two main commands.

- **allocate**, which allocates a new, fixed-sized buffer in graphics memory.
- **buffersplat**, which takes a polygon from one buffer and renders it onto another buffer. **buffersplat** takes a source and destination buffer, and a sequence of point maps, each of which is a mapping from a point on the source board to a point on the destination board. This mapping capability is both powerful and general. It can be used to simulate scaling, translation, or rotation. This is the command that does the majority of the work inside ChalkBoard.

As well as the two principal instructions, there are also commands for deallocation of buffers, saving buffers to disk images, and **colorsplat**, a specialized version of **buffersplat** where the source is a single color instead of a buffer.

8   Compiling ChalkBoard to ChalkBoard IR

When compiling ChalkBoard, we traverse our AST in much the same way as the attribute grammar example above, but instead of passing in the inherited attribute (x, y) many times, we walk over our graph *once*, providing as inherited attributes:

- a basic quality of the required picture argument. In this way, a specific `Board` can know how much it is contributing to the final image;
- any rotations, translations, or scaling performed *above* this node;
- and an identifier for a pre-allocated *target* buffer.

We then have a set of compilation schemes for each possible `Board` type. In general we perform the following compile steps

- `Constant Boards` compile into a single splat onto the target board.
- `Move`, `Scale` and `Rotate` update the inherited attribute context, recording the movement required, and then compile the sub-board with this new context.
- For `Over`, we interpret the child boards according to the type of `Board`. For `Board Bool` and `Board RGBA`, `Over` draws the back (second) board, and then draws the first board on top. For `Board RGB`, `Over` simply compiles the first board.
- For `Fmap` we infer the type of the map by inferring the type of the functional argument to `Fmap`, using the capabilities provided by `O`. We then emit the bridging code for the `Fmap`, compiled from the reified functional argument, and call the relevant compilation scheme for the sub-board's type.

The compilation scheme for `Board Bool` has one extra inherited attribute, a color to use to draw `True` values. The primitive `Polygon`, which is always of type `Board Bool`, is translated into a **colorsplat** of the pre-computed `True` color onto a pre-allocated backing board that is initialized to the `False` color.

The key trick in the compiler is compiling a `Fmap` which translates a `Board Bool` into a `Board RGB` (or `Board RGBA`). For example

```
( Fmap f (Polygon (...) :: Board Bool) ) :: Board RGB
```

f here has type `O Bool -> O RGB`. To compile the inner `Board Bool` syntax tree, we need to compute the `True` (or foreground) color, and `False` (or background) color. To find these colors, we simply apply `f` to `True`, and also apply `f` to `False`, giving the two colors present on the board.

9   Interpreting ChalkBoard IR

The ChalkBoard IR is interpreted by the ChalkBoard Back End (CBBE). This CBBE is run in a separate thread from the rest of ChalkBoard. After it has been initialized, it waits on an `MVar` (a type of concurrency "mailbox" used in concurrent Haskell programs) for lists of CBIR instructions from the compiler.

These CBIR instructions are then expanded and executed inside OpenGL. After these instructions are executed, a specified final board is printed out onto the screen by the CBBE. A new set of instructions can then be passed to the CBBE in order to repeat the process. Any of the boards can also be saved to a file using the `save` CBIR instruction.

The concept of a `Board` in ChalkBoard translates roughly into an OpenGL texture inside the CBBE. For each new buffer that is allocated in the CBIR instructions, a new OpenGL texture is created in the CBBE. These new textures can have a variety of internal formats based on the color depth needed by the board (Luminance, RGB, or RGBA) and either have an initial color specified by the CBIR instruction or an initial image that is read in from a specified image file.

These textures can then be texture-mapped onto one another in order to create the effects of `buffersplat` in the CBIR. The preferred way to do this is using the OpenGL Framebuffer object, or FBO. The FBO saves a lot of overhead by allowing images to be rendered straight into a texture instead of onto the screen, from which images would need to be copied back into a texture. When splatting one board onto another, the back or destination texture is attached to the current color attachment point of the FBO, and then the front or source texture is simply texture-mapped on top of it using the `pointmaps` specified in the CBIR instruction. The resulting image is automatically rendered into the destination texture. There is no additional copying necessary because the effects have already been stored in the destination texture directly.

To support older graphics cards and drivers, an alternate method to using FBOs is also implemented. The main difference between the methods is that drawing in the alternative method must be done to the default screen Framebuffer and then copied back out into the appropriate destination texture using `glCopyTexImage`. Because we use double buffering, the images are drawn to the buffer and then copied out without ever being swapped onto the screen. In this way, the actual step-by-step drawing is still invisible to the user but will take considerably longer than when using FBOs because the resulting image structure must be copied back out into the destination texture.

As an example of the performance difference between the two methods, we wrote a small micro-benchmark, called ChalkMark, to stress test `splatbuffer` by rendering 5000 triangles onto a buffer 100 times. When running ChalkMark on a OSX 10.5 with an NVIDIA GeForce 8600M GT running OpenGL 2.0, the CBBE currently achieves about 38,000 `splatbuffer` commands per second when using an FBO, versus about 11,000 `splatbuffer` commands per second when using the alternative `glCopyTexImage`. Even as we further tune the CBBE, we expect the difference between the two methods to remain this significant. Thankfully, most systems today that would use ChalkBoard should have graphics cards with FBO support, with the `glCopyTexImage` method providing only backwards compatibility.

The `colorsplat` CBIR instruction also uses these two methods for its implementation in the CBBE. It works in much the same way as the `buffersplat` instruction except that a simple, colored polygon is drawn over the destination texture instead of texture-mapping a second source texture onto it. This removes the needless overhead of allocating extra 1x1 texture boards just to use as basic colors.

Though there remains considerable scope for optimizing the use of the OpenGL pipeline, and there also are many improvements that could be made to our ChalkBoard compiler, we have found the current performance is more than sufficient for simple animations.

10 Related Work

Functional image generation has a rich history, and there have been many previous image description languages for functional languages. Early work includes Reade [9], where he illustrates the combinational nature of functional programming using a character picture DSL in ML, resulting in ASCII art, Peter Henderson's functional geometry [11], Kavi Arya's functional animation [12], and more recently Findler and Flatt's slide preparation toolkit [13]. Functional languages are also used as a basis for a number of innovative GUI systems, the most influential one being the Fudgets toolkit [14]. ChalkBoard instead concerns itself with image generation and not GUIs, and intentionally leaves unaddressed the issues of interactivity and interactivity abstractions.

Elliott has been working on functional graphics and image generation for many years resulting in a number of systems, including TBAG [15], Fran [16] Pan[17] and Vertigo [18]. The aims of these projects are aligned with ChalkBoard—making it easier to express patterns (sometimes in 2D, sometimes in 3D) using functional programs and embedded domain specific languages, and to aggressively optimize and compile these embedded languages. Elliott's ongoing work has certainly been influential to us, and ChalkBoard starts from the basic combinators provided by Pan. The main difference from the user's point of view is the adoption of the ability to aggressively optimize and compile these EDSLs for faster execution.

There are a number of imperative style interfaces to graphic systems in Haskell. Hudak [10] used the HGL graphics Library, which exposes the basic imperative drawing primitives of Win32 and X11, allowing students to animate basic shapes and patterns. On top of this imperative base, Hudak shows how to build purely functional graphics and animations. OpenGL, GLUT and other standard graphics systems are also available to Haskell programmers, through FFI layers provided on `hackage.haskell.org`. The issue remains that these libraries behave like imperative graphics libraries.

11 Conclusion and Future Work

We have developed an OpenGL-based accelerator for a simple domain specific language for describing images. The language supports basic shapes, transparency, and color images, and our implementation also provides import and export of images in popular image formats. Our system generates images successfully and quickly, giving a many-fold improvement over our previous implementation of ChalkBoard.

In order to capture our DSL, we needed to invent our observable object O, and create a small, functor-like algebra for it. This idiom appears to be both general and useful, and merits further study. Lifting this idea into the space of applicative functors [8] is an obvious next step.

Our implementation has many possible improvements and enhancements. In the current ChalkBoard compilation scheme, we do not make use of the `buffersplat` primitive, but we expect to do so in the near future as we continue to enhance our compiler. Specifically, we will use data reification [7] to allow the observation of sharing of boards and other intermediate values, and `buffersplat` will allow us to compile this sharing into CBIR. There are a number of interesting compilation tradeoffs to explore here.

We intentionally chose OpenGL as a well-supported target platform. Most modern graphics cards are independently programmable beyond what is offered in OpenGL, through interfaces like OpenCL or CUDA. We use OpenGL because it offers the hardware support for what we specially want—fast polygon rendering—rather than using general computation engines for polygon pushing. In the future, we will consider in what way we can use these additional computational offerings while at the same time retaining the fast polygon support.

We want to use ChalkBoard for drawing educational animations. Right now, a `Board` is a two-dimensional abstract object. Could we make it a three-dimensional object with time as the third dimension, and build on the ideas from functional reactive programming (FRP) [19]? If we limit ourselves to only animations, and not reactivity, could we simplify the current complexities and challenges surrounding FRP events, and build a small animation language on top of ChalkBoard? In particular, we are interested in describing animations that are performed on streaming video sources.

We believe that ChalkBoard is a viable and useful research platform for experimenting with applied functional programming. All the diagrams in this paper that did not require font support were rendered using ChalkBoard. The version of ChalkBoard discussed in this paper is available on the Haskell package server hackage, and development continues on the next version.

Acknowledgments

We would like to thank the members of CSDL at KU, and the IFL referees for useful and detailed feedback. We would especially like to thank Conal Elliott, who both provided a starting point for this work, and extensive feedback and comments about the paper and the research direction.

References

1. Peyton Jones, S. (ed.): Haskell 98 Language and Libraries – The Revised Report. Cambridge University Press, Cambridge (2003)
2. cairo, http://www.cairographics.org/

3. The Glasgow Haskell Compiler, http://haskell.org/ghc/
4. Elliott, C.: Functional images. In: The Fun of Programming. Cornerstones of Computing, Palgrave (March 2003)
5. Gill, A., Hutton, G.: The worker/wrapper transformation. Journal of Functional Programming 19(2), 227–251 (2009)
6. Peyton Jones, S., Vytiniotis, D., Weirich, S., Washburn, G.: Simple unification-based type inference for gadts. In: ICFP 2006: Proceedings of the eleventh ACM SIGPLAN international conference on Functional programming, pp. 50–61. ACM, New York (2006)
7. Gill, A.: Type-safe observable sharing in Haskell. In: Proceedings of the 2009 ACM SIGPLAN Haskell Symposium (September 2009)
8. McBride, C., Patterson, R.: Applicative programing with effects. Journal of Functional Programming 16(6) (2006)
9. Reade, C.: Elements of functional programming. Addison-Wesley, Wokingham (1989)
10. Hudak, P.: The Haskell school of expression: learning functional programming through multimedia. Cambridge University Press, New York (2000)
11. Henderson, P.: Functional geometry. In: LFP 1982: Proceedings of the 1982 ACM symposium on LISP and functional programming, pp. 179–187. ACM, New York (1982)
12. Arya, K.: Processes in a functional animation system. In: FPCA 1989: Proceedings of the fourth international conference on Functional programming languages and computer architecture, pp. 382–395. ACM, New York (1989)
13. Findler, R.B., Flatt, M.: Slideshow: functional presentations. J. Funct. Program. 16(4-5), 583–619 (2006)
14. Carlsson, M., Hallgren, T.: Fudgets: a graphical user interface in a lazy functional language. In: FPCA 1993: Proceedings of the conference on Functional programming languages and computer architecture, pp. 321–330. ACM, New York (1993)
15. Elliott, C., Schechter, G., Yeung, R., Abi-Ezzi, S.: TBAG: A high level framework for interactive, animated 3D graphics applications. In: SIGGRAPH (1994)
16. Elliott, C.: From functional animation to sprite-based display. In: Gupta, G. (ed.) PADL 1999. LNCS, vol. 1551, p. 61. Springer, Heidelberg (1999)
17. Elliott, C., Finne, S., de Moor, O.: Compiling embedded languages. Journal of Functional Programming 13(2) (2003)
18. Elliott, C.: Programming graphics processors functionally. In: Proceedings of the 2004 Haskell Workshop. ACM Press, New York (2004)
19. Elliott, C., Hudak, P.: Functional reactive animation. In: International Conference on Functional Programming (1997)

Implementing Fusion-Equipped Parallel Skeletons by Expression Templates

Kiminori Matsuzaki[1] and Kento Emoto[2]

[1] School of Information,
Kochi University of Technology, Japan
`matsuzaki.kiminori@kochi-tech.ac.jp`
[2] Graduate School of Information Science and Technology,
University of Tokyo, Japan
`emoto@ipl.t.u-tokyo.ac.jp`

Abstract. Developing efficient parallel programs is more difficult and complicated than developing sequential ones. Skeletal parallelism is a promising methodology for easy parallel programming in which users develop parallel programs by composing ready-made components called parallel skeletons. We developed a parallel skeleton library *SkeTo* that provides parallel skeletons implemented in C++ and MPI for distributed-memory environments. In the new version of the library, the implementation of the parallel skeletons for lists is improved so that the skeletons equip themselves with fusion optimization. The optimization mechanism is implemented based on the programming technique called expression templates. In this paper, we illustrate the improved design and implementation of parallel skeletons for lists in the SkeTo library.

Keywords: Skeletal parallelism, fusion transformation, list skeletons, expression templates, template meta-programming.

1 Introduction

Hardware environments for parallel computing are now widely available. The popularization and growth of multicore CPUs call for more parallelism to utilize the potential of the hardware. Developing parallel programs, however, is more difficult and complex than developing sequential ones due to, for example, data distribution, communication, and load balancing.

Skeletal Parallelism [1] is a promising methodology for this problem. In the skeletal parallelism, parallel programs are developed by composing ready-made components, called *parallel skeletons*, which are abstract computational patterns often used in parallel programs. Parallel skeletons conceal many details of parallelism in their implementation and, thus, allow for the development of parallel programs as if they were sequential programs. This paper considers parallel skeletons for data-parallel computations in which large amounts of data are processed in parallel.

M.T. Morazán and S.-B. Scholz (Eds.): IFL 2009, LNCS 6041, pp. 72–89, 2010.
© Springer-Verlag Berlin Heidelberg 2010

Our group has intensively studied skeletal parallelism for data-parallel computations since the late 90's. We have developed several methods for deriving skeletal parallel programs and for optimizing skeletal programs using fusion transformation [2] based on the constructive algorithmic theory [3]. To make these results easily available, we have developed a parallel skeleton library named *SkeTo* [4]: the name is from the abbreviation of <u>*Ske*</u>*leton Library in* <u>*To*</u>*kyo* and it also means helper or supporter in Japanese. Three important features of the SkeTo library are:

- The library is implemented in standard C++ and MPI (Message Passing Interface), and we can widely use the library on distributed-memory environments as well as shared-memory ones. Users who know C++ can use the library without learning another language or library for parallel programming.
- The library provides parallel skeletons for data-parallel computation. Supported data structures are lists (one-dimensional arrays), matrices (two-dimensional arrays), and trees. Parallel skeletons over these data structures have similar interfaces.
- The library provides a mechanism of optimizing skeletal programs based on fusion transformation [5].

The SkeTo library version 0.3beta was released in January 2007. After this release, some problems were found that needed be resolved and the new version 1.0 of the SkeTo library was developed. Two important improvements of the library are:

- With the old version, users had to select the proper skeleton for their specific situation (e.g., a skeleton to overwrite lists). In the new version, selections are automatically done by the library.
- In the old version, the fusion optimization was implemented in OpenC++ [6]– a meta-programming language for C++. OpenC++ is now obsolete. In the new version, the fusion optimization mechanism is implemented using standard C++ in conjunction with the meta-programming technique called *expression templates* [7]. In addition, more powerful fusion rules than those of the old version are implemented.

The SkeTo library is available for several environments. In terms of the OS, it is available for Linux, Mac OS X, and Windows with cygwin; in terms of the Compiler, it is available for GCC versions 3.4 and 4.3, and Intel Compilers 9.1 and 11.1; in terms of the MPI library, it is available for mpich and OpenMPI.

This paper discusses the design and the implementation of the parallel list skeletons in the SkeTo library. The focus is on the self-optimization mechanism implemented with expression templates. The rest of the paper is organized as follows. Section 2 presents the sequential and the parallel definitions of the list skeletons provided in the SkeTo library and discusses how to optimize skeletal programs using fusion transformation. The implementation of the parallel list skeletons is discussed in Section 3. Section 4 evaluates the performance of the SkeTo library using two examples. Related work is reviewed in Section 5 and concluding remarks are presented in Section 6.

$$\mathsf{generate}(f,n) = [f(0), f(1), \ldots, f(n-1)]$$

$$\mathsf{map}(f,[a_0, a_1, \ldots, a_{n-1}]) = [f(a_0), f(a_1), \ldots, f(a_{n-1})]$$

$$\mathsf{zipw}(f,[a_0, a_1, \ldots, a_{n-1}],[b_0, b_1, \ldots, b_{n-1}]) = [f(a_0, b_0), f(a_1, b_1), \ldots, f(a_{n-1}, b_{n-1})]$$

$$\mathsf{reduce}(\oplus,[a_0, a_1, \ldots, a_{n-1}]) = a_0 \oplus a_1 \oplus \cdots \oplus a_{n-1}$$

$$\mathsf{scan}(\oplus, e, [a_0, a_1, \ldots, a_{n-1}], ptr) = [e, e \oplus a_0, \ldots, e \oplus a_0 \oplus a_1 \oplus \cdots \oplus a_{n-2}]$$
$$\text{where } ptr \leftarrow e \oplus a_0 \oplus a_1 \oplus \cdots \oplus a_{n-2} \oplus a_{n-1}$$

$$\mathsf{scanr}(\oplus, e, [a_0, a_1, \ldots, a_{n-1}], ptr) = [a_1 \oplus \cdots \oplus a_{n-2} \oplus a_{n-1} \oplus e, \ldots, a_{n-1} \oplus e, e]$$
$$\text{where } ptr \leftarrow a_0 \oplus a_1 \oplus \cdots \oplus a_{n-2} \oplus a_{n-1} \oplus e$$

$$\mathsf{shift}_{\gg}(e, [a_0, a_1, \ldots, a_{n-1}], ptr) = [e, a_0, \ldots, a_{n-2}] \quad \text{where } ptr \leftarrow a_{n-1}$$

$$\mathsf{shift}_{\ll}(e, [a_0, a_1, \ldots, a_{n-1}], ptr) = [a_1, \ldots, a_{n-1}, e] \quad \text{where } ptr \leftarrow a_0$$

Fig. 1. The sequential definition of list skeletons. Updates of values through pointers are denoted by $ptr \leftarrow a$ to make the definition consistent with the implementation in the SkeTo library.

2   Parallel List Skeletons in the SkeTo Library

The parallel skeletons provided in the SkeTo library are computational patterns in the Bird-Meertens Formalism (BMF) [3] that was originally studied for sequential programming. This section defines the parallel list skeletons from two viewpoints: the sequential definition from the user's point of view and the parallel definition from the implementer's point of view. This sections also discuss how to apply fusion transformation to optimize programs with parallel list skeletons.

2.1   Sequential Definition of List Skeletons

Figure 1 shows some of the list skeletons available in the SkeTo library. Users develop their programs based on this sequential definition.

Skeletons generate, map, and zipw are element-wise computational patterns. Skeleton generate(f, n) returns a list of length n whose elements are the results of the function f applied to the indices $[0, \ldots, n-1]$. Skeleton map(f, as) applies the function f to each element of the list as. Skeleton zipw(f, as, bs) applies function f to each pair of corresponding elements of the lists as and bs.

Skeleton reduce$(\oplus, as)$ computes the reduction of the list as with the associative binary operator $\oplus$. Skeleton scan$(\oplus, e, as, ptr)$ computes accumulation on the list as from the left to the right (also called prefix-sums) with the associative binary operator $\oplus$. The accumulation starts at e, and the fully accumulated result is returned through the pointer ptr. Skeleton scanr$(\oplus, e, as, ptr)$ accumulates from the right to the left.

Skeleton shift$_{\gg}(e, as, ptr)$ (`shiftr` in the program code) returns a list whose elements are shifted to the right, where the leftmost value is e and the original rightmost value is returned through ptr. Skeleton shift$_{\ll}(e, as, ptr)$ (`shiftl` in the program code) is a shift computation from the right to the left.

$\mathsf{generate}(f, n)$
  $= \mathbf{let}\ bs_i = \mathsf{generate}_{\mathrm{local}}(f, \lceil i * n/p \rceil, \lceil (i+1) * n/p \rceil - 1)$ for $i \in [0, p-1]$
    $\mathbf{in}\ [bs_0, \ldots, bs_{p-1}]$

$\mathsf{map}(f, [as_0, \ldots, as_{p-1}])$
  $= \mathbf{let}\ bs_i = \mathsf{map}_{\mathrm{local}}(f, as_i)$ for $i \in [0, p-1]$
    $\mathbf{in}\ [bs_0, \ldots, bs_{p-1}]$

$\mathsf{zipw}(f, [as_0, \ldots, as_{p-1}], [bs_0, \ldots, bs_{p-1}])$
  $= \mathbf{let}\ cs_i = \mathsf{zipw}_{\mathrm{local}}(f, as_i, bs_i)$ for $i \in [0, p-1]$
    $\mathbf{in}\ [cs_0, \ldots, cs_{p-1}]$

$\mathsf{reduce}(\oplus, [as_0, \ldots, as_{p-1}])$
  $= \mathbf{let}\ b_i = \mathsf{reduce}_{\mathrm{local}}(\oplus, as_i)$ for $i \in [0, p-1]$
    $\mathbf{in}\ \mathsf{reduce}_{\mathrm{global}}(\oplus, [b_0, \ldots, b_{p-1}])$

$\mathsf{scan}(\oplus, e, [as_0, \ldots, as_{p-1}], ptr)$
  $= \mathbf{let}\ bs_i = \mathsf{scan}_{\mathrm{local}}(\oplus, \iota_{\oplus}, as_i, c_i)$ for $i \in [0, p-1]$
    $[d_0, \ldots, d_{p-1}] = \mathsf{scan}_{\mathrm{global}}(\oplus, e, [c_0, \ldots, c_{p-1}], ptr)$
    $es_i = \mathsf{map}_{\mathrm{local}}((d_i \oplus), bs_i)$ for $i \in [0, p-1]$
    $\mathbf{in}\ [es_0, \ldots, es_{p-1}]$

$\mathsf{shift}_{\gg}(e, [as_0, \ldots, as_{p-1}], ptr)$
  $= \mathbf{let}\ b_i = last(as_i)$ for $i \in [0, p-1]$
    $[c_0, \ldots, c_{p-1}] = \mathsf{shift}_{\gg \mathrm{global}}(e, [b_0, \ldots, b_{p-1}], ptr)$
    $ds_i = \mathsf{shift}_{\gg \mathrm{local}}(c_i, as_i, NULL)$ for $i \in [0, p-1]$
    $\mathbf{in}\ [ds_0, \ldots, ds_{p-1}]$

Fig. 2. The parallel definition of list skeletons based on the sequential definition given in Figure 1. The subscript "local" indicates that a skeleton is used as a local computation and the subscript "global" indicates that a skeleton is used as a global computation. The definition of $\mathsf{generate}_{\mathrm{local}}$ is a bit different from that in Figure 1. It takes the first and the last indices of the list as input. Function $last$ returns the last element of the given list and $\iota_{\oplus}$ is the unit of the binary operator $\oplus$.

2.2 Parallel Definition of List Skeletons

The SkeTo library is a parallel skeleton library for distributed-memory environments. We adopt the SPMD (Single Program/Multiple Data) computation model in which each process has its own data. In this model, we implement a list as a nested list whose elements are local lists allocated by processes. More concretely, in an environment with p processes we represent a list of n elements $a_0, a_1, \ldots, a_{n-1}$ as follows.

$$[[a_0, \ldots, a_{\lceil n/p \rceil - 1}], \ldots, [a_{\lceil (p-1)*n/p \rceil}, \ldots, a_{n-1}]]$$

The parallel implementation of the list skeletons consists of local computation parts in which each process computes independently with its local lists and of global computation parts for which inter-process communication occurs. Figure 2 shows the definition of the list skeletons for parallel implementation. We omit the definition of scanr (and $\mathsf{shift}_{\ll}$), since it is similar to that of scan (and $\mathsf{shift}_{\gg}$).

Since skeletons generate, map, and zipw are element-wise computational patterns, they can be easily implemented with local computations. Skeleton reduce first performs local reduction on each local list, and then reduces the local results with a global computation. Skeleton scan is implemented in three steps: (1) we compute scan for each local list, (2) compute scan globally on the results of the local scans, and (3) update the results of local scan with local map for each local list. Skeleton shift$_{\gg}$ is implemented by global shift$_{\gg}$ applied to the last elements of local lists followed by local shift$_{\gg}$ applied to each local list.

Note that there exists another three-step implementation of scan that consists of local reduce, global scan, and local scan. This implementation is not used, because applying the fusion transformation to the local scan is, in general, complicated.

2.3   Target of Fusion Optimization

In the skeletal parallelism, users develop parallel programs by composing several skeletons. One potential drawback of such a methodology is the overhead caused by many calls of skeletons with intermediate data passed between skeletons. The fusion transformation is an important optimization technique that removes such overhead, and there have been several studies on this topic [8, 9, 2, 5]. We will review these studies in Section 5.

In the new version of the SkeTo library, we implemented the fusion transformation focusing on realistic and important parts of skeletal programs. The idea is to fuse the local computation parts only, instead of applying the fusion transformation over whole skeletons. As we defined in Figure 2 the skeletons are implemented with local computations and global computations, and we apply the fusion transformation to the consecutive local computations between global computations. Figure 3 shows an example of the targets of the fusion transformation. It is worth noting that almost all the skeletal programs to which the fusion mechanism of the old version of the SkeTo library can be applied to can be optimized. Moreover, programs can be optimized using the scan and shift skeletons.

Now the targets of the fusion transformation are formalized. First, in the implementation of the shift$_{\gg}$ and shift$_{\ll}$ skeletons the global shift computation is moved before the local shift computation. Based on this fact and on the definition of skeletons in Figure 2, observe that the local computations between global computations have a specific form: almost element-wise computations (map, zipw, shift$_{\gg}$, and shift$_{\ll}$) occur in some order first and then scanning on local lists (reduce or scan) may follow. Therefore, there is a fusion transformation implementation for this specific form. Implementation details are given in Section 3.

The fusion transformation considered here is known as the loop-fusion optimization. It is worth noting that loop-fusion often makes a program faster when the loop computations are rather small. Sometimes, however, loop fusion makes the program slower due to the increased number of registers needed.

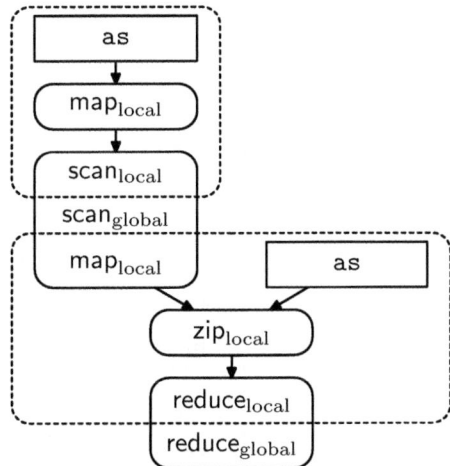

Fig. 3. Two targets of the fusion transformation (denoted by dashed lines). After the fusion transformation, the number of local computations (loops) decreases from 5 to 2. You may think that this example is artificial, but this combination of skeletons comes from parallelization of a very common form of recursive functions on lists [10].

3   Implementation of Parallel List Skeletons in the SkeTo Library

Before discussing the implementation details, example programs to compute the variance of n values $[a_0, \ldots, a_{n-1}]$ (where $a_i = i^5$ mod 100) using the following definition below are displayed.

$$ave = \sum_{i=0}^{n-1} a_i / n$$
$$var = \sum_{i=0}^{n-1} (a_i - ave)^2 / n$$

Figure 4 shows a program with simple for-loops, Figure 5 shows a program with the SkeTo library, and Figure 6 shows a program with the STL library.

3.1   Interface

Distributed List Structure. In the SkeTo library, distributed lists are provided as instances of the template class `dist_list`. Data distribution is concealed in the constructors of the `dist_list` class and users do not need to know how the elements of a list are distributed to the processes.

One difference of the new implementation from the previous one is that the real buffer of a distributed list is managed with its reference count in another class `dist_list_buffer` to which the `dist_list` class has a pointer. With this change, we can implement automatic allocation/release of memory and automatic dispatching to specialized skeletons that overwrite the results on the inputs. We illustrate the difference with an example. In the previous version, users had to call `delete` explicitly to release the memory used by the distributed lists as follows:

```
#include <iostream>
using namespace std;
const int n = 10000000;

int main(int, char**) {
  int *as = new int[n];
  double ave = 0;
  for (int i = 0; i < n; ++i) {
    as[i] = i*i*i*i % 100;
    ave += as[i];
  } ave /= n;

  double var = 0;
  for (int i = 0; i < n; ++i) {
    var += (as[i]-ave) * (as[i]-ave);
  } var /= n;

  cout << var << endl;
  delete [] as;
}
```

Fig. 4. A program using for-loops

```
#include <iostream>
#include <sketo/sketo.h>
#include <sketo/list_skeletons.h>
const int n = 10000000;

using namespace std;
using namespace sketo;
using namespace sketo::list_skeletons;

struct gen
  : public functions::base<int (int)> {
  int operator()(int i) const {
    return i*i*i*i % 100;
  }
};

int sketo::main(int, char**) {
  dist_list<int> as;
  as = generate(n, gen());
  double ave
    = reduce(plus<double>(), as) / n;

  double var
    = reduce(plus<double>(),
        map(functions::square<double>(),
          map(bind2nd(minus<double>(), ave),
            as))) / n;

  sketo::cout << var << endl;
}
```

Fig. 5. A program using the SkeTo library

```
#include <iostream>
#include <vector>
#include <functional>
#include <algorithm>
#include <numeric>
using namespace std;

const int n = 10000000;

struct gen {
  mutable int index;
  gen() : index(0) {};
  double operator()() const {
    const int i = index++;
    return i*i*i*i % 100;
  }
};

struct minus_ave_sqr {
  double ave;
  minus_ave_sqr(double ave) : ave(ave) { }
  double operator()(double x) const {
    return (x - ave) * (x - ave);
  }
};

int main() {
  vector<double> as(n);

  generate(as.begin(), as.end(), gen());
  double ave
    = accumulate(as.begin(), as.end(),
                 0.0, plus<double>()) / n;

  transform(as.begin(), as.end(),
            as.begin(),
    minus_ave_sqr(ave));
  double var
    = accumulate(as.begin(), as.end(),
                 0.0, plus<double>()) / n;

  cout << var << endl;
}
```

Fig. 6. A program using STL

```
dist_list<int> *as = new dist_list<int>(array, size);
dist_list<int> *bs = list_skeletons::map(f, as);
   ...
delete bs;
delete as;
```

In the new version of the SkeTo library, the `dist_list` class is responsible for memory management and, thus, programmers can simplify as follows:

```
dist_list<int> as(array, size);
dist_list<int> bs = list_skeletons::map(f, as);
   ...
```

Parallel Skeletons. The parallel list skeletons that manipulate distributed lists are defined in the name space `list_skeletons`. The interfaces of the parallel list skeletons are essentially the same as before.

In the SkeTo library, the argument functions for parallel skeletons are function objects (objects that implement an `operator()` method). With function objects instead of function pointers, compilers can find the concrete definition of the functions and optimize the function calls by inline expansion. The inline expansion works quite well when programs are the composition of several small components. Function objects passed to parallel skeletons are instances of classes that inherit one of the template classes `sketo::functions::base` for the declaration of the types of the arguments and the return value. For example, a function object that takes a value of type A and returns a value of type B should inherit the template class `sketo::functions::base<B (A)>`. These base classes are implemented in a similar way to the `boost::function`. The reason for reimplementation is that `boost::function` cannot be inline-expanded due to its implementation. For the same reason, anonymous functions, `boost::lambda`, have problems of efficiency. It is worth noting that the function objects provided by `<functional>` in STL are available in SkeTo.

The most important change to the interface of parallel list skeletons is that we only provide a single function for each skeleton. In the previous implementation, we provided two or more functions for a skeleton. For example, for the map skeleton there were three functions: normal `map` function with two arguments, `map` function with three arguments, and specialized implementation `map_ow` for overwriting. In the new version, we unify those implementations into a single interface. In fact, based on the reference count in `dist_list_buffer` and the expression template technique, the library dispatches skeleton calls to specific implementations. The details of the implementation with expression templates are shown in the next subsection.

To illustrate the differences consider the following example. In the previous version, to overwrite the results of `map` onto its inputs a specialized version of the `map` skeleton, namely `map_ow`, had to be used as follows:

```
list_skeletons::map_ow(f, as);
list_skeletons::map_ow(g, as);
v = list_skeletons::reduce(plus, 0, as);.
```

With the new version the code is written as follows:

```
as = list_skeletons::map(f, as);
as = list_skeletons::map(g, as);
v = list_skeletons::reduce(plus, as);.
```

The library automatically selects the specialized code. Furthermore, since the result of the map is dist_list, we can also write it in the following nested way:

```
v = list_skeletons::reduce(plus,
      list_skeletons::map(g,
        list_skeletons::map(f, as)));.
```

3.2   Optimization Mechanism by Expression Templates

The new version of the SkeTo library uses expression templates [7] to implement fusion transformations and uses overwriting for memory reuse. This section introduces the expression template technique and illustrates how the optimization mechanisms are implemented.

Expression Templates. This subsection introduces the meta-programming technique called expression templates [7]. This technique has been used to implement efficient libraries for linear-algebraic computations [11] and for domain-specific regular expressions.

When an expression in C++ is evaluated, the sub-expressions are evaluated one by one. Consider evaluating the following code where the variables A, B, C and D are vectors:

```
D = A + B - C;
```

Usually, the sub-expression A + B is evaluated first which generates, E, an intermediate vector. Then the subtraction, E - C, is computed which also generates, F, another intermediate vector. Finally, the vector F is assigned to D.

The use of the expression template technique generates certain structures representing the computation (often tree structures like abstract syntax trees) and delay the computation until the results are required. By delaying the computation, efficient code can be generated for the whole expression. In the example above, an instance of template type plus<vec,vec> is generated for the sub-expression A + B, then the right-hand side of the expression is given as an instance of template type minus<plus<vec,vec>,vec>, and finally the member function

```
vec::operator=(minus<plus<vec,vec>,vec>)
```

is called. Proper code is generated for these member functions with the help of the template structures. In the example above, a fast implementation corresponding to the following loop is generated:

```
for (int i = 0; i < n; i++) { D[i] = A[i] + B[i] - C[i]; }.
```

Implementation of Fusion Transformation. In Section 2.3, we stated that the target of the fusion transformation is a set of consecutive local computations between global computations. Due to the lack of type inference in C++, in the new version of the SkeTo, we apply the fusion transformation to local computations that are written as a single expression. For example, in the following code from Figure 5

```
double var
  = reduce(plus<double>(),
      map(functions::square<double>(),
        map(bind2nd(minus<double>(), ave), as))) / n;
```

the two `maps` and the `reduce` are the target of the fusion transformation.

In the implementation, template types for local map, local zipw, local shift$_{\gg}$, and so on are defined. For example, the template object for local map, `ls_mapobj`, is defined as follows:

```
template <typename F, typename AS>
struct ls_mapobj {
  F f;
  const AS as;
  ls_mapobj(const F &f, const AS &as) : f(f), as(as) { }

  typedef typename F::result_type element_type;
  element_type local_get(int i) const { return f(as.local_get(i)); }

    ...
};.
```

This template object stores the function object and the argument list, and the computation of the `map` skeleton is executed in the member function `local_get`. The `map` skeleton just generates this template object as follows:

```
template <typename F, typename AS>
_impl::ls_mapobj<F, AS> map(F f, const AS& as) {
  return _impl::ls_mapobj<F, AS>(f, as);
}.
```

The computation of a parallel skeleton is delayed until either reduce, scan, scanr or an assignment to a list occurs. For example, in the implementation of reduce, the computation of skeletons is triggered through the member function `local_get` as shown in the following code:

```
A result = as.local_get(0);
{
  const int n = as.get_local_size();
  for (int i = 1; i < n; ++i) {
    result = oplus(result, as.local_get(i));
  }
}.
```

To illustrate how the fusion transformation with expression templates is done consider, once again, the sample code above. The skeleton `reduce` takes a value of type

```
ls_mapobj<G,ls_mapobj<F,dist_list<double> > >
```

where **F** represents the type of bind2nd(minus<double>(),ave), and **G** represents the type of functions::square<double>(). Then, in the computation of
reduce, the local computation represented by two ls_mapobjs are fused to the
local reduction because the local_get functions of the two ls_mapobj are called
in a nested way. After fusion optimization and inline expansion, the main loop
of the generated code becomes the same as the following simple loop:

```
double result = (as[0] - ave) * (as[0] - ave);
for (int i = 1; i < n; ++i) {
  result = result + (as[i] - ave) * (as[i] - ave);
}.
```

The performance effects of the fusion transformation are discussed in Section 4.
    The current implementation of the fusion transformation for programs includ-
ing shift$_\gg$ or shift$_\ll$ has room for improvement. For example, for the following
code

```
bs = map(f, shiftr(e, as));
```

the current implementation generates code corresponding to the following loop.

```
for (int i = 0; i < n; ++i) {
  bs[i] = f( (i==0) ? e : as[i-1] );
}
```

However, the following loop is faster in many cases.

```
bs[0] = f(e);
for (int i = 1; i < n; ++i) {
  bs[i] = f( as[i-1] );
}
```

This improvement of the fusion transformation is a part of our future work.

Implementation of Specialized Skeletons. Overwriting the results of parallel skeletons onto their inputs is an important optimization in terms of memory
consumption and the cost of memory allocation/release. The implementation of
this optimization is also attained by expression templates.
    A single line of the skeletal programs usually has the following form.

```
as = skeleton_calls;
```

With the expression templates, the right-hand side *skeleton_calls* forms a tree
structure representing the skeleton calls. The following template member function was added to dist_list

```
template <typename BS> void operator=(const BS &bs);
```

and the dispatch mechanism was implemented in the member function.
    The results of skeletons are overwritten when all the following conditions hold
(where **as** denotes the distributed list on the left-hand side):

1. The buffer is already allocated for **as**.
2. The length of **as** is the same as that of resulting list of the right-hand side.
3. The reference count in **as** is greater by one than the number of occurrences of **as** on the right-hand side. Note that the reference count of **as** increases if it appears on the right-hand side, and this condition means that **as** does not share the array with other variables.
4. The tree structure has no shift$_\gg$/shift$_\ll$ applied to **as** except for the root.

Note that in condition 4 we permit the inclusion of scan and scanr because they allocate another distributed list.

Revealing Errors in Programs Developed with Expression Templates.
Expression templates are an important programming technique for implementing efficient libraries. However, a problem occurs when we use expression templates for implementing a skeleton library: unreadable error messages appear when we fail to compile template programs. It is worth noting that the following discussion is relevant to the use of GCC. The Intel Compiler checks errors before expanding expression templates and, thus, the following "tricks" are unnecessary.

When using expression templates for linear-algebraic computations, the primary operators used in user programs are + and * and, as such, programs have fewer errors. However, in skeletal parallel programming, users can specify any function for parallel skeletons and thus user programs tend to have errors. For example, in the code displayed in Figure 5, a programmer may mistakenly pass a unary function, like square<double>(), as the first argument to bind2nd. This single mistake causes 20 lines of error messages. A sample error message line is a line:.

```
sketo/list_skeletons_with_fusion.h: In member function 'typename F::
result_type sketo::_impl::ls_mapobj<F, AS>::local_get(int) const [
with F = sketo::functions::square<double>, AS = sketo::_impl::
ls_mapobj<std::binder2nd<sketo::functions::square<double> >, sketo::
dist_list<double> >]': .
```

Note that this error is detected inside the library code even though the bug is in the user code. Users not familiar with the implementation details of the SkeTo library cannot determine the reason for this annoying error message.

To resolve this problem, we provide another implementation of the SkeTo library that does not optimize skeletal programs by expression templates. Users can easily switch the implementations: defining a macro __SKETO_NO_FUSION__ at the preprocessing stage is enough and no change to the program code is needed. The bug can easily be found with this alternative library implementation. For the above example, the error messages are reduced to 13 lines and the bug can directly be identified in:

```
variance.cpp:26: error: no matching function for call to 'map(std::
binder2nd<sketo::functions::square<double> >, sketo::dist_list<
double>&)'
```

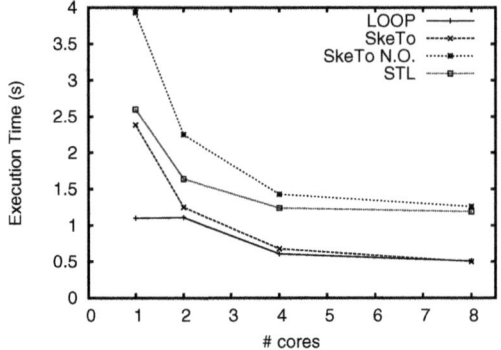

Table 1. The execution time for computing variance (in seconds)

#cores	1	2	4	8
LOOP	1.10	1.11	0.61	0.51
SkeTo	2.38	1.25	0.68	0.50
SkeTo N.O.	3.93	2.25	1.43	1.26
STL	2.60	1.64	1.24	1.19

Fig. 7. The execution time for computing variance

4 Experiments

To evaluate the performance of the SkeTo library, experiments with computing variance (Figures 4, 5, and 6), the bracket matching problem [10], and the N-queen problem were conducted.

Variance computation was used to evaluate the sequential performance, the speed-up, and the overhead of the parallel list skeletons. In the experiments, a list of length 200,000,000 was used. The experiments were carried out on a desktop PC with two Intel Xeon E5430 (2.66GHz, quad-cores) CPUs and 8 GByte memory. The compiler and MPI library were GCC 4.4.0 and mpich 1.2.7p1. Figure 7 and Table 1 show the results of experiments. LOOP indicates the program with simple loops in Figure 4 parallelized with OpenMP, SkeTo indicates the program with the SkeTo library in Figure 5, SkeTo N.O. indicates the same program as SkeTo but no optimization is applied, and STL indicates the program with STL in Figure 6 parallelized with GCC libstdc++ parallel mode [12]. With the fusion optimization using expression templates, the program utilizing SkeTo is optimized so that it achieves almost the same performance as the simple for-loops with OpenMP. It is worth noting that the SkeTo library and the program in Figure 5 are also available on distributed-memory environments. The program without fusion optimization and the program with STL are slower due to the overhead caused by multiple list traversals. Note that the relatively small speedups in this example are due to memory bandwidth saturation.

The bracket matching problem [10] was used to investigate the effects of the fusion optimization using expression templates. The outline of the skeletal program for this problem is the same as that in Figure 3, but the concrete function objects for skeletons are a bit more complicated. The complete definition can be found in [10]. The main part of the program is the first map and scan: the function g'_2 for map is

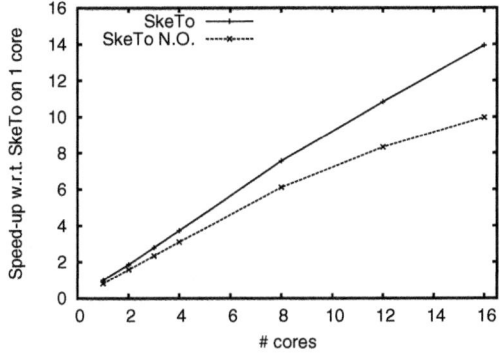

Table 2. The execution time for the bracket matching problem (in seconds)

# core	1	4	8	16
SkeTo	12.26	3.29	1.62	0.88
SkeTo N.O.	15.21	3.94	2.01	1.23

Fig. 8. The speedup for the bracket matching problem

$$g'_2(a) = \textbf{if } isOpen(a) \textbf{ then } ([a], 1, 0)$$
$$\textbf{elseif } isClose(a) \textbf{ then } ([\,], 0, 1)$$
$$\textbf{else } ([\,], 0, 0)$$

and the operator $\otimes$ for scan is

$$(cs_1, n_1, m_1) \otimes (cs_2, n_2, m_2) = \textbf{if } m_1 \geq n_2 \textbf{ then } (cs_1, n_1, m_1 - n_2 + m_2)$$
$$\textbf{else } (cs_1 +\!\!+ drop(m_1, cs_2), n_1 + n_2 - m_1, m_2)$$

where the operator $+\!\!+$ concatenates two lists and the function $drop(m_1, cs_2)$ drops the first m_1 elements from the list cs_2.

In the experiment, the string length is 100,000,000, the different types of brackets is 4, and the maximum nesting of brackets is 10. The hardware environment is a cluster of four PCs with an Intel Core2Quad 2.4GHz CPU and 4 GByte memory connected with Gigabit Ethernet. The compiler and library used are Intel C++ Compiler 9.0 and MPICH 1.2.7p1. The optimized version and the non-optimized version of the skeletal program were executed varying the number of cores from 1 to 16. Table 2 shows the results of the experiments and Figure 8 plots the speed-up with respect to the execution of the optimized version on one core. The optimized version is 20% faster than the non-optimized version independent of the number of cores.

Finally, experiments to evaluate the scalability of the SkeTo library using the 18-Queens problem are presented. The hand-written code using MPI and C developed by Kise et al. [13] (qn24b) and a program with list skeletons using the SkeTo library (SkeTo) are used as benchmarks. The environment is a cluster of PCs with dual Xeon 2.4GHz CPUs and 2GByte memory connected with Gigabit Ethernet, GCC 4.1.2, and mpich 1.2.7p1. Figure 9 and Table 3 show the empirical results.

From these results, we can see that both programs achieve good speedups. In this example, nonoptimized version runs as fast as the optimized version, since

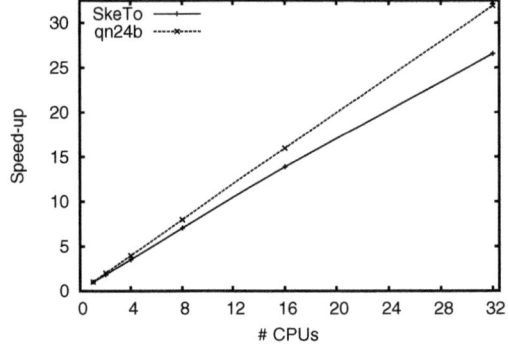

Table 3. The execution time for
18-Queens problems (in seconds)

#CPU	1	4	16	32
SkeTo	554	157	39.9	20.9
qn24b	596	149	37.3	18.7

Fig. 9. The speed-up for 18-Queens problem

almost all the execution time is spent in a single map skeleton. The program
with the SkeTo library shows a bit worse scalability. This is due to the static
scheduling policy of the SkeTo library: the program with the SkeTo library runs
a bit faster on 1 CPU, but the loads may be ill-balanced on many CPUs. In
the future version of the SkeTo library we would like to integrate dynamic load-
balancing.

5   Related Work

Parallel Skeleton Libraries

Several parallel skeleton libraries have been implemented. Since the idea of skeletal parallel programming is closely related to functional programming, there are
several implementations based on functional languages such as Haskell [14], Template Haskell [15], and SML [16].

There are also several implementations or widely used imperative languages
like C, C++, and Java developed for efficiency reasons. For example, Muskel [17]
and eSkel [18] provide parallel skeletons mainly for task-parallel computations;
Muesli [19] provides a two-tier model of task- and data-parallel skeletons; Intel TBB (Thread Building Blocks) [20] is now being widely used for multicore
parallel programming. Among these, Muesli is the skeleton library most related
to the SkeTo library. It provides data-parallel skeletons for lists and matrices
implemented in C++ and MPI (the new version of Muesli also uses OpenMP)
and some task-parallel skeletons. Compared with Muesli, the SkeTo library offers
the advantages of matrix skeletons that are defined based on the theory of constructive algorithmics [21], tree skeletons [22], and the optimization mechanism
based on the fusion transformation.

Instead of developing a new library, providing a parallel implementation to
an existing standard library is another approach to skeletal parallelism. For example, DatTel [23] and MCSTL [12] are parallel implementations for STL (the

standard template library) in C++. In particular, the latter is now integrated into GCC with the name "libstdc++ parallel mode," and is used in the experiments in Section 4.

Optimization of Skeletal Programs by Fusion Transformation

The fusion transformation is an important optimization technique that removes overhead caused by too many skeleton calls with intermediate data between them. There have been several studies on this topic [2, 5, 8, 9, 24, 25].

In the framework proposed by Aldinucci et al. [8], many transformation rules are used to optimize skeletal programs. They considered not only simple rules like map-map fusion, but also complex rules like fusing scan and reduce under certain conditions on operators. The number of optimization rules, however, easily becomes too large and it is unrealistic to implement all of them.

In the previous version of the SkeTo library [5], we implemented a fusion optimization mechanism based on normal forms that characterize data generation/consumption. The fusion rules on those normal forms were proposed in [2]. Though this method is simple and rather easy to implement, the fusion transformation often fails for scan and shift skeletons. Note that the fusion optimization by the expression templates covers almost all the cases that the fusion mechanism in the old version can be applied to.

Single assignment C (SAC) [25] is a programming language with high level array operations. The SAC compiler has a powerful fusion optimization mechanism called with-loop-folding [24], which combines consecutive array operations into a singe one. The basic idea for the fusion transformation is almost the same: to fuse almost element-wise computations. Since the optimization was implemented in the SAC compiler, it supports more powerful optimizations such as high-dimensional arrays, more complicated data movement, and changing the size of arrays.

Expression Templates

In the new implementation of the SkeTo library, we implemented the fusion transformation by the expression template technique. Expression templates are often used in efficient implementations for linear algebraic computation and in domain-specific computations such as those for regular expressions. For the linear algebraic computation, Blitz++ [11] and the uBLAS library in the Boost library[1] are two well-known implementations. As a research-level implementation, NT2 [26] implemented several nontrivial optimizations for parallel linear-algebraic computation with expression templates.

6 Conclusion

This paper discusses the new design and implementation of the parallel list skeletons of the SkeTo library. Based on the parallel definition of the list skeletons, we

---

[1] http://www.crystalclearsoftware.com/cgi-bin/boost_wiki/
wiki.pl?Effective_UBLAS

formalized the target of the fusion transformation as consecutive local computations between global computations. The optimization mechanism in the new version of the SkeTo library was implemented using expression templates. The presented experiments confirm the good performance of the SkeTo library and, in particular, the good performance of the fusion optimization implemented in the new library.

As we stated in Section 3.2, the results of the fusion transformation for the computations with shift skeletons are not the best ones. Emoto et al. [9] proposed an optimization method for those computations with shift skeletons. Implementing this optimization for the SkeTo library is a part of our future work.

References

1. Cole, M.: Algorithmic Skeletons: Structural Management of Parallel Computation. Research Monographs in Parallel and Distributed Computing. MIT Press, Cambridge (1989)
2. Hu, Z., Iwasaki, H., Takeichi, M.: An accumulative parallel skeleton for all. In: Le Métayer, D. (ed.) ESOP 2002. LNCS, vol. 2305, pp. 83–97. Springer, Heidelberg (2002)
3. Bird, R.S.: An introduction to the theory of lists. In: Logic of Programming and Calculi of Discrete Design. NATO ASI Series F, vol. 36, pp. 5–42. Springer, Heidelberg (1987)
4. Matsuzaki, K., Iwasaki, H., Emoto, K., Hu, Z.: A library of constructive skeletons for sequential style of parallel programming. In: InfoScale 2006: Proceedings of the 1st international conference on Scalable information systems. ACM International Conference Proceeding Series, vol. 152. ACM Press, New York (2006)
5. Matsuzaki, K., Kakehi, K., Iwasaki, H., Hu, Z., Akashi, Y.: A fusion-embedded skeleton library. In: Danelutto, M., Vanneschi, M., Laforenza, D. (eds.) Euro-Par 2004. LNCS, vol. 3149, pp. 644–653. Springer, Heidelberg (2004)
6. Chiba, S.: A metaobject protocol for C++. In: Proceedings of OOPSLA 1995, Tenth Annual Conference on Object-Oriented Programming Systems, Languages, and Applications. SIGPLAN Notices, vol. 30, pp. 285–299. ACM Press, New York (1995)
7. Veldhuizen, T.L.: Expression templates. C++ Report 7(5), 26–31 (1995); Reprinted in Lippman, S. (ed.): C++ Gems
8. Aldinucci, M., Gorlatch, S., Lengauer, C., Pelagatti, S.: Towards parallel programming by transformation: the FAN skeleton framework. Parallel Algorithms and Applications 16(2-3), 87–121 (2001)
9. Emoto, K., Matsuzaki, K., Hu, Z., Takeichi, M.: Domain-specific optimization strategy for skeleton programs. In: Kermarrec, A.-M., Bougé, L., Priol, T. (eds.) Euro-Par 2007. LNCS, vol. 4641, pp. 705–714. Springer, Heidelberg (2007)
10. Hu, Z., Takeichi, M., Iwasaki, H.: Diffusion: Calculating efficient parallel programs. In: Proceedings of the 1999 ACM SIGPLAN Workshop on Partial Evaluation and Semantics-Based Program Manipulation (1999)
11. Veldhuizen, T.L.: Arrays in Blitz++. In: Caromel, D., Oldehoeft, R.R., Tholburn, M. (eds.) ISCOPE 1998. LNCS, vol. 1505, pp. 223–230. Springer, Heidelberg (1998)
12. Singler, J., Sanders, P., Putze, F.: The multi-core standard template library. In: Kermarrec, A.-M., Bougé, L., Priol, T. (eds.) Euro-Par 2007. LNCS, vol. 4641, pp. 682–694. Springer, Heidelberg (2007)

13. Kise, K., Katagiri, T., Honda, H., Yuba, T.: Solving the 24-queens problem using MPI on a PC cluster. Technical Report UEC-IS-2004-6, Graduate School of Information Systems, The University of Electro-Communications (2004)
14. Klusik, U., Loogen, R., Priebe, S., Rubio, F.: Implementation skeletons in Eden: Low-effort parallel programming. In: Mohnen, M., Koopman, P. (eds.) IFL 2000. LNCS, vol. 2011, pp. 71–88. Springer, Heidelberg (2001)
15. Hammond, K., Berthold, J., Loogen, R.: Automatic skeletons in Template Haskell. Parallel Processing Letters 13(3), 413–424 (2003)
16. Scaife, N., Horiguchi, S., Michaelson, G., Bristow, P.: A parallel SML compiler based on algorithmic skeletons. Journal of Functional Programming 15(4), 615–650 (2005)
17. Aldinucci, M., Danelutto, M., Dazzi, P.: Muskel: an expandable skeleton environment. Scalable Computing: Practice and Experience 8(4), 325–341 (2007)
18. Benoit, A., Cole, M., Gilmore, S., Hillston, J.: Flexible skeletal programming with eSkel. In: Cunha, J.C., Medeiros, P.D. (eds.) Euro-Par 2005. LNCS, vol. 3648, pp. 761–770. Springer, Heidelberg (2005)
19. Kuchen, H.: A skeleton library. In: Monien, B., Feldmann, R.L. (eds.) Euro-Par 2002. LNCS, vol. 2400, pp. 620–629. Springer, Heidelberg (2002)
20. Reinders, J.: Intel Threading Building Blocks: Outfitting C++ for Multi-core Processor Parallelism. O'Reilly Media, Inc., Sebastopol (2007)
21. Emoto, K., Hu, Z., Kakehi, K., Takeichi, M.: A compositional framework for developing parallel programs on two-dimensional arrays. International Journal of Parallel Programming 35(6), 615–658 (2007)
22. Matsuzaki, K.: Efficient implementation of tree accumulations on distributed-memory parallel computers. In: Shi, Y., van Albada, G.D., Dongarra, J., Sloot, P.M.A. (eds.) ICCS 2007, Part II. LNCS, vol. 4488, pp. 609–616. Springer, Heidelberg (2007)
23. Bischof, H., Gorlatch, S., Leshchinskiy, R.: Generic parallel programming using C++ templates and skeletons. In: Lengauer, C., Batory, D., Consel, C., Odersky, M. (eds.) Domain-Specific Program Generation. LNCS, vol. 3016, pp. 107–126. Springer, Heidelberg (2004)
24. Scholz, S.-B.: With-loop-folding in SAC — condensing consecutive array operations. In: Clack, C., Hammond, K., Davie, T. (eds.) IFL 1997. LNCS, vol. 1467, p. 72. Springer, Heidelberg (1998)
25. Scholz, S.B.: Single assignment C — efficient support for high-level array operations in a functional setting. Journal of Functional Programming 13(6) (2003)
26. Falcou, J., Sérot, J., Pech, L., Lapresté, J.T.: Meta-programming applied to automatic SMP parallelization of linear algebra code. In: Luque, E., Margalef, T., Benítez, D. (eds.) Euro-Par 2008. LNCS, vol. 5168, pp. 729–738. Springer, Heidelberg (2008)

Arity Raising in Manticore

Lars Bergstrom and John Reppy

University of Chicago, Chicago IL 60637, USA
{larsberg,jhr}@cs.uchicago.edu

Abstract. Compilers for polymorphic languages are required to treat values in programs in an abstract and generic way at the source level. The challenges of optimizing the boxing of raw values, flattening of argument tuples, and raising the arity of functions that handle complex structures to reduce memory usage are old ones, but take on newfound import with processors that have twice as many registers. We present a novel strategy that uses both control-flow and type information to provide an arity raising implementation addressing these problems. This strategy is *conservative* — no matter the execution path, the transformed program will not perform extra operations.

1 Introduction

Arity is the number of arguments that a function accepts. The arity raising transformation takes a function of n arguments and turns it into a function of $\geq$ arguments. By increasing the number of arguments to a function, we increase the opportunity for the compiler to store values associated with those arguments in registers instead of in heap-allocated data. Reducing the amount of heap-allocated data both reduces pressure on the garbage collector and removes overhead associated with writing and reading data in memory.

There are two major sources of extra memory allocations that we focus on removing.

1. Raw data, such as integers and floating-point numbers, stored in a heap objects
2. Datatypes and tuples, which package up a set of data into a single structure in memory

Both of these sources of memory allocations and memory access have been shown to be very expensive by Tarditi and Diwan [1]. In fact, the overhead associated with reading and writing a uniform representation and extra checks to see if the garbage collector needs to run often cost more than the garbage collection process itself. In their work, using a simulator to collect instruction counts, they showed that 19-46% of the execution time of a program in Standard ML of New Jersey was spent in tasks related to storage management.

The first source of extra memory allocations is commonly known as *boxing*. By storing raw data into heap objects, the rest of the system does not need to worry about the format of the raw object. The garbage collector treats all values in registers and the stack as pointers and can trace them uniformly. Polymorphic functions operate on values of any type without taking special action based on the underlying object type. But this uniform treatment comes at a cost — allocating and accessing raw data in the heap can

M.T. Morazán and S.-B. Scholz (Eds.): IFL 2009, LNCS 6041, pp. 90–106, 2010.

be very expensive, especially for small and frequently used data. Our implementation of arity raising determines where it is safe to pass the raw object value instead and removes the creation of the box object.

The second source of memory allocations is tuples and datatypes. If the user has created a very deeply nested set of datatype definitions or tuples but functions commonly only need few pieces of data deep within that datatype, it can be expensive to create and traverse the whole structure just to handle those few pieces of data. Our implementation of arity raising determines when only a few pieces of a datatype are being used and allocates and passes just those pieces, rather than the entire structure.

This paper describes a strategy for arity raising that allows the compiler to safely increase the number of parameters to a function and remove allocations due to both boxing operations and data structures. This strategy is *conservative* — it will not change the program in a way that could degrade the performance by introducing extra operations. We restrict ourselves to transforming expressions along a code path without branches. Those transformations move expressions and eliminate matching allocation and selection pairs.

After presenting some preliminary notation we use in our arity raising strategy, in Section 3 we describe the analysis of function bodies. This analysis provides information on when it is useful to transform data stored in heap objects into directly passed parameters. In Section 4, we show how to use the gathered information to transform function definitions and call sites. Following an example of the analysis and transformation, we discuss implementation details of this arity raising strategy within the Manticore compiler. We present performance measurements of our implementation in Section 7 then cover the substantial related work and conclude.

2   Preliminaries

We use the direct style intermediate representation in Figure 1 for this presentation. We assume that all bound variables are unique and that associated with each application call site is a *program point*, labeled with a superscript l, that is a unique label for the expression. Booleans, tuples, and functions are the only values that variables can take on in this language. Integers may only be used in selections.

We assume the presence of the maps in Figure 2, computed using a control-flow analysis, to build this graph. Our implementation uses a control-flow analysis similar to that presented by Serrano [2], which provides sufficient information to implement these maps.

$\mathcal{F}$ maps each function identifier to the list of all program points (call sites) if they are known. If a function identifier g has an unknown call site, then $\mathcal{F}(g)$ is $\emptyset$. A function *escapes* if it has any potentially unknown call sites and $\mathcal{F}$ maps those functions to $\emptyset$. We cannot safely perform a translation on any functions with unknown call sites.

$\mathcal{C}$ lists the set of functions that can be called at a given program point or $\emptyset$ if the set is unknown. A call site with unknown target functions can not be transformed.

$\mathcal{A}$ maps a function to the set of all the functions that could potentially share call sites with it. This map can be computed from the $\mathcal{F}$ and $\mathcal{C}$ maps provided by control-flow analysis.

$$\begin{array}{llr}
Exp \ni e ::= & x & \text{variable or function name} \\
& | \quad \text{fun } g(\boldsymbol{x}) = e_1 \text{ in } e_2 & \text{function binding} \\
& | \quad \text{let } x = e_1 \text{ in } e_2 & \text{local variable binding} \\
& | \quad \text{if } x \text{ then } e_1 \text{ else } e_2 & \text{conditional} \\
& | \quad g^l(\boldsymbol{x}) & \text{application (labeled)} \\
& | \quad \langle \boldsymbol{x} \rangle & \text{tuple creation} \\
& | \quad \#i(x) & \text{tuple selection} \\
& | \quad b & \text{boolean}
\end{array}$$

$$i \in \mathbb{N} \qquad\qquad\qquad\qquad\qquad\qquad \text{literal integers}$$

$$l \in \mathbb{L} \qquad\qquad\qquad\qquad\qquad\qquad \text{labels}$$

$$b \in \{\text{true, false}\} \qquad\qquad\qquad\qquad \text{boolean values}$$

Fig. 1. Direct style intermediate representation

$$\begin{array}{ll}
\mathcal{F} : \text{FunID} \rightarrow 2^{\mathbb{L}} & \text{Function call sites} \\
\mathcal{C} : \mathbb{L} \rightarrow 2^{\text{FunID}} & \text{Called functions by call site} \\
\mathcal{A} : \text{FunID} \rightarrow 2^{\text{FunID}} & \text{Functions sharing call sites} \\
\mathcal{U} : \text{VarID} \rightarrow \mathbb{N} & \text{Variable use count}
\end{array}$$

Fig. 2. Maps computed by static analysis

The use count of a variable is the number of times that the variable occurs in any position other than its binding occurrence. The map $\mathcal{U}$ provides the use count of a variable.

3   Signature Analysis

The signature analysis phase of this optimization contains almost all of the complexity. Control-flow analysis is run over the whole program before we begin execution. Any function with unknown call sites is ignored. For all functions with only known call sites, we gather information from the body of the function and then compute a signature based on whether or not call sites are shared with other functions.

3.1   Gathering Information

An *access path* is a series of tuple selection operations performed on a parameter. Access paths are zero-based and the selections occur in left-to-right order. The access path 0.1.2 means to take the first parameter to the function, select the second item from it, and then select the third item from that. The *variable map*

$$\mathcal{V} : \text{var} \rightarrow \text{path}$$

maps a variable to an access path. The notation $\mathcal{V}_f$ refers to the map $\mathcal{V}$ restricted to those variables defined within the function f. The initial value for each variable is .

$$\mathbb{V}[\![\,]\!] \; : \; Exp \rightarrow Unit$$
$$\mathbb{V}[\![\text{fun } g(\boldsymbol{x}) = e_1 \text{ in } e_2]\!] = \forall x_i \in \boldsymbol{x} \; (\mathcal{V}(x_i) := i); \mathbb{V}[\![e_1]\!] \; ; \; \mathbb{V}[\![e_2]\!]$$
$$\mathbb{V}[\![\text{let } x = \#i(y) \text{ in } e_2]\!] = \begin{cases} \mathcal{V}(x) := \mathcal{V}(y).i; \mathbb{V}[\![e_2]\!] & \text{when } \mathcal{V}(y) \neq \emptyset \\ \mathbb{V}[\![e_2]\!] & \text{otherwise} \end{cases}$$
$$\mathbb{V}[\![\text{let } x = e_1 \text{ in } e_2]\!] = \mathbb{V}[\![e_1]\!] \; ; \; \mathbb{V}[\![e_2]\!]$$
$$\mathbb{V}[\![\text{if } x \text{ then } e_1 \text{ else } e_2]\!] = \mathbb{V}[\![e_1]\!] \; ; \; \mathbb{V}[\![e_2]\!]$$
$$\mathbb{V}[\![e]\!] = ()$$

$$\mathcal{P}_f(p) = \sum_{x | \mathcal{V}_f(x) = p} \left(\mathcal{U}(x) - | \{y \mid x \prec y \text{ and } \mathcal{V}(y) \neq \emptyset\} | \right)$$

Fig. 3. Algorithm to compute variable and path maps

The *path map* $\mathcal{P}_f$ maps an access path to a count of the number of times that path is directly used. The path map $\mathcal{P}_f$ is specific to function f, as access paths are relative to the parameters of the function and have a different meaning within different scopes. The path map is equal to the use count of the variable associated with that path minus any uses of that variable as the target of a selection.

To illustrate these definitions, consider the following intermediate representation for the function f:

```
fun f(x) =
  let a = #0(x)
  let b = #1(a)
  in b
...
```

The intermediate representation for the function f above has the following variable and path maps:

$$\mathcal{V} = \{x \mapsto 0, a \mapsto 0.0, b \mapsto 0.0.1\}$$
$$\mathcal{P}_f = \{0 \mapsto 0, 0.0 \mapsto 0, 0.0.1 \mapsto 1\}$$

The variable map indicates that x is the first parameter, a is the first slot of the first parameter and that b is the second slot of the first slot of the first parameter. And the path map indicates that only the variable b is used outside of tuple selection expressions.

The imperative map $\mathcal{V}$ is filled in by the algorithm $\mathbb{V}$ in Figure 3. Where a more specific case appears earlier in the algorithm, that case is to be run in place of the more general one later. The most important two cases are function definition and variable binding where the right hand side is a selection. The operation $\prec$ is a binary operator that is true if the first access path is a prefix of the second. For example, the access path 0.1 is a prefix of 0.1.3 but is not a prefix of 0.2. The map $\mathcal{P}$ is defined directly.

Consider the algorithm $\mathbb{V}$ applied to the example function f at the beginning of this section. The maps $\mathcal{V}$ and $\mathcal{P}_f$ are initially empty. Analysing the function binding, we add all of the parameters to the map $\mathcal{V}$, binding them to their corresponding index. The function binding for f defines a single parameter, x, so the variable map is set to $\{x \mapsto 0\}$. At each local variable binding whose right hand side is a selection, the path represented by that selection statement and base variable is entered in the map $\mathcal{V}$ as corresponding to that variable. After processing the two `let` bindings within the body of `f`, the variable map $\mathcal{V} = \{x \mapsto 0, a \mapsto 0.0, b \mapsto 0.0.1\}$. The map $\mathcal{P}_f$ is now valid on those three paths, returning the path map described earlier.

3.2 Computing Signatures

The function's signature is a list of all arguments passed to the function.[1] Given the maps $\mathcal{V}$ and $\mathcal{P}$, we can compute an individual function's ideal arity-raised signature and final arity-raised signature. A function's ideal signature is the signature that promotes the variables corresponding to selection paths that are used in the function's body up to parameters — but only if another parameter is not a prefix of the proposed new parameter. This ideal signature is a list of of selection paths. A function's final signature is a list of access paths, sorted in lexical order. The final signature of a function also differs from the ideal signature in that it is the same as all other functions that it shares a signature with.

The ideal signature reduces the list of selection paths because if one variable's path is a prefix of another variable's path, the variable that is a prefix will already require the calling function to do an allocation of all of the intermediate data. For example, in the function `usesTwo` below, it may be worth promoting the variable `first` to a parameter, but we will not also promote the variable `deeper` to a parameter. Promoting `deeper` will not open up any opportunities to remove allocated data from any callers of the `usesTwo` function, but will introduce more register pressure. There is a possibility that we could avoid a memory fetch if there was a spare register and we could directly pass `deeper` instead of performing a selection from `first`, but since our algorithm is conservative and aggressive promotion results in huge numbers of parameters in practice, we will not promote variables like `deeper`.

```
fun usesTwo (param) =
  let first = #1(param)
  let deeper = #2(first)
  in otherFun (first, deeper)
```

The ideal signature for a function `f` is denoted by σ_f and is defined as follows:

$$\sigma_f = \{\, p \mid p \in \rho_f \wedge (\nexists q \in \rho_f)(q \prec p) \,\}$$

where $\rho_f = \{\, p \in \text{rng}(\mathcal{V}_f) \ \wedge \ \mathcal{P}_f(p) > 0 \,\}$ is the list of all of the access paths corresponding to variables in the function `f` with non-zero use counts after substracting their uses in tuple selections. The ideal signature is computed by selecting all of the paths that do not have a prefix in ρ_f.

The map $\mathcal{S}$ is from a set of function identifiers to either a new signature or $\emptyset$, indicating that the function will not have its parameter list or any passed arguments transformed.

We build up the map $\mathcal{S}$ by using the $\mathcal{A}$ map provided by control-flow analysis to determine the set of all functions that share call sites and computing the merged signature from their ideal signatures. The merged signature of two ideal signatures is a

---

[1] In the implementation of Manticore, the signature also includes the current exception handler.

set consisting of the shortest prefix paths between the two signatures and is defined as follows:

$$\sigma_1 \uplus \sigma_2 = \{\, p \mid p \in \sigma_1 \wedge (\nexists q \in \sigma_2)(q \preceq p)\,\} \cup \{\, p \mid p \in \sigma_2 \wedge (\nexists q \in \sigma_1)(q \preceq p)\,\}$$

Note, however, that the merged signature may not be safe. Consider the pair of functions below, usesFirst and usesSecond, and assume that they share a call site.

```
fun usesFirst(param) =
  let first = #1(param)
  in first
fun usesSecond(param) =
  let second = #2(param)
  in second
```

They will have the following ideal signatures:

$$\sigma_{\text{usesFirst}} = \{0.1\}$$
$$\sigma_{\text{usesSecond}} = \{0.2\}$$

And therefore their merged signature is: $\sigma_{\text{usesFirst}} \uplus \sigma_{\text{usesSecond}} = \{0.1, 0.2\}$

Unfortunately, there is no guarantee that it is safe to perform the merged selections at all of the unshared call sites. For example, assume usesFirst is called in the following way:

```
let x = <2.0>
in usesFirst (x)
```

Then adding a selection of a second element as required by the shared signature would result in the following unsafe code after transformation:

```
let x = <2.0>
let first = #1(x)
let second = #2(x)
in usesFirst (first, second)
```

Since there is no second element in the allocated argument tuple, the transformation will have introduced an unsafe selection.

In an untyped setting, for any path that is in one signature to be safe, it needs to be a prefix of or equal to a path in the other signature. If either of the sets σ'_1 or σ'_2 below are non-empty, we cannot compute a common signature for this pair of functions using this algorithm.[2] In that case, the map $\mathcal{S}$ will instead return a final signature corresponding to the default calling convention.

$$\sigma'_1 = \{\, p \mid p \in \sigma_1 \wedge (\nexists q \in \sigma_2)(p \preceq q \vee q \preceq p)\,\}$$
$$\sigma'_2 = \{\, p \mid p \in \sigma_2 \wedge (\nexists q \in \sigma_1)(p \preceq q \vee q \preceq p)\,\}$$

---

[2] See the implementation notes in Section 6 for how we avoid this limitation in Manticore through the use of type information.

4   Transformation

Each new function signature requires the code to be transformed in three places.
Figure 4 shows the transformation process on this intermediate representation via the $\mathbb{T}$
transformation.

For each function that is a candidate for arity raising, we transform the parameter
list of the function definition to reflect its new signature. That new signature is made up
of the variables corresponding to the paths that are part of the final signature in $\mathcal{S}$. The
parameters are ordered by the lexical order of the paths as returned by $\mathcal{S}$.

The parameter to the transformation ys is the set of variables that have been lifted
to parameters of functions. We add variables to this set at any function definition where
we add a variable to the parameter list. When we encounter a variable binding for a
member of the set ys, we skip that binding since the variable is already in scope at the
parameter binding.

At each location where the function is called, we replace the call's argument list
with a new set of arguments selected from the original ones based on the new signature.
There is one procedure not defined: in the case of a call to a function that is being arity
raised, we construct a series of let bindings for the new arguments based on the final
signature of the functions sharing that call site, represented by the variable sels.

For example, if the function f has an entry in the map $\mathcal{S}$ with a value of $[0.0, 0.1.0]$,
then a call to the function f will be transformed from

$$\mathbb{T}[\![]\!] : (Exp \times Vars) \rightarrow Exp$$

$$\mathbb{T}[\![\mathrm{fun}\ f(x) = e_1\ \mathrm{in}\ e_2]\!]ys = \begin{cases} \mathrm{fun}\ f(x) = \mathbb{T}[\![e_1]\!]ys \\ \quad \mathrm{in}\ \mathbb{T}[\![e_2]\!]ys & \mathrm{when}\ \mathcal{S}(f) = \emptyset \\[2ex] \mathrm{fun}\ f(z) = \mathbb{T}[\![e_1]\!]z \cup ys & \mathrm{where}\ z = \{z|(\exists p)(p \in \mathcal{S}(f) \\ \quad \mathrm{in}\ \mathbb{T}[\![e_2]\!]ys & \quad \wedge\ \mathcal{V}(z) = p)\} \end{cases}$$

$$\mathbb{T}[\![\mathrm{let}\ x = e_1\ \mathrm{in}\ e_2]\!]ys = \begin{cases} \mathbb{T}[\![e_2]\!]ys & \mathrm{when}\ x \in ys \\[2ex] \mathrm{let}\ x = \mathbb{T}[\![e_1]\!]ys & \mathrm{otherwise} \\ \quad \mathrm{in}\ \mathbb{T}[\![e_2]\!]ys \end{cases}$$

$$\mathbb{T}[\![\mathrm{if}\ x\ \mathrm{then}\ e_1\ \mathrm{else}\ e_2]\!]ys = \mathrm{if}\ x\ \mathrm{then}\ \mathbb{T}[\![e_1]\!]ys$$
$$\mathrm{else}\ \mathbb{T}[\![e_2]\!]ys$$

$$\mathbb{T}[\![f^l(x)]\!]ys = \begin{cases} f^l(x) & \mathrm{when}\ \mathcal{C}(l) = \emptyset \vee \mathcal{S}(\mathcal{C}(l)) = \emptyset \\[2ex] \mathrm{let\ new} = sels & \mathrm{where}\ sels = \mathcal{S}(\mathcal{C}(l))\ \mathrm{paths} \\ \quad \mathrm{in}\ f(\mathrm{new}) \end{cases}$$

$$\mathbb{T}[\![\langle x \rangle]\!]ys = \langle x \rangle$$
$$\mathbb{T}[\![\#i(x)]\!]ys = \#i(x)$$
$$\mathbb{T}[\![x]\!]ys = x$$
$$\mathbb{T}[\![b]\!]ys = b$$

Fig. 4. Algorithm to arity raise functions

```
f(arg)
```

into

```
let a1 = #0(arg)
let t1 = #1(arg)
let a2 = #0(t1)
in f(a1, a2)
```

Transformation of the code is performed in a single pass over the intermediate representation.

5   An Example

To better understand the intermediate representation, what the optimization looks at and attempts to remove, and what the desired generated code looks like, we present an example that exhibits both of the types of memory allocations listed in the introduction. Raw floating point numbers are boxed and there is a user-defined type. This code defines an ML function that takes a pair of parameters — a datatype with two reals, and another real. The function then extracts the first item from the datatype and adds it to the second parameter. The second member of the datatype is unused.

```
datatype dims = DIM of real * real;
fun f(DIM(x, _), b) = x+b;
f (DIM(2.0, 3.0), 4.0)
```

This code transforms into the following intermediate representation, as presented in Figure 1 but augmented with reals and the addition operator. Temporary variables have been given meaningful names in the example to aid understanding.

```
fun f(params) =
  let dims = #0(params)
  let fourB = #1(params)
  let four = #0(fourB)
  let twoB = #0(dims)
  let two - #0(twoB)
  let six = two+four
  in <six>
let twoB = <2.0>
let threeB = <3.0>
let fourB = <4.0>
let dims = <twoB, threeB>
let args = <dims, fourB>
in f (args)
```

This intermediate representation is clearly too naive to generate efficient code from. Note that we use the same mechanism, allocation, to box raw values, to allocate tuples, and to allocate datatypes. This similarity, which is manifest in the Manticore intermediate representation, allows our arity raising algorithm to treat all three mechanisms uniformly. Even though boxing of types, tuples, and datatype definitions will ultimately have different output from the code generator, uniform treatment in the intermediate representation enables optimizations in arity raising and elsewhere in the compiler.

The function f above has the following variable and path maps:

$$\mathcal{V} = \left\{ \begin{array}{l} \mathtt{params} \mapsto 0, \mathtt{dims} \mapsto 0.0, \ \mathtt{fourB} \mapsto 0.1, \\ \mathtt{four} \mapsto 0.1.0, \ \mathtt{twoB} \mapsto 0.0.0, \ \mathtt{two} \mapsto 0.0.0.0 \end{array} \right\}$$

$$\mathcal{P}_{\mathtt{f}} = \{0 \mapsto 0, \ 0.0 \mapsto 0, \ 0.1 \mapsto 0, \ 0.1.0 \mapsto 1, \ 0.0.0 \mapsto 0, \ 0.0.0.0 \mapsto 1\}$$

Since there is only one function and its call site is immediate, the control-flow analysis information is not too interesting. The ideal signature for this function is:

$$\sigma_{\mathtt{f}} = [0.1.0, 0.0.0.0]$$

After running the transformation $\mathbb{T}$, the code is now:

```
fun f(two, four) =
  let val six = two+four
  in <six>
let twoB = <2.0>
let threeB = <3.0>
let fourB = <4.0>
let dims = <twoB, threeB>
let args = <dims, fourB>
let dims' = #0(args)
let fourB = #1(args)
let four = #0(fourB)
let twoB = #0(dims')
let two = #0(twoB)
in f (two, four)
```

After Manticore's standard local cleanup phase to remove redundant allocation and selection pairs and unused variables, we have the following intermediate code:

```
fun f(two, four) =
  let six = two+four
  in <six>
f(2.0, 4.0)
```

6   Implementation

Manticore [3] is a compiler for a parallel programming language based on Standard ML. Arity raising is performed on the weakly typed, continuation-passing style (CPS) intermediate representation. Unlike the direct style representation, the CPS representation of the program treats both function calls and returns uniformly. This uniform treatment allows arity raising to remove allocations not only on arguments to functions, but also from values returned in the original source program.

After types are inferred on the original source program, we both preserve and check them through each transformation in our intermediate representation. Monomorphic types are preserved exactly, but polymorphic types are weakened to an unknown type.

This type information is sufficient to provide a better solution to the *incompatible paths* problem mentioned during Section 3. In Manticore, we first compute the merged signature with all functions that share call sites. Instead of then removing all unique selection paths, as presented earlier in this paper, we check the type of the provided argument at each call site to ensure that the selection path is both safe and has the same representation. The selection path is safe if the selection path is guaranteed to be valid. For example, the selection path 0.1 is valid in the type ((int * int) * any) but is not a safe selection into an argument with type (any * any). The selection path has the same representation if the type of the data selected has the same representation format. For example, since raw floating point numbers have a different representation than raw integers, even though the selection path 0.1 is valid in the types ((int * int) * any) and ((int * float) * any), it would be unclear whether the argument should be passed as an integer in a general-purpose register or in a floating-point register. The selection path 0 would be used instead in this case, as the tuple types (int * int) and (int * float) share the same representation.

We are also less conservative in Manticore with branches than we presented in Section 1, where we stated that no transformations are performed inside of the arms of conditional branches. If a conditional statement is a direct check against a property of a selection from a parameter path, then we do not permit any paths derived from that path to be added into the maps, but we do allow analysis to continue within the arms of the conditionals. Consider the following function, which extracts two parameters, performs a conditional check on one, and then performs some other operations.

```
fun f(params) =
  let x = #0(params)
  let y = #1(params)
  in if null? x
    then ...
    else ...
```

Within the arms of the conditional, if there are further selections to the paths corresponding to the variables x and y, only selections through the variable y will be added to the variable map. We conservatively assume that, unless the parameter type guarantees that the selection is safe, the conditional may be protecting operations based on the runtime structure of the data.

7   Results

We performed two studies on a set of four benchmarks. The first study investigates the reduction in allocated bytes of memory across the default ML function calling convention without any arity raising, an *argument-only* form of arity raising similar to what is used in most other strongly-typed functional language implementations, and the full arity raising algorithm presented in this paper. The second study examines the impact on program runtime across these three arity raising strategies.

7.1   Experimental Method

Our test machine has four quad-core AMD Opteron 8380 processors running at 2.5GHz. Each core has a 512KB L2 cache and shares 6MB cache with the other cores of the processor. The system has 32GB of RAM and is running Debian Linux (kernel version 2.6.31.1-amd64).

7.2   Benchmarks

We evaluated the three strategies on the benchmarks listed in the table below. For each benchmark, this table provides the size, in lines of code, and a small description of the type and shape of data manipulated. Since we cannot perform arity raising on any functions that the control-flow analysis determines may escape, we also provide the number of functions eligible for arity raising and the number of functions that escape. Some of the escaping functions are due to imprecision in the control-flow analysis, but many more are due to passing functions to our C runtime for storage in the scheduling queues used to implement Manticore's parallel language features.

Benchmark	Size	Eligible	Escaping	Description
barnes-hut	323	504	97	Floating point with datatypes
life	181	106	39	Integers and list operations
mandelbrot	91	228	55	Loop-heavy floating point
quickhull	138	366	76	Floating point with heavy random access
raytracer	548	308	55	Floating point with trivial parallelism

The Barnes-Hut benchmark [4] is a classic N-body problem solver. Each iteration has two phases. In the first phase, a quadtree is constructed from a sequence of mass points. The second phase then uses this tree to accelerate the computation of the gravitational force on the bodies in the system. Our benchmark runs 20 iterations over 1,000,000 particles. Our version is a translation of a Haskell program [5].

Life is a simulation of Conway's game of life. This benchmark is an example of code that this arity raising algorithm cannot optimize — the code operates over lists of tupled integers. Since there are no explicit, deep data structures to remove and access to individual data elements is guarded in conditionals, we cannot promote the data to arguments.

Mandelbrot renders a 3000 × 3000 image of the Mandelbrot set. This benchmark has a very tight set of inner loops over floating point values that take most of the runtime and benefits heavily from arity raising, since loops are implemented as function calls and floating points values are boxed and stored in memory rather than registers in the default ML calling convention.

The Quickhull benchmark determines the convex hull of 20,000,000 points in the plane. This algorithm is interesting for Manticore because while it is trivially parallel, the parallel subtasks are not guaranteed to be of equal work sizes. This code is based on the algorithm presented in [6].

The Raytracer benchmark renders a 1000 × 1000 image in parallel as two-dimensional sequence, which is then written to a file. The original program was written in ID [7] and is a simple ray tracer that does not use any acceleration data structures.

7.3   Conventions

The default calling convention in the tables below is the default calling convention specified in the user's program. All arguments are tupled and passed as a single value to the function.

The argument-only calling convention is a straightforward, type-directed translation of the function's argument tuple from a single value into the set of tupled items. This calling convention does not remove any nested tupling.

The full calling convention is the result of the arity raising strategy presented in this paper.

7.4   Allocation

The table below shows the raw allocation data in megabytes (2^{20} bytes) allocated along with percentage improvements over the default calling convention. Smaller numbers are better, and the two percentages reported are $\frac{mb_{arg-only}}{mb_{default}}$ and $\frac{mb_{full}}{mb_{default}}$, where $mb_{arg-only}$ is the argument-only arity raising algorithm, $mb_{default}$ is the default ML calling convention, and mb_{full} is the full arity raising algorithm presented in this work. In all benchmarks, argument-only allocates fewer bytes than the default convention, and the full arity raising algorithm allocates even fewer.

Benchmark	Default	Arg-Only	Full	$\frac{mb_{arg-only}}{mb_{default}}$	$\frac{mb_{full}}{mb_{default}}$
barnes-hut	325,435	298,755	282,196	91.8%	86.7%
life	32,581	32,130	31,364	98.6%	96.2%
mandelbrot	200,421	125,136	57,558	62.4%	28.7%
quickhull	72,790	67,577	62,136	92.8%	85.4%
raytracer	369,958	273,952	273,890	74.0%	74.0%

Barnes-hut and quickhull have some opportunities to perform arity raising on tight inner loops, but the use of parallel language constructs around the tight loops as mentioned in this section's introduction prevents the optimization of several inner functions. Life operates on lists of data, providing almost no opportunities to optimize the code. However, our transformation does no harm to the generated code for life. Mandelbrot has significant opportunities for optimization due to the large number of values passed around in small structures within functions that call each other in a tight loop. Both argument-only and the full strategy turn a signficiant number of the intermediate structures into values passed in registers. The raytracer's functions generally operate over either an individual data structure or a single vector at a time. Since there is only one level of allocation to remove, the full arity raising strategy does not show significant benefit over the argument-only convention.

7.5   Execution Time

The table below shows the execution time in seconds along with percentage improvements over the default calling convention. Again, smaller numbers are better, and the two percentages reported are $\frac{t_{arg-only}}{t_{default}}$ and $\frac{t_{full}}{t_{default}}$, where $t_{arg-only}$ is the argument-only arity raising algorithm, $t_{default}$ is the default ML calling convention, and t_{full}

is the full arity raising algorithm presented in this work. In all benchmarks, argument-only runs faster than the default convention, and the full arity raising algorithm runs even faster.

Benchmark	Default	Arg-Only	Full	$\frac{t_{arg-only}}{t_{default}}$	$\frac{t_{full}}{t_{default}}$
barnes-hut	10.660	10.644	10.473	99.8%	98.2%
life	4.193	4.171	4.002	99.5%	95.4%
mandelbrot	5.027	4.427	4.152	88.1%	83.6%
quickhull	4.720	4.667	4.432	98.9%	93.9%
raytracer	7.78	7.186	6.489	92.4%	83.4%

For all of the benchmarks, small reductions in allocated bytes result in small reductions in runtime, and larger reductions in allocated bytes result in larger reductions in runtime. One interesting case, though, is the speedup on the raytracer benchmark of the full arity raising algorithm over the argument-only algorithm despite a very small reduction in the number of bytes allocated. This speedup is because there are a few core functions used in inner loops whose heap-allocated parameters were turned into raw parameters. Though the values passed to these functions were only being allocated infrequently, because the functions are called with the same data repeatedly, removal of the memory access results in a significant performance improvement.

8 Related Work

Optimizations to reduce the amount of overhead introduced by the language or execution model abound. Boxing optimizations change programs to deal with raw values directly instead of either storing them in an altered format or in a heap-allocated structure, introducing coercions between a boxed and unboxed format and increasing the amount of knowledge the generated code has about the specific type of the values in the program.

Datatype flattening reduces the overhead introduced by structuring raw data into heap-allocated objects. In cases where a set of values is placed into an object in the heap just to be passed to a method and subsequently pulled back out into their raw forms, avoiding the intermediate allocation saves a significant amount of overhead.

The related work over the last twenty years has mostly used either type or control-flow to drive their optimizations and most has addressed either the problem of optimizing boxing or flattening datatypes. Our presented work is unique because it uses both type and control-flow information and, by treating boxes and datatypes identically, both flattens datatypes and optimizes boxing. Our work also looks at data usage patterns within called functions, which has to this point been ignored.

8.1 Boxing Optimizations

One of the earliest pieces of formal work on the correctness of a system that handles boxed and unboxed versions of raw data types in the same program was done by Leroy [8]. He introduced operators for boxing and unboxing and extended the type system to handle either boxed values or unboxed values. He then showed how to construct a version of the program that has changed all monomorphic functions — the functions where the raw type is known — to use unboxed values. Calls to his `box` and `unbox` operations (called `wrap` and `unwrap` in this paper) are introduced around polymorphic functions, as anywhere that the type is unknown the value must be in the uniform, boxed representation. Leroy then showed that the version of the program that purely used boxed types computes the same thing as the version of the program that uses a mixed representation. This strategy of mixed representations driven purely by the type system was then directly implemented in their compiler.

Complementary work by Peyton-Jones et al. lifted `box` and `unbox` operations into the source language (Haskell) as well as the intermediate representation [9]. They showed a significant number of transformations that can be performed in an ad-hoc manner within the compiler once the boxing information is available — not only canceling matched pairs of coercions, but also avoiding repeated coercion of the same value. Since they were working with a lazy language, they also provided several valuable insights into the interaction of strictness analysis and unboxed types. Most importantly, whenever an argument is strict (always going to be evaluated), it is safe to change that from a boxed to an unboxed argument, as it will be available at the time of the call. If the argument were not strict, then we would need to instead have an unboxed slot so that we could hold the code that will lazily produce the value instead.

Henglein also made all of the boxing and unboxing operations explicit in the intermediate representation of his program [10]. He then provides a set of reduction rules that move coercions to places that are considered more formally optimal by his framework. By moving coercions until `box` and `unbox` operations are adjacent, it is possible to cancel out the pair of coercions. Depending on the order of the cancellations, this order choice corresponds to either keeping the data in its raw unboxed form or leaving the data in boxed form. Keeping data in raw form is good for monomorphic function calls, which can take arguments in raw form. Keeping data in boxed form is good for polymorphic function calls in this framework, as polymorphic calls required raw types in boxed form in order to dispatch properly. This work did not address which strategy was preferred, nor did this work provide an implementation or benchmarks. Unfortunately, this notion of optimality is based on the static number of coercions in the program, and even the decisions of whether to optimize first for raw form arguments or first for boxed form arguments is based on static determination of the number of polymorphic versus monomorphic functions in the program. Dynamic execution behavior is not considered in this framework.

A few years later, Thiemann revisited the theoretical work done by Henglein and provided a deterministic set of reduction relations for determining coercion placement [11]. In particular, he chose a strategy of attempting to push unboxings toward calls in tail position. Since his work is primarily on the intermediate representation, this strategy ensured that there would be a register available to hold the value and that it would not have to be spilled (and thus boxed).

Ignoring type information, work by Goubault performs intraprocedural data-flow analysis to cancel nearby `box` and `unbox` pairs [12]. While this strategy seems like it would intuitively be much worse than the previous whole program approach, Goubault also introduced a method called *partial inlining*. This method takes the bit of wrapper code that includes the box or unbox operations, which occur at the start of the called function and moves them into the caller. By moving those operations out of the called function, if there was an operation that can now be cancelled in the calling function, this allows that pair of operations to be canceled. While this strategy was not implemented, this work is important because it pushed the idea of splitting out the prologue and epilogue of a function and inlining them at the call sites.

Serrano uses a control-flow analysis approach based on 0CFA to gather information about data values and where they are used [13]. Where functions are called monomorphically, he specializes the functions to use raw types. In practice on a wide set of examples, he saw significant speedups and complete removal of boxing, in many cases. This optimization worked very well for the untyped scheme language he was compiling and produced results similar to those reported for type-directed approaches.

Also ignoring type information is the work on the placement of box and unbox operations is work by Faxén [14]. His work performs whole-program control-flow analysis (CFA) and does the usual cancelling of matched coercion operations. He also uses the CFA information to identify potential sensitive locations in the program (like loops) where moving a box or unbox operation that was not inside of the sensitive area into that area could cause a major change in performance. By respecting the control-flow of the program, his implementation did not exhibit some of the significant reductions in performance that were shown by the previous works on coercion placement when the benchmark included a mix of polymorphic and monomorphic functions.

Attempting to tie up the argument between the type directed and control-flow directed work is a paper comparing practical results in the implementation of the Objective Caml compiler by Leroy[15]. He provided performance data showing that a combined strategy, using the type information in restricted area based on a control-flow analysis (provided by an analysis similar to sub-0CFA with $n = 1$[16]) provided the best results. Relying exclusively on type information lead to extremes in either moving or not moving the coercion operators and results in performance that is worse than doing nothing at all on certain benchmarks. By preserving types during compilation, they could be used when the coercion optimization were going to be applied within functions.

The TIL compiler by Tarditi and Morrisett used a combination of explicit representation of coercions, type dispatch in polymorphic functions, and compiler optimizaitons to remove boxing [17]. The compiler keeps around type information throughout the compilation process. After inlining, it is possible to have a call that boxes and then uses the type dispatch of the polymorphic function immediately in sequence, which their compiler then removes. Since TIL is a whole-program compiler and inlined very aggressively, it was so effective at removing all boxing on the small benchmarks they used that it is hard to tell if this approach would scale to larger programs [18]. Regardless, they got extremely good results with a primarily type-directed approach.

8.2 Arity Raising

Hannan and Hicks produced some of the earliest formal work on the correctness of arity raising [19]. They showed that if a type system captures pairs in its types, then functions that take a single argument that is a pair can be transformed to instead take two arguments (consisting of the individual elements of the pair), all of the call sites can be fixed up, and the program still computes the same value. This transformation was very straightforward and did arity raising whenever it was possible, in a purely type directed manner. Like this work, they rely on the type system to determine where arity raising is safe. Unlike our work, they flatten all types that it is possible to flatten without regard for what the function uses.

Recently, Ziarek et al. showed an enhanced arity raising transformation for MLTon [20]. The MLTon compiler performs a full defunctorization, monomorphisation, and defunctionalization of the program. This set of transformations means that there are no polymorphic functions left at the time that arity raising is being performed. Their approach to arity raising involves passing both the original version of the argument and all of the flattened arguments (relying on useless variable elimination to remove the original version). They provide and compare three different strategies for arity raising: *flatten-all* flattens every data type completely into arguments, *argument-only* just flattens the first level of the argument to functions, and *bounded* attempts to flatten tuples up to a fixed depth only if they were created in the calling function. This heuristic is similar to our combination of control-flow analysis and target usage to determine which parts of the data structure to flatten; we never leave the original version of the argument around, however, as our analysis guarantees that we pass the necessary substructures of the data to the called function. This work has been implemented and benchmarked in the context of MLTon, but is not part of the standard distribution.

Bolingbroke and Peyton-Jones came up with a new intermediate representation for their implementation of Haskell, GHC, that is strict [21]. By translating laziness into thunks, lazy evaluation is captured in a function and then forced at any use site. Now, strictness analysis is not required for the classic optimizations discussed earlier in this and the previous section on boxing — they can be used as-is. Their proposal for arity raising uses only lexically apparant arguments and type information available at the call site. They perform neither control-flow analysis nor defunctionalization, so they will not be able to handle higher-order arguments in a rich way. This work has not yet been implemented.

9 Conclusion

We have presented a strategy for arity raising that is *conservative* and have described its implementation in the Manticore compiler. Our benchmark results show that this strategy is effective at reducing the number of bytes allocated and the runtime for several types of programs. Programs without opportunities for arity raising are not adversely affected.

References

1. Tarditi, D., Diwan, A.: Measuring the cost of storage management. In: LASC, pp. 323–342 (1994)
2. Serrano, M.: Control flow analysis: a functional languages compilation paradigm. In: SAC 1995, pp. 118–122. ACM, New York (1995)

3. Fluet, M., Rainey, M., Reppy, J., Shaw, A., Xiao, Y.: Manticore: A heterogeneous parallel language. In: DAMP 2007, pp. 37–44. ACM, New York (January 2007)
4. Barnes, J., Hut, P.: A hierarchical o(n log n) force calculation algorithm. Nature 324, 446–449 (1986)
5. GHC: Barnes Hut benchmark written in Haskell,
   http://darcs.haskell.org/packages/ndp/examples/barnesHut/
6. Barber, C.B., Dobkin, D.P., Huhdanpaa, H.: The quickhull algorithm for convex hulls. ACM Transactions on Mathematical Software 22(4), 469–483 (1996)
7. Nikhil, R.S.: ID Language Reference Manual. Laboratory for Computer Science. MIT, Cambridge (July 1991)
8. Leroy, X.: Unboxed objects and polymorphic typing. In: POPL 1992, pp. 177–188. ACM, New York (1992)
9. Peyton Jones, S.L., Launchbury, J.: Unboxed values as first class citizens in a non-strict functional language. In: Hughes, J. (ed.) FPCA 1991. LNCS, vol. 523, pp. 636–666. Springer, Heidelberg (1991)
10. Henglein, F., Jørgensen, J.: Formally optimal boxing. In: POPL 1994, pp. 213–226. ACM, New York (1994)
11. Thiemann, P.J.: Unboxed values and polymorphic typing revisited. In: FPCA 1995, pp. 24–35. ACM, New York (1995)
12. Goubault, J.: Generalized boxings, congruences and partial inlining. In: First International Static Analysis Symposium, Namur, Belgium (September 1994)
13. Serrano, M., Feeley, M.: Storage use analysis and its applications. In: ICFP 1996, pp. 50–61. ACM Press, New York (1996)
14. Faxén, K.F.: Representation analysis for coercion placement. In: Hermenegildo, M.V., Puebla, G. (eds.) SAS 2002. LNCS, vol. 2477, pp. 499–503. Springer, Heidelberg (2002)
15. Leroy, X.: The effectiveness of type-based unboxing. In: Workshop on Types in Compilation, Amsterdam. ACM SIGPLAN, Boston College Computer Science Dept. Technical Report BCCS-97-03 (June 1997)
16. Ashley, J.M., Dybvig, R.K.: A practical and flexible flow analysis for higher-order languages. ACM Trans. Program. Lang. Syst. 20(4), 845–868 (1998)
17. Tarditi, D., Morrisett, G., Cheng, P., Stone, C., Harper, R., Lee, P.: TIL: a type-directed optimizing compiler for ML. In: PLDI 1996, pp. 181–192. ACM, New York (1996)
18. Tarditi, D., Morrisett, G., Cheng, P., Stone, C., Harper, R., Lee, P.: TIL: a type-directed, optimizing compiler for ML. SIGPLAN Not. 39(4), 554–567 (2004)
19. Hannan, J., Hicks, P.: Higher-order arity raising. In: ICFP 1998, pp. 27–38. ACM, New York (1998)
20. Ziarek, L., Weeks, S., Jagannathan, S.: Flattening tuples in an SSA intermediate representation. Higher-Order and Symbolic Computation 21(3), 845–868 (2008)
21. Bolingbroke, M.C., Peyton Jones, S.L.: Types are calling conventions. In: HASKELL 2009, pp. 1–12. ACM, New York (2009)

Symbiotic Expressions

Robert Bernecky[1], Stephan Herhut[2], and Sven-Bodo Scholz[2]

[1] Snake Island Research Inc
Toronto, Canada
bernecky@snakeisland.com
[2] University of Hertfordshire, U.K.
{s.a.herhut,s.scholz}@herts.ac.uk

Abstract. We introduce *symbiotic expressions*, a method for algebraic simplification within a compiler, in lieu of an SMT solver, such as Yices or the Omega Calculator. Symbiotic expressions are compiler-generated expressions, temporarily injected into a program's abstract syntax tree (AST). The compiler's normal optimizations interpret and simplify those expressions, making their results available for the compiler to use as a basis for decisions about further optimization of the source program. The expressions are symbiotic, in the sense that both parties benefit: an optimization benefits, by using the compiler itself to simplify expressions that have been attached, lamprey-like, to the AST by the optimization; the program being compiled benefits, from improved run-time in both serial and parallel environments.

We show the utility of symbiotic expressions by using them to extend the SAC compiler's With-Loop-Folding optimization, currently limited to Arrays of Known Shape (AKS), to Arrays of Known Dimensionality (AKD). We show that, in conjunction with array-based constant-folding, injection and propagation of array extrema, and compiler-based expression simplification, symbiotic expressions are an effective tool for implementing advanced array optimizations. Symbiotic expressions are also simpler and more likely to be correct than hard-coded analysis, and are flexible and relatively easy to use. Finally, symbiotic expressions are synergistic: they take immediate advantage of new or improved optimizations in the compiler. Symbiotic expressions are a useful addition to a compiler writer's toolkit, giving the compiler a restricted subset of the analysis power of an SMT solver.

1 Introduction

Compilers use a variety of algebraic expression analysis techniques to make code optimization decisions. For example, loop fusion in SISAL [1,2,3] requires that two loops have the same bounds; an array-bounds-check removal in Fortran must determine if an index vector lies entirely within the array from which it selects; the array language SAC's With-Loop-Folding (WLF) optimization [4,5] must compute the intersection of two index-vector sets. Although these operations are often straightforward for humans to solve by inspection, a compiler may require

M.T. Morazán and S.-B. Scholz (Eds.): IFL 2009, LNCS 6041, pp. 107–124, 2010.
© Springer-Verlag Berlin Heidelberg 2010

some effort to achieve the same end. Common compiler-based approaches for performing this task include *ad hoc* analysis code, tailor-made for each specific optimization, such as [6], or use of an existing SMT solver, such as Yices [7] or the Omega Library [8,9]. In order to motivate a different approach to the problem, consider an Nth-difference array computation, used for signal processing or time-series analysis or, with $N = 1$, to compute delta-modulation values from a digitized audio signal, X, written as the SAC expression:

```
X - (genarray( [N], 0) ++ drop(-N, X))
```

That is, create a zero-vector of length N; catenate to it the original vector X after dropping its last N elements; then subtract that from X. Instead of performing these operations piecemeal, each creating array-valued intermediate results, we would like the compiler's WLF optimization to fuse those operations into a single loop. To do this, the optimizer has to prove that the shape of the catenate result matches the shape of X. In certain limited contexts, idiom recognition can detect common code patterns of this sort. However, in the more general case, the compiler must solve algebraic expressions involving array shapes and values, using standard rules of arithmetic on arrays, distributive law, associative law, de Morgan's laws, Boolean algebra, array versions of constant and value propagation, constant folding, common sub-expression elimination, etc. A common compiler design approach here is to restrict the domain of an optimization to fixed-shape arrays, and to simple index expressions. The required algebraic analysis is then hard-coded into the optimization itself.

Going beyond this point with hard coding is tedious, it does not generalize, and is not good software engineering. Although SMT solvers can often simplify these expressions, there are a few problems with that approach. First, there is an impedance mismatch between the intermediate language (IL) of the compiler and the API of the solver: the relevant IL data must be converted to a form acceptable to the solver, and when the solver finishes, its results must be converted back to IL form. Second, and somewhat harder, is the question of exactly what data should be provided to the solver. In the above example, we would need information about the argument and result shapes of a number of functions, potential values of parameters, etc. The task of deciding exactly what metadata–array shapes, index vector bounds, etc.–have to be passed to the solver can be nearly as difficult as solving the problem itself. Finally, it is difficult to use partial results generated by an SMT solver, since the answers tend to be of the yes-no variety: results from partial constraint resolution are not easy to exploit. Given this, we decided to tackle the problem in a different way.

Our solution entailed some modest extensions to the SAC constant-folding (CF) optimizations, to include some of the constraint resolution capabilities used in SMT solvers. Traditional constant folding comprises simple term-rewriting rules, such as replacing the vector expression ([2,3,4] + 4) by [6,7,8]. The SAC compiler extends traditional constant folding to arrays in several ways, shown in Figure 1. Symbolic constant simplification (SCS) simplifies array-valued expressions on Boolean, arithmetic, and other functions. Constant Folding also performs removal of run-time guards and compiler-internal primitives, in the form of SAA-constant folding (SAACF). This is driven by SAA-derived array rank and shape information [10]. Structural-constant constant folding (SCCF) replaces an array expression by its elements when those parts are arrays, and eliminates indexed references to array-valued intermediate results, thereby implementing array contraction [2].

Type	Expression	Result
SCS	`Array + 0`	`Array`
SCS	`Array - Array`	`genarray(shape(Array), 0)`
SCS	`Vec * VecOfZeros`	`VecOfZeros`
SCS	`BoolArray | FALSE`	`BoolArray`
SCS	`BoolArray | TRUE`	`genarray(shape(BoolArray), TRUE)`
SCS	`max( Array, Array)`	`Array`
SCS	`Array <= Array`	`genarray(shape(Array), TRUE)`
SCCF	`sel( [2], [a, b, c, d]`	`c`
SCCF	`[a, b] ++ [c, d]`	`[a, b, c, d]`
SCCF	`X = modarray( M, iv, V)`	`z = V`
	`z = sel( iv, X)`	`...`
SAACF	`take( shape(Vec), Vec)`	`Vec`

Fig. 1. Array-based constant folding examples

The remainder of this paper is structured as follows: Section 2 introduces *Symbiotic Expressions*, an alternate solution, within our limited context, to an SMT solver, introduces *array extrema*, and presents a running example of our solver injecting, propagating, simplifying, and exploiting symbiotic extrema expressions; Section 3 offers an example of using symbiotic extrema expressions to implement a new optimization, Algebraic With-Loop Folding (AWLF), including the performance characteristics of the new optimization; Section 4 presents the impact of symbiotic expressions within the compiler itself; Section 5 discusses related work; we end with our conclusions and future work in Section 6.

2   Symbiotic Expression Design and Implementation

The SAC compiler's optimizers are heavy-duty array tools, including associative law (AL), arithmetic simplification (AS), array constant folding (CF), common-subexpression elimination (CSE), constant propagation (CP), distributive law (DL), value propagation (VP), and many others.

The availability of such capabilities led us to conjecture that the SAC compiler, with some enhancements, might be powerful enough to perform the algebraic simplifications required by new optimizations. Our idea was to have the compiler inject appropriate algebraic expressions and/or SAC source code into the Abstract Syntax Tree (AST) of the program being compiled, run them through the optimizer cycle, and then see if the expressions had been simplified enough to guide further optimization.

Our proposed approach offered several potential advantages over an SMT solver. First, the entire metadata question became a non-issue, because all information needed by the compiler-based solver was directly available as AST nodes. Second, if our approach worked, it would constitute a generic technique that could be used for other algebraic expression simplification work within the compiler, giving it on-going, extensible value. Third, any new optimizations within the compiler would themselves become available for use by the rest of the compiler, perhaps improving the performance of symbiotic-expression-based optimizations that have no apparent connection to the new optimization.

We now describe the design and implementation of *Symbiotic Expressions*, and how we have used such expressions to implement Algebraic With-Loop Folding (AWLF), an extended array optimization. We use a trivial SAC program as a running example, to illuminate salient steps of the compiler's actions.

2.1   Running Example

Our running example is a trivial SAC program that computes a vector of the first N integers, then reverses that vector and displays the result. This could be written as `print(reverse(iota(N)))`, using SAC standard libraries, but inasmuch as we want to highlight the code simplification process, we provide the required functions as source code. We start with the program shown in Figure 2. Our goal in the example is to have the compiler fold with-loops into a single, data-parallel with-loop, and to perform other beneficial code improvements.

The fundamental structure of interest here is the SAC *with-loop*, a data-parallel array comprehension construct comprising two basic components: the first is a *shape* descriptor, such as `genarray(s,c)`, that specifies creation of an array with frame shape s, and cell shape c, to produce a result of shape shp++shape(c), with sub-array c as the contents of its cells. For example, with : `genarray([2,3], 42)` creates an array of shape [2,3], populated with 42. The second component is zero or more *generators* that specify the contents of sub-arrays within that array. For example, adding the generator (`[0,0] <= i <= [0,1]`) : 666 creates a two-row matrix, in which each row is [666, 42].

2.2   Symbiotic Expressions

Symbiotic Expressions are compiler-generated expressions, written in SAC itself or the IL, that are attached, lamprey-like, as AST nodes near relevant primitives. The compiler simplifies these expressions in exactly the same way that it simplifies the rest of the AST, because the injected expressions are indistinguishable from other AST nodes. Unlike the lamprey, however, symbiotic expressions, once simplified, are exploited by the compiler's optimizers to improve code even further. This benefits the "host" AST and the compiler, hence the term *symbiotic*.

We represent symbiotic expressions as primitive functions with an arbitrary number of arguments, the first of which becomes the result of the function, allowing us to insert symbiotic expressions into the AST with the assurance that data flow will preserve them over optimizations. Remaining arguments have

```
use Array:{-,<,shape,sel};
int main()
{ N = StdIO::readInt();
  ints = iota(N);
  z = reverse(ints);
  StdIO::print(z);
  return(0);
}

inline int[.] reverse( int[.] v)
{ lim = shape(v) - 1;
  z = with { ( [0] <= [j] < shape(v) ) : v[lim - j];
      } : genarray( shape(v), 0 );
  return( z);
}

inline int[.] iota( int y)
{ z = with { ( [0] <= [k] < [y]) : k;
      } : genarray( [y], 0 );
 return(z);
}
```

Fig. 2. Running example source code

semantic meaning only in the context of their application: their expressions are simplified by the optimizers, but the compiler is otherwise unaware of them. We might re-implement symbiotic expressions using just one primitive function, attaching, as the second argument, a tag that would identify the particular type of symbiotic expression being computed.

Symbiotic expressions are removed from the AST by a post-optimizer traversal and by dead code removal (DCR), so they have no detrimental impact on code generation. In this regard, they are merely code annotations, similar in spirit to the PHI functions of Static Single Assignment form [11]. The code that was optimized, thanks to the presence of symbiotic expressions, of course, remains optimized. Now, we discuss the injection, propagation, simplification, and exploitation of symbiotic expressions in slightly more detail.

2.3   Extrema

We introduced *extrema* into the SAC compiler to allow us to analyze array shapes and index vector sets. Extrema are expressions, attached to index vector descriptors, that give estimates of the minimum and maximum values of an array, to be used in a manner similar to integer range analysis [6]. For instance, the index scalar j in the reverse function has a minimum value of the vector [0] and a maximum value of shape(v). For compatibility with the compiler's internal canonical representation for with-loop bounds, the maximum extremum is greater by one than the actual maximum index value, which is shape(v)-1.

2.4   Extrema Injection

The SAC compiler uses a functional AST, in the sense that all of AST nodes must be connected by data flow to the main computation, or they are deemed dead, to be deleted from the AST by DCR. Hence, symbiotic expressions that are inserted into the AST must be hooked into it functionally, so that they will be preserved over optimizations; we discuss this requirement in [12].

Extrema are associated with-loop induction variables as arguments to an internal primitive function, `_attachextrema_`, that serves to preserve the extrema via data flow, and to associate extrema values with each variable. The `reverse` function, after introduction of extrema, is shown in Figure 3. By this time, any compiler optimizations on `j` can exploit its extrema. However, the index operation, `v[idx]`, which could exploit extrema, has no extrema on `idx` as yet; that information becomes available later, through extrema propagation.

```
inline int[.] reverse(int[.] v)
{ lim = shape(v) - 1;
  lb = [0];
  ub = shape(v);
  z = with { (lb <= [j] < ub) {
          j = _attachextrema_(j, lb, ub);
          idx = lim - j;
          el = v[idx];
          } : el;
        } : genarray(shape(v), 0 );
  return(z);
}
```

Fig. 3. IL after expression injection

2.5   Extrema Propagation

In order to be useful, extrema must be propagated from their origins to the referents of the variables with which they are associated. In our example, `idx` is offset from the with-loop's index vector, `j`. When one of a primitive function's arguments has extrema, the compiler's *extrema propagation* phase will inject symbiotic expressions to compute extrema for the primitive, attaching them to the AST as was done for with-loop index vectors. From a Hoare logic perspective, extrema propagation thus derives post-conditions for primitive operations given an existing pre-condition. In our example, the vector index offset computation (`lim-j`) meets this criterion, so two subtraction expressions are created, to compute the new extrema for `idx`, using `lim` and the extrema of `j` as arguments. The resulting expressions are injected into the AST as shown in Figure 4, then subjected to the compiler's normal optimizations, where they will be simplified, hopefully enough to be exploited by the compiler.

```
inline int[.] reverse(int[.] v)
{ lim = shape(v) - 1;
  lb = [0];
  ub = shape(v);
  z = with { (lb <= [j] < ub) {
          j = _attachextrema_(j, lb, ub);
          idx = lim - j;
          maxidx = lim - lb + 1;
          minidx = lim - (ub - 1);
          idx = _attachextrema_(idx, minidx, maxidx);
          el = v[idx];
          } : el;
        } : genarray(shape(v), 0 );
  return(z);
}
```

Fig. 4. IL after expression propagation

2.6 Symbiotic Expression Simplification and Exploitation

Symbiotic expression simplification is performed entirely by compiler optimization cycles. We will summarize the process as it operates on our running example. With-loop invariant removal (WLIR) moves maxidx and minidx out of the with-loop; array-based Constant Folding (CF) removes the idempotent subtraction of vector zero in maxidx; Constant Folding (CF) reduces the addition and subtraction of one to zero, ultimately leading to shape(v) as value of maxidx. Constant and Value Propagation (CVP) replaces maxidx by ub, making maxidx dead code, removed by Dead Code Removal (DCR), giving the IL shown in Figure 5.

```
inline int[.] reverse(int[.] v)
{ lim =  shape(v) - 1;
  lb = [0];
  ub = shape(v);
  minidx = lim - (ub - 1);
  /* minidx: ((shape(v)-1) - (shape(v)-1)) */
  z = with { (lb <= [j] < ub) {
          j = _attachextrema_(j, lb, ub);
          idx = lim - j;
          idx = _attachextrema_(idx, minidx, ub);
          el = v[idx];
          } : el;
        } : genarray(shape(v), 0 );
  return(z);
}
```

Fig. 5. IL after optimization cycle 1

At this point, Algebraic With-Loop Folding Inference (AWLFI) injects code, slightly more complex than that shown in Figure 6, to compute the intersection of the with-loop bounds in `iota()` that generated v with `idx`'s index set extrema, using the `_attachintersect_` primitive to attach the calculation to the AST, in a manner similar to guards [12] and integer range analysis [6]. As with `_attachextrema_`, this primitive uses data flow to associate its first argument with its result; the remaining arguments act as annotations to be simplified by the optimizers, and provide a mechanism to let the AWLF traversal find the requisite intersection information for the subsequent index operation. Figure 7 shows how in SaC a symbiotic expression can be written.

Concurrently, AL, AS, and DL rearranged the terms comprising `minidx`, from:

```
((shape(v)-1) - (shape(v)-1))
```

to:

```
((shape(v)-shape(v)) + (1-1))
```

Next, CF replaces both terms by [0], and later eliminates the addition. Since `lb` is also [0], CF replaces `minint` by [0]. The term `maxint` is similarly simplified,

```
inline int[.] reverse(int[.] v)
{ lim =  shape(v) - 1;
  lb = [0];
  ub = shape(v);
  minidx = lim - (ub - 1);
  z = with { (lb <= [j] < ub) {
          j = _attachextrema_(j, lb, ub);
          idx = lim - j;
          idx = _attachextrema_(idx, minidx, ub);
          minint = sacprelude:partitionIntersectMin(lb, minidx);
          maxint = sacprelude:partitionIntersectMax(ub, ub);
          idx = _attachintersect_(idx, minint, maxint);
          el = v[idx];
          } : el;
        } : genarray shape(v), 0 );
  return( z);
}
```

Fig. 6. IL after array intersection computation insertion

```
inline int[.] partitionIntersectMax( int[.] idxmin, int[.] bound1)
{
  dif  = _sub_VxV_( idxmin, bound1);
  p = _ge_VxS_( dif, 0);
  z = _mesh_VxVxV_( p, idxmin, bound1);
  return(z);
}
```

Fig. 7. SAC-defined symbiotic expression function

first to max(shape(v),shape(v)), and then to shape(v), giving the IL shown
in Figure 8. At this point, the intersect terms minint and maxint match the
extrema of idx, which satisfies the needs of AWLF.

```
inline int[.] reverse( int[.] v)
{ lim =  shape(v) - 1;
  lb = [0];
  ub = shape(v);
  z = with { ( lb <= [j] < ub) {
          j = _attachextrema_( j, lb, ub);
          idx = lim - j;
          idx = _attachextrema_( idx, lb, ub);
          idx = _attachintersect_( idx, lb, ub);
          el = v[idx];
          } : el;
        } : genarray( shape(v), 0 );
  return( z);
}
```

Fig. 8. IL after constant folding

The intersect calculation is the information AWLF needs to replace v[idx]
with the cell computation body from iota(). In this trivial case, the code body
is merely the with-loop's induction variable, so we end up, after extrema and
dead code deletion, with the single, well-optimized with-loop shown in Figure 9.

```
inline int[.] reverse( int[.] v)
{ lim =  shape(v) - 1;
  lb = [0];
  ub = shape(v);
  z = with { ( lb <= [j] < ub) {
          el = lim - j;
          } : el;
        } : genarray( shape(v), 0 );
  return( z);
}
```

Fig. 9. IL at completion

3   Algebraic With-Loop Folding

Now that we understand what symbiotic expressions are, and how they work,
we shall see how well they work in practice. With-loop folding (WLF) is the
fundamental loop optimization in the SAC compiler. It enables APL-like array
operations to be combined into a single data-parallel loop, eliminating array-
valued intermediate results and increasing the parallelism available within the

program being compiled. WLF operates only on Arrays of Known Shape (AKS)–
the arrays of Fortran 77–but many array language applications deal with Arrays
of Known Dimension (AKD), but unknown shape. Although the AKS and AKD
versions of code may be nearly identical, AKD performance can be much worse
than AKS performance, because the compiler may not be able to deduce exact
shapes of all arrays. This led us to write a new optimization, *algebraic with-loop folding* (AWLF), able to fold AKS and AKD arrays by using symbiotic-expressions to perform the partial symbolic evaluation of algebraic with-loop
index sets and their set intersections required by the optimization. We then
conducted a series of experiments to quantify the relative performance of AWLF
against WLF.

3.1   Experimental Setup

We evaluated the utility of symbiotic expressions by measuring their effective-ness in performing AWLF *vs.* WLF, and also by measuring the performance
of each optimization on AKS *vs.* AKD arrays. Our platform was a 4GB AMD
Opteron 165, running at 1.8GHz, running Ubuntu 8.10, gcc 4.3.2 and sac2c
product Build #16338 (www.sac-home.org). We used CPU time measurements,
taken with PAPIEX [13,14], as our metric for this paper.

3.2   Experimental Findings and Performance

First, we compared the performance of AWLF *vs.* WLF on AKS array problems,
which gives the edge to WLF, because WLF exploits knowledge of fixed-shape
arrays. Figure 10 shows CPU-time ratios for AWLF *vs.* WLF on AKS-based
benchmarks, taken from the APEX test suite [15]. Our hope was that AWLF
would approach the same level of performance as WLF. Measured performance
levels turned out to be mixed, but quite respectable, for about two-thirds of
the tests. The benchmarks in which AWLF performs poorly, such as `logd2AKS`
and `primesAKS`, include those that require *with-loop partition slicing*, a WLF
optimization that we have not yet completely implemented in AWLF. In general,
we deem these results acceptable, as we understand the areas where AWLF is
deficient and we are taking corrective measures.

We then turned to the performance of AWLF on AKD arrays. Since these
arrays frequently appear in applications such as data base queries, stock ex-change trading histories, stock market portfolio analysis, etc., we consider AKD
performance to be at least as important as AKS performance. The benchmark
programs for AKS and AKD are, essentially, identical. They differ only in that
the AKD versions hide the problem size from the compiler, preventing it from
inferring array shapes, as it does for the AKS versions. As with the AKS exper-iments, we measured CPU times, shown in Figure 11, as the speedup of AWLF
over WLF[1]. Here, the benefits of AWLF emerge, showing most benchmarks
slightly faster under AWLF than under WLF; several are considerably faster.

---

[1] We have intentionally restricted the y-axis scales on these charts, so that detail near
the bottom remains clear.

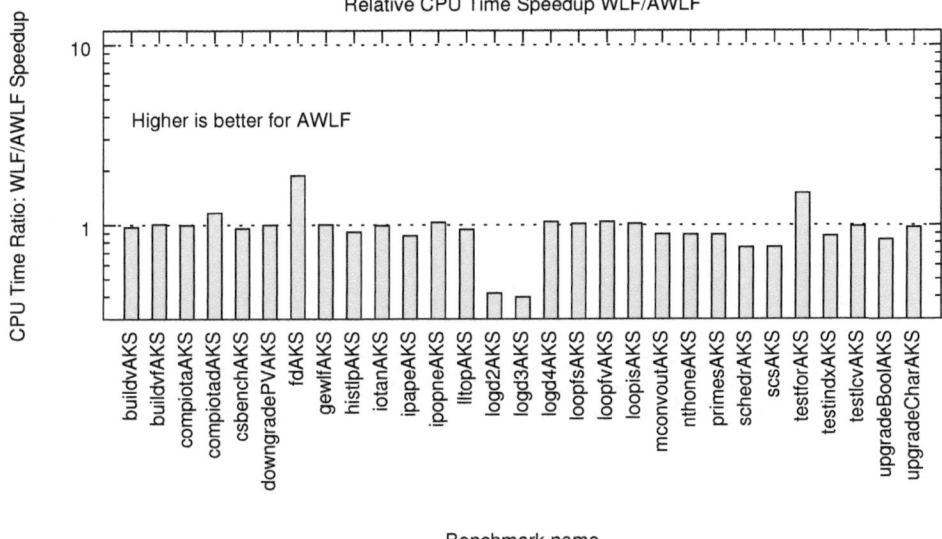

Fig. 10. APEX AKS CPU time performance WLF *vs.* AWLF

The remaining problem areas in AWLF are attributable to two factors. First, the uncompleted implementation of with-loop partition slicing affects some benchmarks. Because AWLF makes use of Symbolic Array Attribute (SAA) [10] information, it is implemented in a different optimimzation cycle from WLF. Both optimization cycles can be enabled independently; eventually, we will de-support the WLF cycle. This problem does not, therefore, detract from the inherent benefits of symbiotic expressions and AWLF.

We wanted to measure the performance of AWLF on AKS data *vs.* AKD data. Ideally, both problems would execute with the same speed, except for degradation due to the need to pass array shapes into, and out of, functions. Hence, if all results showed 100% for relative AKS and AKD performance, we could claim success in masking the differences between AKS and AKD problems in AWLF. The reality, is slightly different. Figure 12 presents the relative CPU time measurements for AWLF operating on AKS and AKD problems; WLF measurements are provided for comparison purposes. AWLF nearly always matches or exceeds WLF performance, in the sense of making performance of AKD-based problems approach AKS-based ones. If AWLF matches WLF performance on a benchmark, it means either that the benchmark is essentially entirely AKS-based, or that AWLF is missing some potential folding opportunities.

It is clear that AWLF often performs better, offering AKD performance that rivals AKS. Both optimizations, for reasons we do not yet understand, occasionally do better on AKD problems than on AKS problems. These are the places where the bar dips below 100%. The cause is likely some code unrelated to WLF and AWLF, because these optimizations have no code in common.

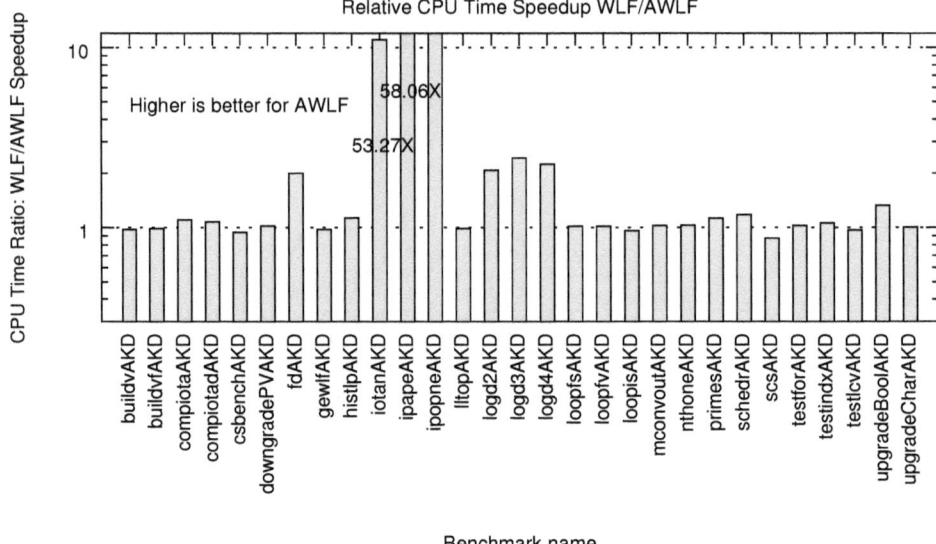

Fig. 11. APEX AKD CPU time performance WLF *vs.* AWLF

Cache performance generally improves with AWLF over WLF, as can be seen in Figure 13 and Figure 14. L1 cache performance under AWLF is, with two exceptions, either identical to, or superior to, that under WLF, sometimes by one or more orders of magnitude. L2 cache performance shows similar results.

4   Compiler Impact

Given the poor theoretical worst-case performance of SMT solvers such as Yices and Omega, it is reasonable to ask how well the SAC compiler performs when it solves symbiotic expressions. We do not know, as we have not yet made any controlled experiments to measure it, but we have observed that the SAACYC optimization cycle runs more trips when it is solving those expressions. The cost of our injected symbiotic expressions is, at least, several extra operations per primitive involved in the chain between index vector creation and index vector use, those operations being the ones that compute the new index vector extrema and attach them to the AST. Multiple injections may be inserted and solved concurrently, so the number of additional optimization cycles probably is not as bad as it could be. Also, since the injected expressions have a tendency to be quite simple, they are evaluated relatively quickly. Even so, their resolution may require several iterations of the optimization cycle.

If the increased iteration count becomes a problem in practice, we might want to consider introducing *micro-optimization cycles*, which we conceive of as allowing a subset of optimizations to be explicitly invoked on a specific user-defined function. The observation here is that optimizations such as CF, AS,

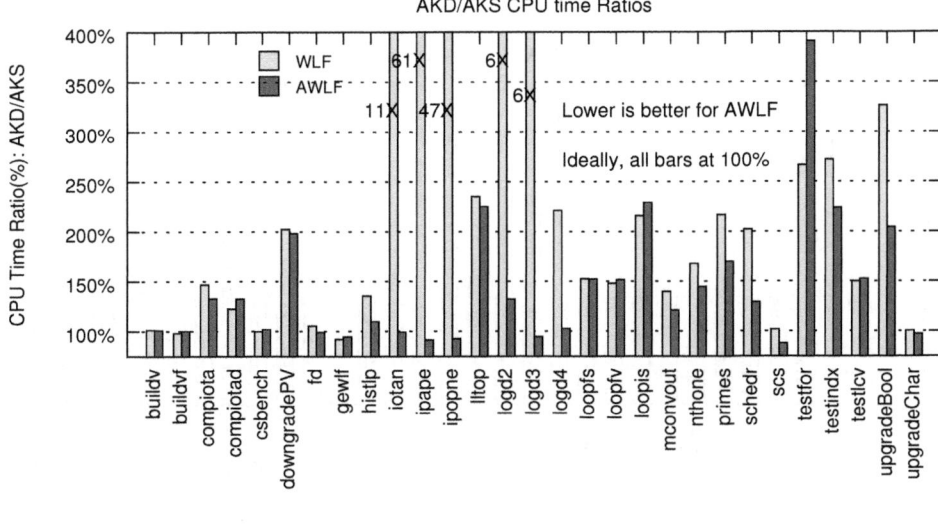

Fig. 12. APEX CPU time performance AKD *vs.* AKS

DL, AL, VP, and CSE are useful for simplifying our symbiotic expressions used in AWLF, other optimizations, such as those that manipulate with-loops, are not, and could be omitted in a micro-optimization cycle.

In terms of compiler complexity, the work required to support symbiotic expressions was minimal, partly due to the excellent structure of the SAC compiler as a research tool. Adding new primitives to the SAC compiler is merely a matter of adding an entry to one table, and defining the relationship between the function result and its arguments, basically a cut-and-paste operation. Simple abstract syntax tree traversals were added to introduce, propagate, exploit, and delete the two new compiler primitives and extrema. This was facilitated by Stephan Herhut's creation of XML code that allows new compiler traversals to be added with just a few lines of XML. Exploitation of extrema required more effort, since it has to drive the entire AWLF optimization. Introduction and propagation of extrema is straightforward; deletion of extrema is trivial.

In [16], which discusses some data flow problems similar to those in [12], the authors state "A refinement-style representation also obscures optimization opportunities by introducing multiple names for the same value." The SAC compiler uses pattern-matching to chase back across multiple assignments, etc., so this problem was largely solved for us already. Trivial changes were required to several optimizations to make them skip over the extrema and intersect primitives, usually no more than a name change in a pattern-matching function, from one that traces back over assign chains, to one that traces back over both assign chains and attach primitives.

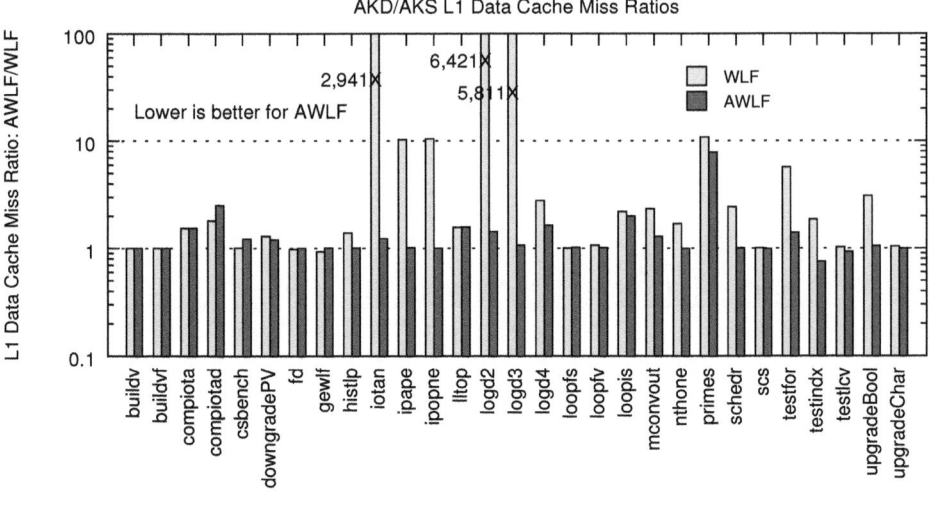

Fig. 13. APEX L1 cache performance AKD *vs.* AKS

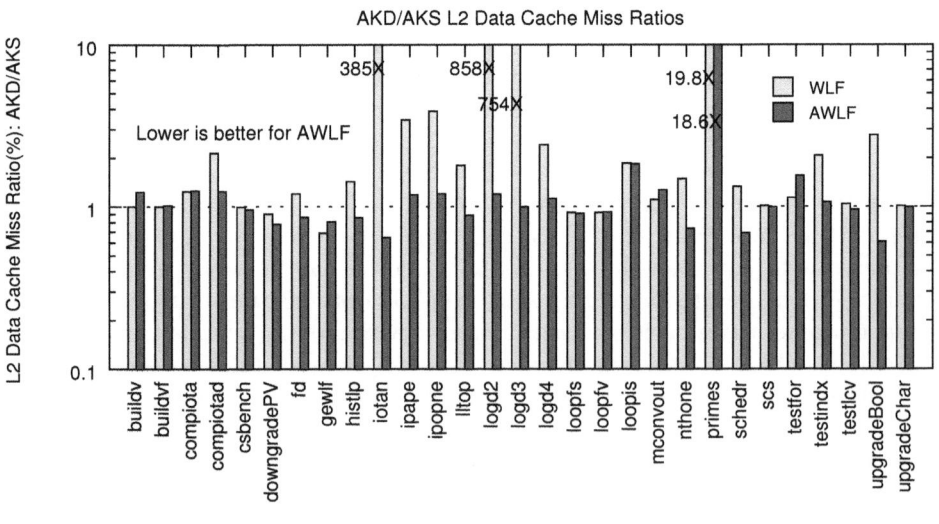

Fig. 14. APEX L2 cache performance AKD *vs.* AKS

Most compiler traversals merely ignore primitives that are not relevant to them, so the new primitives did not present any significant problems. The semantics of the new primitives are very simple, from the standpoint of most of the compiler; they can be thought of as idempotent functions whose result is their first argument; remaining arguments are, essentially, annotations, even though they are the symbiotic expressions that are simplified by the compiler.

Two WLF-related problems surfaced during the course of our experiments. First, we noticed that AKD matrix products on character data, `ipapeAKD` and `ipopneAKD`, performed about fifty times slower under WLF than under AWLF. We considered discarding these benchmarks from our test suite, because they reflect a performance problem that seems to go beyond WLF: other matrix product codes, such as `ipddAKD`, do not have this problem. However, the very presence of such performance problems makes it clear that the ease of using built-in optimizations to simplify algebraic expressions, rather than hand-crafting hard-coded analysis, has payoffs beyond mere convenience for the compiler writer. Hard-coded solutions may harbor code faults that only rarely raise their ugly heads. Such faults are usually only found by careful examination of generated IL code using a debugger to trace the cause of the fault.

Second, the `dtb` class of APEX benchmarks do not appear here because the WLF tests crashed the SAC compiler, due to an erroneously detected array bounds violation in WLF array offset computation. The AWLF code does not exhibit this failure. Again, this demonstrates the virtue of using existing optimizations to do the heavy lifting for new ones.

5   Related Work

Presently, we have not investigated the use of symbiotic expressions in other compiler contexts nor the use of array-based constant folding in other compiler projects. However, APL interpreters have always included special-case code to detect algebraic identities, such as those shown in the introduction. Many of the array-based constant-folding optimizations in SAC have their roots in APL.

In part, the extrema work was inspired by, and is a generalization of, earlier work on Symbolic Array Attributes. Whereas SAA annotates AST array descriptors with array dimension and shape information, extrema annotate them with array value information; both methods then exploit the optimization process itself to enable further optimizations; SAA information can, therefore, also be considered symbiotic expressions, in the sense described here.

The main aim of the introduction of SAA expressions was to enable optimizations that require shape equalities as well as shape information across function boundaries. After optimization, again in the spirit of symbiotic expressions, unused shape information is eliminated from the syntax tree.

The symbiotic expressions introduced in this paper are a generalization of the SAA approach, albeit applied in a rather different context. While making shape information explicit can be seen as a change in representation that facilitates further optimizations, extrema information adds new context information about the range of values possible at runtime. This information is attached and propagated for selected values only, rather than for all values. Furthermore, the constraints of interest here are not just equalities, but also inequalities of all sorts. In our experience, simplification of shape expressions requires, for the purposes of AWLF, exploitation of both SAA and extrema information.

The use of symbiotic expressions to narrow the range of index values in array comprehensions has parallels with refinement types [17,18], also referred to as predicate sub-typing [19]. Similar to refinement types, we annotate type information with predicates–the minimal and maximal value of an index vector at runtime. However, other than in refinement type systems, these refinements are annotated automatically by the compiler and exploited only for the optimizations. Also, we do not use symbiotic expressions to prove user-defined properties of programs. The main difference of our approach is that our annotations are regular SaC expressions. They are neither encoded in the type system itself nor are they a specific extension for refinement types. This allows us to reuse existing optimizations, opposed to requiring a specialized SMT solver.

For the same reasons, symbiotic expressions are not dependent types. However, symbiotic expression might be useful in the context of dependent types to prove user-annotated constraints and infer type information.

6   Conclusions and Future Work

Symbiotic expressions are source language or IL expressions. They are inserted into the AST by the compiler, simplified by its optimization phases, then the results are used by the compiler in further optimization, or for other desired purposes, after which they are deleted from the AST, so they do not appear in run-time code. Symbiotic expressions are a completely general approach for letting a compiler use itself to solve its own problems, whatever they may be.

Our use of symbiotic expressions to implement AWLF within the SaC compiler has paid off well. The optimization worked correctly, essentially, from day zero; the injection and propagation of symbiotic expressions was simple and straightforward. It is a general approach that is applicable to many common compiler problems.

Our success with symbiotic expressions suggests that, even if a compiler may not have all the power of an SMT solver, our approach can be of use in other contexts where SMT-like solvers or hand-coded expression simplifiers are used today. Specifically, symbiotic expressions should be usable in almost any compiler environment, including imperative, object-oriented, or functional settings. The main contribution of our approach is that it makes all of the AST metadata available in a common framework, where it is directly shared by optimizers and other compiler components. We suggest that extending the optimization capabilities of compilers to allow them to act as tightly integrated SMT solvers would offer even greater benefits than we have obtained already.

Several benefits accrued from our use of symbiotic expressions to implement AWLF. First, AWLF often brings AKD problem performance very close to AKS performance. Second, AWLF significantly reduces cache miss rates over WLF. Third, because with-loops are the fundamental unit of parallel execution in SAC AWLF increases the size of data-parallel code blocks and reduces the number of parallel synchronization barriers. Since AWLF is able to fold more with-loops than WLF, AWLF increases the available parallelism in AKD-dominated programs over WLF. Although space limitations preclude detailed discussion of parallel performance measurements or performance against Fortran dialects, we note that the logd2 benchmark executed in 1493msec under Fortran 95, 433msec under Fortran 77, and 295msec under SAC in a serial environment.

We have begun to apply symbiotic expressions to the partial evaluation of run-time guards. This project has the potential to increase significantly the number of guards that can be statically removed from SAC programs. Also, as we noted in [12], guards can allow many optimizations to be performed in the absence of precise information about the arrays upon which they operate. These *guarded optimizations*, or *optimistic optimizations*, can create the desirable situation whereby introduction of safety features, such as array bounds checking, can materially speed programs up, rather than slow programs down.

We have not yet tried to scale symbiotic expressions beyond annotating and exploiting range information for index values. It would be interesting to investigate if our approach can be extended to provide some or all of the power of full refinement types. This would require more general annotations and a more powerful optimization-based solver. To determine whether this would bring our approach on a par with SMT-solver based solutions remains future work.

Acknowledgements

We thank the anonymous referees for their thoughtful comments and insights.

References

1. Cann, D.C.: Compilation Techniques for High Performance Applicative Computation. PhD thesis, Computer Science Department, Colorado State University (1989)
2. Bacon, D.F., Graham, S.L., Sharp, O.J.: Compiler transformations for high-performance computing. ACM Computing Surveys 26, 345–420 (1994)
3. Padua, D., Wolfe, M.: Advanced Compiler Optimizations for Supercomputers. ACM Comm. 29, 1184–1201 (1986)
4. Scholz, S.B.: Single Assignment C — efficient support for high-level array operations in a functional setting. Journal of Functional Programming 13, 1005–1059 (2003)
5. Scholz, S.B.: With-loop-folding in SAC–Condensing Consecutive Array Operations. In: Clack, C., Hammond, K., Davie, T. (eds.) IFL 1997. LNCS, vol. 1467, pp. 72–92. Springer, Heidelberg (1998)
6. Rugina, R., Rinard, M.: Symbolic bounds analysis of pointers, array indices, and accessed memory regions. In: PLDI 2000 Conference Proceedings, pp. 182–195. ACM, New York (2000)

7. Dutertre, B., de Moura, L.: The yices smt solver. Technical report, SRI International (2006)
8. Pugh, W.: A practical algorithm for exact array dependence analysis. CACM 35, 102–115 (1992)
9. Kelly, W., Maslov, V., Pugh, W., Rosser, E., Shpeisman, T., Wonnacott, D.: The OMEGA library, version 1.1.0 interface guide. Technical report, University of Maryland (1996)
10. Trojahner, K., Grelck, C., Scholz, S.B.: On Optimising Shape-Generic Array Language Programs using Symbolic Structural Information. In: Horváth, Z., Zsók, V., Butterfield, A. (eds.) IFL 2006. LNCS, vol. 4449, pp. 1–18. Springer, Heidelberg (2007)
11. Cytron, R., Ferrante, J., Rosen, B.K., Wegman, M.N., Zadeck, F.K.: An efficient method for computing static single assignment form. In: Conference Record of the Sixteenth Annual ACM Symposium on Principles of Programming Languages, pp. 23–35 (1989)
12. Herhut, S., Scholz, S.B., Bernecky, R., Grelck, C., Trojahner, K.: From contracts towards dependent types: Proofs by partial evaluation. In: Chitil, O., Horváth, Z., Zsók, V. (eds.) IFL 2007. LNCS, vol. 5083, pp. 254–273. Springer, Heidelberg (2008)
13. Browne, S., Deane, C., Ho, G., Mucci, P.: Papi: A portable interface to hardware performance counters. In: HPCMP Users Group Conference, U.S Department of Defense (1999)
14. Mucci, P.: Papiex - execute arbitrary application and measure hardware performance counters with papi (2009)
15. Bernecky, R.: APEX: The APL Parallel Executor. Master's thesis, University of Toronto (1997)
16. Menon, V.S., Glew, N., Murphy, B.R., McCreight, A., Shpeisman, T., Tabatabai, A.-R., Petersen, L.: A verifiable SSA program representation for aggressive compiler optimization. In: POPL 2006 Conference Proceedings, pp. 397–408. ACM, New York (2006)
17. Freeman, T., Pfenning, F.: Refinement types for ml. SIGPLAN Not. 26, 268–277 (1991)
18. Xi, H., Pfenning, F.: Dependent Types in Practical Programming. In: POPL 1999, pp. 214–227. ACM Press, New York (1999)
19. Rushby, J., Owre, S., Shankar, N.: Subtypes for specifications: Predicate subtyping in PVS. IEEE Transactions on Software Engineering 24, 709–720 (1998)

Stream Fusion on Haskell Unicode Strings

Thomas Harper

Oxford University Computing Laboratory
Oxford, United Kingdom

Abstract. Prior papers have presented a fusion framework called stream fusion for removing intermediate data structures from both lists and arrays in Haskell. Stream fusion is unique in using an explicit datatype to accomplish fusion. We demonstrate how this can be exploited in the creation of a new Haskell string representation *Text*, which achieves better performance and data density than *String*. *Text* uses streams not only to accomplish fusion, but also as a way to abstract away from various underlying representations. This allows the same set of combinators to manipulate Unicode text that is stored in a variety of ways.

1   Introduction

Lists are the primary workhorse data structure of functional programming. In the programming language Haskell[1], strings are represented using the built-in list type. This allows programmers to use standard polymorphic list combinators to build complex string manipulation functions in the same way that they would manipulate other lists. Haskell programmers often take advantage of this by composing list functions to form "pipelines" for transforming lists (and strings). For example:

$$return \cdot words \cdot map \; toUpper \cdot filter \; isAlpha \ll readFile \; f$$

This program reads in a file, filters out the non-alphabetic characters, converts the remaining characters to uppercase, and then tokenises them. It exemplifies Haskell's ability to create concise yet powerful programs through the composition of modular functions. It is also, however, extremely inefficient. Haskell's *String*s are much larger than, for example, their C counterparts. To address these inefficiencies, there is an alternative to *String* in the Haskell core libraries called *ByteString*. *ByteString* addresses *String*'s inefficiencies and achieves greater performance, but it does so at the cost of support for non-ASCII characters. We are introducing a new data type, *Text*, to fill in the gap left between these two approaches. *Text* addresses the performance issues associated with *String* while maintaining Unicode support.

The *Text* type is an array-based string representation that is faster and more compact than *String*. Its API is based on Haskell's list library, which means that it can be used as a drop-in replacement for *String*. Figure 1 shows the speed-up achieved by using *Text*s to run the example program from above. The main contribution of this paper is a faster, more compact string representation

M.T. Morazán and S.-B. Scholz (Eds.): IFL 2009, LNCS 6041, pp. 125–140, 2010.
© Springer-Verlag Berlin Heidelberg 2010

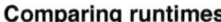

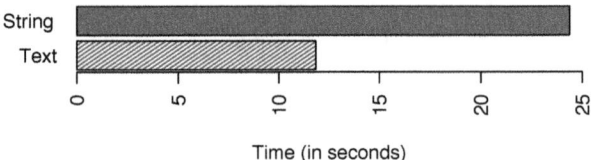

Fig. 1. Sample comparison of *Text* and *String* runtimes

for Haskell that incorporates Unicode support. We implement Haskell's list API over *Texts*. Like *ByteString*, we use *stream fusion* to remove intermediate data structures. Our use of stream fusion demonstrates how to exploit it in a novel way. Our API implementation uses the *Stream* type as an abstraction over more complex underlying representations. As we will show, this is an important aspect of how we implemented the API for *Text*.

The rest of the paper is organised as follows: Section 2 provides some important background information. It discusses Haskell's *String* type and its advantages and disadvantages. It presents some information on the Unicode standard and Unicode encoding standards. It also provides a short introduction to stream fusion. Section 3 discusses the internal structure of the *Text* datatype and how it addresses the inefficiencies of *String*. Section 4 describes the API for *Text* and how it uses stream fusion in its implementation. Section 5 presents and discusses some benchmarks of *Text* in comparison with both *String* and *ByteString*. Section 6 discusses some of the related fusion and string alternative efforts. Section 7 presents our conclusions and proposals for further work.

2   Background

2.1   The *String* and *ByteString* Types

Haskell defines *String* using the built-in list and *Char* types:

type *String* = [*Char*]

There are many benefits to this design. It is consistent with the notion that a string is a list of individual characters and allows us to manipulate them as we would other lists. Haskell's polymorphic list library contains functions that encapsulate a variety of common recursion patterns. Programmers can compose these functions to create modular programs where each of the individual components can be reused. *Strings* are also Unicode-compliant. This elegance, however, comes with a price. Figure 2 shows the structure of *String*. Using the Haskell list type as the basis for *String* means that it uses a series of *Cons* cells to store values. In the case of *String*, each of these *Cons* cells points to both a heap-allocated *Char* and then the next *Cons* cell in the list. Each heap-allocated object has a word-sized (either 32-bit or 64-bit) header. All pointers are also word-sized. Each

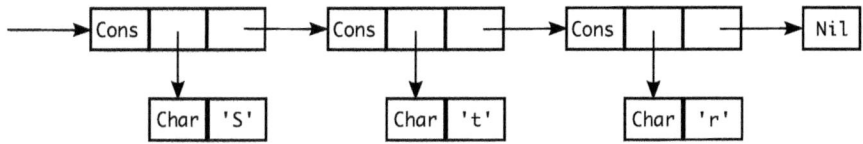

Fig. 2. The low-level structure of a *String*

Char is also word-sized. This amounts to a string representation that requires 20 bytes per character on a 32-bit system where only 8 to 32 bits are needed [2].[1]

Coutts et al. [3] created a new string type, *ByteString*, which offers better density and performance than *String*. In order to overcome *String*'s memory and performance drawbacks, *ByteString* uses a strict, array-based representation. The underlying structure of this representation is shown in Figure 3. This array structure eliminates the need for memory-consuming pointers and headers for each character. It only uses 8 bits for each character instead of *String*'s 32 bits. This compactness, while desirable, also sacrifices support for Unicode characters, leaving a rather large gap between the performance of ASCII text and Unicode text in Haskell. As a strict data structure, the creation of intermediate *ByteStrings* would have a severe impact on performance. To address this problem, the authors of *ByteString* introduced a new fusion technique which they called *stream fusion* [4]. This technique, which we also employ, is explained briefly in Section 2.3.

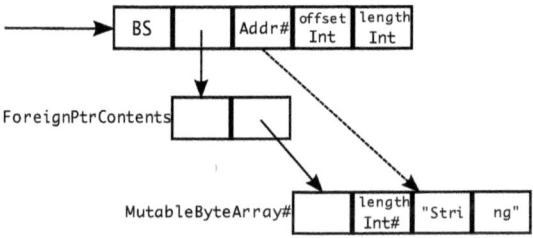

Fig. 3. The low-level structure of a *ByteString*

2.2   Unicode

Unicode is a world standard for representing text in nearly all of the world's modern and historical writing systems [5], including, for example, Cyrillic, Arabic, and East Asian scripts. The Unicode Standard also specifies three encoding systems for Unicode code points: UTF-8, UTF-16, and UTF-32. Of these, UTF-8 and UTF-16 are *variable-width*, and UTF-32 is *fixed-width*. For variable-width

---

[1] For ASCII characters, each repeated character only requires an additional 12 bytes because GHC pre-allocates and shares ASCII characters.

encodings, decoding a Unicode stream into Unicode code points involves some binary arithmetic.

UTF-8 is a byte-oriented encoding in which each code point requires between one and four bytes depending on its value (the larger the code point value, the more bytes required). This encoding is the most compact, using only one byte for the smallest code points. It is also backward compatible with ASCII (that is, a UTF-8 document consisting only of those characters in ASCII will be exactly the same). The price for UTF-8's compactness is increased overhead in decoding. Outside of traditional ASCII characters (i.e. any code point above U+7F[2]), it is necessary to reconstruct code points from two or more bytes for many commonly used characters (e.g. every character in the Cyrillic alphabet or Arabic alphabets).

UTF-16 is a 16-bit-word-oriented encoding. Characters are encoded using one or two words. Two adjacent words that are used to represent a character together are a *surrogate pair*. In comparison with UTF-8, UTF-16 is less compact; the minimum space required for a code point is 16 bits rather than 8. What this costs in space, however, is gained in efficiency. The range of code points that fit into one UTF-16 word is U+0000 to U+FFFF. This range is known as the Basic Multilingual Plane which includes all writing systems currently in use around the world as well as some writing systems no longer used.[3]. This means that surrogate pairs occur rarely in modern language documents. Those code points that are stored in only one 16-bit word are stored as raw values; no arithmetic is required to decode them.

Of the three encodings, UTF-32 is the simplest. It represents each code point as a 32-bit number. A code point requires at most 21-bits to represent its value, so UTF-32 can represent any of them without any splitting or arithmetic. While this is the most straightforward implementation of Unicode, it is also the most inefficient in terms of space. All common (and even many obscure) code points take up two to four times as much space as necessary.

Although UTF-8 is the most compact encoding, *Text* uses UTF-16 due to its much lower overhead. In the case of ASCII characters, this does represent a greater use of space that is strictly necessary. However, given the fact that UTF-8 also requires 16 bits for any non-Basic Latin character, UTF-16 represents a similar solution with far less overhead, especially for non-Latin-based scripts.

2.3 Stream Fusion

Stream fusion is a technique for removing intermediate data structures that appear from the composition of recursive functions. These data structures are created when one function passes data on to the next. They are then discarded, waiting to be garbage collected. Depending on the situation, this can have a

---

[2] Unicode code points are usually represented as "U+" prefixed to the hexadecimal form of the number.

[3] The exception to this is about 40,000 of the "Han Unification" characters used for East Asian languages. These are rarely used or are obscure.

significant impact on performance. Although other techniques have been implemented in Haskell[6,7], the use of stream fusion for *ByteString* has demonstrated that it is well-suited to fusing arrays. In contrast, other common fusion systems are generally adapted for fusing lists. Here, we give an overview of the stream fusion material published by Coutts et al., whose papers provide a more in-depth explanation of the technique.

Stream fusion differs from other fusion strategies in using an explicit data type:

data *Stream a* = ∃*s*. *Stream* (*s* → *Step s a*) *s*
data *Step s a* = *Done* | *Yield a s* | *Skip s*

A *Stream* is a co-recursive form of a list, where each element of the list may be yielded one at a time. It contains a stepper function, which is used to unfold the *Stream*, and an initial seed to pass to the stepper function. The results of the stepper function cover three possibilities. The *Yield* constructor produces an element and a new seed. The *Done* constructor signals the end of the list. The case of *Skip* allows a new seed to be produced without yielding a value. This is important in allowing us to define functions that have potentially non-productive steps (e.g. *filter*). The central idea of stream fusion is that instead of recursive functions over data structures, we can define non-recursive ones over streams. We can then convert our data structures to and from streams to achieve the desired transformation.

Data structures are converted to and from streams by the functions *stream* and *unstream*. The *stream* function converts a data structure into a *Stream*. It creates a new *Stream* with a stepper function that yields successive values of the data structure until its end, finally yielding *Done*. For example, the *stream* function over lists is

```
stream :: [a] → Stream a
stream s0 = Stream next s0
  where
    next [] = Done
    next (x : xs) = Yield x xs ·
```

The way to convert back to our original structure is with *unstream*. This function actually applies a *Stream*'s stepper function recursively to each successive seed until it encounters *Done*. For lists, the *unstream* function is

```
unstream :: Stream a → [a]
unstream (Stream next s0) = unfold s0
  where unfold s = case next s of
    Done      → []
    Skip s'   → unfold s'
    Yield x xs → x : unfold xs ·
```

Functions over streams transform it by modifying the definition of its stepper function. This is done by defining a new function that calls the original stepper

$$mapS :: (a \rightarrow b) \rightarrow Stream\ a \rightarrow Stream\ b$$
$$mapS\ (Stream\ next\ s0) = Stream\ next'\ s0$$
    where
        $next'\ s = $ **case** $next\ s$ **of**
            $Done$ $\rightarrow Done$
            $Skip\ s'$ $\rightarrow Skip\ s'$
            $Yield\ a\ s' \rightarrow Yield\ (f\ a)\ s'$

$$filterS :: (a \rightarrow Bool) \rightarrow Stream\ a \rightarrow Stream\ a$$
$$filterS\ p\ (Stream\ next\ s0) = Stream\ next'\ s0$$
    where
        $next'\ s = $ **case** $next\ s$ **of**
            $Done$ $\rightarrow Done$
            $Skip\ s'$ $\rightarrow Skip\ s'$
            $Yield\ a\ s'\ |\ p\ x$ $\rightarrow Yield\ a\ s'$
                       $|\ otherwise \rightarrow Skip\ s'$

Fig. 4. Some examples of stream functions

function and pattern matching on each of the three *Step* constructors. Figure 4 shows the stream version of some common list functions. The function *filterS* is particularly notable in demonstrating the use of the *Skip* constructor. In the case where the predicate p is not satisfied the *Yield* is replaced with a *Skip* which discards the value and only keeps the seed. This allows the stepper function to be productive without yielding an element we wish to discard.

It is important to note that stepper functions are non-recursive. When a stream is unfolded, *all* the transformations are applied to a yielded element before producing a new one. This merges what would be several recursive traversals over a structure into a single recursive unfold of a stream. In general, fusible functions on streamable data structures are defined in terms of their analogous stream transformers: *stream* and *unstream*. A fusible function defined in terms of streams tends to have the following structure:

$$f\ x = unstream \cdot fS \cdot stream$$

where *fS* is the stream transformation analogue of f. Functions that only consume streams have no *unstream*, and functions that only produce streams will have no *stream*. When two fusible functions f and g are composed as $f \cdot g$, they can be inlined to form

$$unstream \cdot fS \cdot stream \cdot unstream \cdot gS \cdot stream$$

In the middle of this function, there is an instance of unfolding a stream, only to create a new one. Eliminating occurrences of *stream* · *unstream* yields the program:

$$unstream \cdot fS \cdot gS \cdot stream$$

Removing this portion of the program produces a new program that is equivalent. The occurrence of *stream · unstream* would have created an intermediate data structure, only to convert it to new stream. Instead, the original stream is transformed twice and then unfolded. To accomplish this fusion automatically, we specify the following rewrite rule:

⟨**stream/unstream fusion**⟩ $\forall s.\ stream\ (unstream\ s)\ \mapsto s$

This rule can be specified in GHC using compiler directives [8], which allows us to apply it automatically during compilation.

3 The *Text* Data Type

The first step in creating *Text* is to design its underlying datatype. The purpose of the *Text* datatype is to store Unicode text more efficiently than *String*. Having seen the effectiveness of array-based storage, we use this approach in *Text*. Using an array removes the numerous pointers and *Cons* cells that account for so much of the space consumed by a *String*. We can also remove the pointers to elements, and their associated headers, by using an array of unboxed elements. Finally, we can decrease the minimum size of a character by utilising a Unicode encoding instead of representing them as raw code points. In this case, we chose UTF-16. The reason for this decision is not arbitrary; UTF-16 achieved better performance in benchmarks that dealt with large amounts of non-ASCII test, most likely because of its simpler arithmetic [9]. We consider such a case to be a major use of this library and therefore an important factor.

The result is the following definition of *Text*:

data *Text = Text* !(*UArray Int Word16*) !*Int* !*Int*

Text is an unboxed array of 16-bit words indexed by integers. The other integers are offset and length fields. These fields allow "free" creation of substrings merely by modifying these fields and pointing to the original string's array. The exclamation points are strictness annotations which prevent these fields from being calculated lazily; since the underlying array is strict anyway, any laziness will only introduce inefficiencies. Figure 5 shows the underlying structure of *Text*. The use of *Word16* reflects our use of UTF-16, which is based on converting 1 or 2 16-bit words into a Unicode code point. Even in the worst case, *Text* still only requires 32 bits instead of *Strings* 20 bytes.

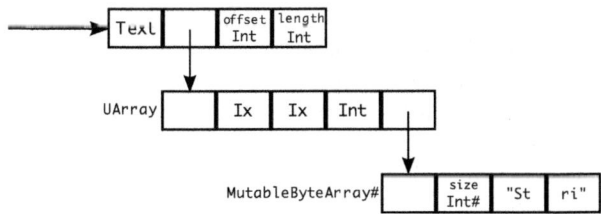

Fig. 5. The low-level structure of a *Text*

The switch from a list-based representation to an array-based one alters the complexity of some fundamental string operations. Some operations are now faster and consume less memory. Indexing is now a constant time operation, allowing for easy reads in the middle of the string. Because of the length and offset fields, operations involving substring creation (e.g. *take* and *drop*) do not require any additional space. Functions that construct strings, however, require more resources than before. Both *cons* and *concat* require all of its inputs to be copied into a new array. This shifts *cons* from a constant time operation to linear one, and *concat* has gone from being linear in the length of its first argument to linear in the length of *both* arguments combined. The impact of these design decisions is also measured in Section 5.

4   Fusion and the *Text* API

In Section 2, we introduced the *Stream* datatype, along with the associated functions *stream* and *unstream*. These functions allowed us to use transformers over *Stream* as transformers over a target data structure. The use of *stream* and *unstream* allows us to syntactically identify and remove intermediate data structures from a program automatically.

In order to take advantage of stream fusion, all we need to do is implement *Text* versions of *stream* and *unstream*. The *stream* function must define a stepper function and seed that will traverse an array. Slightly more complicated is *unstream*, which needs to unfold the stream and place the yielded elements in an array. This entails allocating an array of the appropriate size. The initial solution to this problem was to start with a small array, allocating a new array that was double the size of the original when needed. The cost of copying, however, quickly overtook any performance gains. Instead, we added a strict *Int* field to *Stream*. This field holds the length of the array from which the stream was created, allowing the *unstream* to make a good guess of what the string size will be. Copying can still be performed if necessary but is avoided in most cases. Functions that modify the length of a string (e.g. *cons*,*concat*,*take*,*drop*) can modify this length field.

The crucial question in streaming *Text*s is how to manipulate them. In prior implementations of stream fusion, the elements of the underlying data structure are simply turned into a *Stream* of the same elements. This logic would lead us to converting *Text*s to *Stream Word16*s. This would mean that programmers would have to deal with encoding and decoding UTF-16 values themselves, which is highly undesirable. The idea is to abstract away from the underlying representation in our API, thus letting programmers deal with *Char*s. Therefore, we need to implement *stream* and *unstream* so that they not only create a *Stream*, but decode and re-encode UTF-16 values.

The first function, *stream*, decodes a UTF-16 array and creates a *Stream* from the result. This function is shown in Figure 6. This function creates a *Stream Char* whose stepper function *next* both decodes and streams elements of the array. The seeds for this function are indices of the array. This implementation makes some

```
stream :: Text → Stream Char
stream (Text arr off len) = Stream next off len
    where
        end = off + len
        next !i
            | i ⩾ end                    = Done
            | n ⩾ 0xD800 ∧ n ⩽ 0xDBFF = Yield (chr2 n n2) (i + 2)
            | otherwise                  = Yield (unsafeChr n) (i + 1)
            where
                n  = unsafeAt arr i
                n2 = unsafeAt arr (i + 1)
```

Fig. 6. The *stream* function for *Text*

important assumptions about the input *Text*. First, it assumes that all elements are *valid* UTF-16 values. This eliminates the need to perform certain bounds checks. The only condition we check about the elements is whether or not they are the beginning of a surrogate pair. If they are, it is assumed the following element is a valid second member of a surrogate pair. Finally, we use *unsafeAt* and *unsafeChr*, which assume that the values they are given are valid indices and character values, respectively. Making these assumptions cuts down significantly on the number of bounds checks we need to perform. For large strings, doing these for every character has a significant impact on performance. We allow ourselves to take these for granted by assuming that all *Text*s are always valid UTF-16 streams. We can do this because we do full Unicode checks when *Text*s are created from other sources, and then control the manipulation of *Text*s through our API.

The *unstream* function needs to convert a *Char* back into its UTF-16 equivalent. This is shown in Figure 7. This function allocates an array based upon length information given in the *Stream*. It then converts each character into one or two *Word16*s according to the UTF-16 standard. We again make the assumption of safety of our characters and do not perform full Unicode bounds checking. We can assume this rather safely because, unless the programmer is doing something tricky, *Char* will not contain an invalid Unicode code point. Furthermore, we manually track the bounds of the allocated array so that bounds checking does not need to be done with every write by the array API functions (hence *unsafeWrite*).

Together, these two functions perform all of the Unicode encoding and decoding necessary for string manipulation. This decision makes it easy to find and eliminate bottlenecks in our code. All of the encoding overhead is concentrated in only these two functions. Because stream fusion requires writing transformations over an explicit datatype, the usual stream transformers will work with a streamed *Text*. The only modifications we make are to restrict the type of certain functions (elements of a *Text* are always characters, and there are no nested *Text*s) and modify our length field where appropriate.

```
unstream :: Stream Char → Text
unstream (Stream next0 s0 len) = x 'seq' Text (fst x) 0 (snd x)
  where
    x :: ((UArray Int Word16), Int)
    x = runST ((unsafeNewArray_ (0, len + 1) :: ST s (STUArray s Int Word16))
        ≫= (λarr → loop arr 0 (len + 1) s0))
    loop arr !i !max !s
      | i + 1 > max = do
          arr' ← unsafeNewArray_ (0, max * 2)
          case next0 s of
            Done → liftM2 (,) (unsafeFreezeSTUArray arr) (return i)
            _    → copy arr arr' ≫ loop arr' i (max * 2) s
      | otherwise = case next0 s of
        Done   → liftM2 (,) (unsafeFreezeSTUArray arr) (return i)
        Skip s' → loop arr i max s'
        Yield x s'
          | n < 0x10000 → do
            unsafeWrite arr i (fromIntegral n :: Word16)
            loop arr (i + 1) max s'
          | otherwise → do
            unsafeWrite arr i l
            unsafeWrite arr (i + 1) r
            loop arr (i + 2) max s'
        where
          n = ord x; m = n − 0x10000
          l = fromIntegral ((shiftR m 10) + (0xD800))
          r = fromIntegral ((m .&. (0x3FF)) + (0xDC00))
```

Fig. 7. The *unstream* function for *Text*

Placing our decoding and encoding functionality in the stream conversion functions has another benefit: the stream fusion rewrite rule removes intermediate data structures *and* reduces the number of decodings/encodings that take place within a program automatically. This concept is key to the abstraction that we wish to achieve from the underlying data structure. Once we have a definition for *stream* and *unstream*, we no longer care about the data representation that is being used in *Text* when writing transformations. Regardless of the encoding of the characters, or the structure of the underlying sequence, the string manipulation functions are identical.

This abstraction has useful implications. Suppose that we want to use a function from some other library that only gives us *Strings*. For our *Text* library to work, we have to convert it first. For this, we use the *pack* function.

```
pack :: String → Text
pack str = (unstream (stream_list str))
  where
    stream_list s0 = Stream next s0 (length xs)
      where
```

$$next \; [\,] \quad\quad = Done$$
$$next \; (x : xs) = Yield \; x \; xs$$

The *pack* function allows us to convert a *String* into a *Text* using streams. It uses its own *stream_list* function, which is actually just the list version of *stream*. We then use *unstream*, which has already been heavily optimised, to write out the stream to a *Text*. Using streams here doesn't just make the function concise, though. If we transform a *Text* created using *pack*, we can fuse any intermediate *Texts* that are created. This means that in such a pipeline, only the final output *Text* is created, even though the input to the pipeline is a *String*.

Another example of where this is exploited is in file I/O. One of the benefits of *ByteString* is its extremely fast file I/O. To take advantage of this, we implement stream fusion over *ByteStrings* as well. Unlike the original implementation of *ByteString* fusion, though, we don't treat *ByteString* as an array of characters but rather as an array of bytes. We then implement the functions *encode* and *decode*, which read to and write from *ByteStrings*. Again, we do so using streams so that conversions do not result in unnecessary *Texts* being written. In addition, we implement the arithmetic to encode/decode *all* possible Unicode encoding standards. This is an example of where Unicode validation takes place when creating *Texts*. Because it involves reading from an external source, we must also check to make sure all the Unicode characters are valid and insert fallback characters if necessary.

The use of stream fusion also allows for easy expansion of the API, for example by an end-user of the library. As described in Section 2.3, transformations are composed of *stream*, *unstream*, and a stream transformer. Programmers can easily define their own stream transformers and compose them with *stream* and/or *unstream* as necessary to define their own fusible functions. The fusion can be applied to them as it is to any pre-defined function.

While stream fusion is an extremely useful abstraction, there are some instances where exploiting the low-level data structure can achieve better performance. For example, the length and offset fields allow us to create a version of *tail* that does not require copying:

$$unfused\_tail :: Text \rightarrow Text$$
$$unfused\_tail \; (Text \; arr \; off \; len)$$
$$\quad | \; len \leqslant 0 \quad\quad = errorEmptyList \; \texttt{"tail"}$$
$$\quad | \; n \geqslant 0 \; xD800 \; \wedge$$
$$\quad\quad n \leqslant 0 \; xDBFF = Text \; arr \; (off + 2) \; (len - 2)$$
$$\quad | \; otherwise \quad\;\; = Text \; arr \; (off + 1) \; (len - 1)$$
$$\textbf{where}$$
$$\quad n = unsafeAt \; arr \; off$$

By checking whether the first character is a surrogate pair or not, we can decide whether to move the offset by one or two characters and have a *Text* with the desired contents without the copying of the *Stream* version. It isn't fusible, though. We would prefer a way to automatically choose the best version of *tail* for a given situation. This can be accomplished with the following rule:

⟨**tail/unfused**⟩ $\forall t. \; unstream \; (tailS \; (stream \; t)) \; \mapsto \; unfused\_tail \; t$

136   T. Harper

This rule states that any occurrence of *tailS* that is not fused with another stream transformer should be converted to our low-level definition of *unfused_tail*. If a call to *tail* were fusible, it would not directly follow a call to *stream* because stream fusion would have removed this call. Now, we have GHC choosing the most appropriate function for us. This technique is useful for a variety of functions where totally decoding or copying the string is not strictly necessary, such as *init*, *last*, and *append*.

5 Performance

As a more compact and more efficient version of *String*, it is expected that *Text* should be much faster than *String*. This is generally the case. Compared to *String*, *Text* usually achieves much better performance. In comparison with *ByteString*, the extra overhead of Unicode encoding and decoding means that, for ASCII text, *ByteString* is still faster (and, at 8-bits per character, more compact). Figure 8 shows the runtimes for each of the three string representations for some common functions. Although both *Text* and *ByteString* generally outperform *String*, the runtimes of the *cons* function exhibit some of inherent disadvantages of using an array-based string representation. Unlike lists, implementations of *cons* over *Text*s require copying the source array completely, resulting in a linear time operation instead of a list's constant time one. Similar functions, such as *append*, suffer from similar problems.

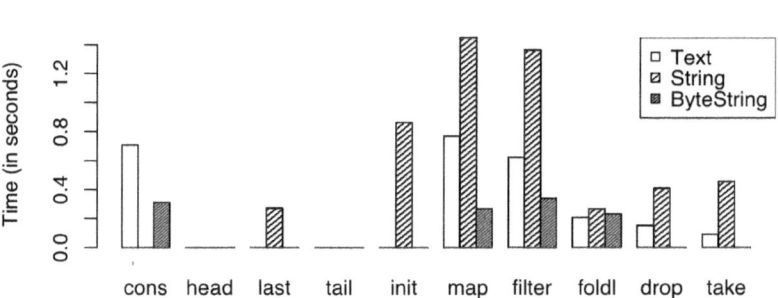

Fig. 8. Benchmarks: ASCII Text

Figures 9 and 10 show the performance of *String* versus *Text* for different sets of Unicode text. Figure 9 shows benchmarks for Unicode text in the Basic Multilingual Plane. The performance figures are very similar to the ASCII ones. This is to be expected, as ASCII text is treated the same as other low-numbered Unicode code points in UTF-16.

Figure 10 shows the performance of *Text* and *String* with text solely from the Supplementary Multilingual Plane (SMP). The SMP consists of more rarely used characters such as musical and mathematical notations. In general, a document will very rarely contain more than a relatively small number of these characters.

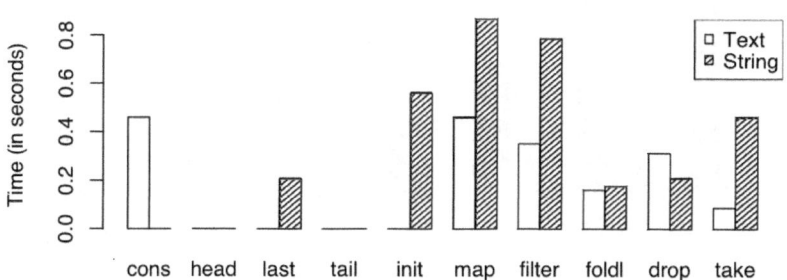

Fig. 9. Benchmarks: BMP Text

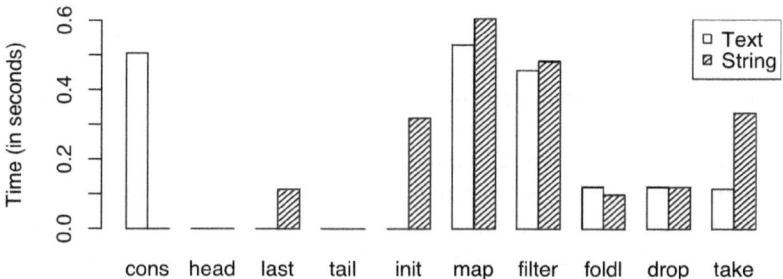

Fig. 10. Benchmarks: SMP Text

This benchmark represents a "worst case" of dealing with a document that exclusively uses such characters. This has a critical impact on performance because all SMP characters require two UTF-16 code points and must be assembled and disassembled when being streamed and unstreamed. In this case, *Text* slows down nearly to the performance of *String*, although still outperforms it in most cases. This shows that, in a worst case scenario, *Text* still scales well and can outperform *String*.

The benchmarks above show that *Text* outperforms *String* in single transformations, but fusion is an important aspect of this library. Figure 11 shows the performance of *Text* versus *String* in a variety of common fusion patterns. These benchmarks compare *Text* using stream fusion with *String* using *foldr/build* fusion. The figures show that *Text* significantly outperforms *String* in these situations. This figure is perhaps the most crucial, as string manipulation functions are more likely to be pipelined than called singly.

These benchmarks reveal that *Text* usually outperforms *String*, but that the low-level differences between the two must be considered when using *Text*. The inherent differences between arrays and lists makes some operations differ with

Benchmarks: Fusion

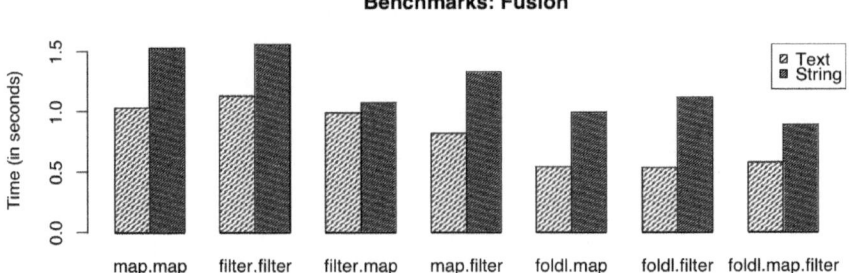

Fig. 11. Fusion Benchmarks

respect to complexity. This performance can sometimes be regained by fusion. The *Stream* version of these slower functions can easily fuse with other functions. In such a case there is very little *extra* cost associated with performing them, because the *Text* is already being copied. For example, *cons x · map f xs*, *cons* will not have the same impact on performance as it does in isolation.

Text is therefore most useful for manipulating strings, for example from user input or a file. Its performance becomes less desirable when constructing strings through concatenation and similar operations.

Another consideration is the strictness of *Text*. In programs that use file I/O, a lazy data structure will only read data into memory as necessary. Consider the example program in Section 1. Although *Text*'s runtime was better, the maximal memory consumption was actually much smaller in *String*. This is because, in *String*, new data can only be read in by *readFile* as it was consumed by *foldl*, but in *Text* the entire file is read in, and then consumed. For more discussion of lazy *Texts*, see Section 7.

6   Related Work

Although stream fusion was chosen as the fusion framework for this particular library, there are other related fusion frameworks that have been implemented in Haskell:

foldr/build. The *foldr/build* fusion framework is currently used in GHC for fusing lists [6]. It uses *foldr* with its traditional definition to consume lists and a function called *build* to produce them. This makes some functions, such as *filter*, much more straightforward to implement. It cannot, however, fuse zips.

destroy/unfoldr. The *destroy/unfoldr* fusion system [7] is the most similar to stream fusion. Like stream fusion, *destroy/unfoldr* uses the notion of co-data to produce a list, but using the well-known list function *unfoldr*. Compared with stream fusion, *destroy/unfoldr* has similar fusion capabilities, being able to express left folds and zips. However, unlike stream fusion, it requires recursion for *filter*-like functions, which affect the compiler's ability to perform certain optimisations and can drastically impact performance.

Neither of these frameworks uses an explicit data type. This unique characteristic of stream fusion is what makes it such a desirable candidate for our library, because we can clearly separate the conversion between *Char*s and *Word16*s using the *Stream* datatype.

Stream fusion also already appears in the Haskell library *ByteString* [3]. As previously mentioned, it has helped *ByteString* achieve (and sometimes beat) the performance of similar programs written in C. *ByteString* also uses a *ForeignPtr* for its underlying data structure, making it accessible to code in other languages (notably C). There is also an implementation of stream fusion over Haskell lists [4].

7 Conclusions

Stream fusion is already a known and successful fusion framework, but we have exploited a useful aspect of it in the creation of *Text*. By treating stream fusion's *Stream* type as an abstraction from underlying representations, we have used the stream fusion framework as tool for designing a library over strings that is independent of various low-level representations. In doing so, stream fusion not only prevents the creation of intermediate *Text*s in a string transformation pipeline, it also prevents unnecessary conversion between different encodings and data structures.

There is still plenty of work being done for *Text*. Since the completion of this project, Bryan O'Sullivan has continued to maintain and refine *Text*. His major contributions to the project have been to replace *UArray* with a lower level (and thus faster and smaller) data type and to create a lazy version of *Text*. He has done this by using a list of array chunks. He has also achieved 93% QuickCheck [10] coverage of API functions, weeding out several subtle issues. He has also shifted certain list API functions so that integer-based indexing is less used (e.g. instead of returning the index of the first occurrence of 'c', split at the first occurrence of 'c'), which is more efficient. The most recent version of *Text* is available in the Hackage database.

The performance of *Text* is generally better than that of *String*, and provides a fast way to transform Unicode text in a functional style. Its current array-based representation limits its flexibility in creating strings efficiently, and so while the API abstracts away from its low-level representation, this still must be considered when using *Text* to achieve the best performance. However, it may be possible to use more sophisticated persistent data structures to create a more versatile *Text* with even better performance.

Text's array-based structure also has some drawbacks with respect to persistence. Currently, substrings can be created by modifying the length and offset fields of an existing *Text*. While this has the benefit of allowing constant-time substring creation, it does not take into account the size of the substring relative to its parent string. A very small substring may keep a much larger string from garbage collection. We also have many operations with undesirable complexities for building strings. We wish to investigate the possibility of using another data structure for the underlying representation of *Text*. A possible candidate is to use finger trees [11] of arrays to create a fusible rope [12]. This would make the library better suited to manipulating *and* building strings.

References

1. Peyton-Jones, S.: The Haskell 98 Report (2002)
2. The GHC Team: The Glorious Glasgow Haskell Compilation System User's Guide, Version 6.12.1
3. Coutts, D., Stewart, D., Leshchinskiy, R.: Rewriting Haskell Strings. In: Hanus, M. (ed.) PADL 2007. LNCS, vol. 4354, pp. 50–64. Springer, Heidelberg (2006)
4. Coutts, D., Leshchinskiy, R., Stewart, D.: Stream Fusion: From Lists to Streams to Nothing At All. In: ICFP 2007. ACM, New York (October 2007)
5. The Unicode Consortium: The Unicode Standard, Version 5.2.0 (2010)
6. Gill, A., Launchbury, J., Peyton-Jones, S.: A Short Cut to Deforestation. In: ICFP 1993, pp. 223–232. ACM, New York (1993)
7. Svenningsson, J.: Shortcut fusion for accumulating parameters & zip-like functions. In: ICFP 2002, pp. 124–132. ACM, New York (2002)
8. Petyon-Jones, S., Tolmach, A., Hoare, T.: Playing by the Rules: Rewriting as a practical optimisation technique in GHC. In: Haskell Workshop, ACM SIGPLAN, pp. 203–233 (2001)
9. Harper, T.: Fusion on Haskell Unicode Strings, Master's Thesis, University of Oxford (2008)
10. Claessen, K., Hughes, J.: QuickCheck: a lightweight tool for random testing of Haskell programs. In: ICFP 2000. ACM, New York (2000)
11. Hinze, R., Paterson, R.: Finger trees: a simple general-purpose data structure. Journal of Functional Programming 16(2) (2006)
12. Boehm, H.J., Atkinson, R., Plass, M.: Ropes: an Alternative to Strings. Software: Practice and Experience 25(12), 1315–1330 (1995)

Nested and Dynamic Contract Boundaries*

T. Stephen Strickland and Matthias Felleisen

PLT @ Northeastern University
{sstrickl,matthias}@ccs.neu.edu

Abstract. Previous work on software contracts assumes fixed and statically known boundaries between the parties to a contract. Implementations of contract monitoring systems rely on this assumption to explain the nature of contract violations and to assign blame to violators. In this paper, we explain how to implement arbitrary, nested, and dynamic contract boundaries with two examples. First, we add nestable contract regions to a static, first-order module system. Second, we show that even a dynamic, higher-order, and hierarchical module system can be equipped with software contracts that support precise blame assignment.

1 Contracts for Modules

PLT Scheme [1] comes with a widely used contract system for specifying behavioral (functional) properties of module exports and imports. Roughly speaking, a behavioral software contract imposes restrictions on the domain and range of a function that flows from one module to another. If the function does not produce the kind of values promised in a contract, the run-time monitoring system raises a contract exception and blames the server module for exporting an ill-behaved function. Conversely, if the client module applies an imported function to values that fail to satisfy the domain contract, the run-time system blames the client for not living up to its promises.

Unlike other systems for monitoring behavioral software contracts [2, 3, 4, 5, 6, 7, 8, 9, 10, 11, 12, 13, 14, 15, 16, 17], PLT Scheme's contract system does not restrict contracts to first-order functions and methods. Instead, programmers may formulate contracts for all kinds of values, including higher-order values [18]. The module system, however, is restrictive. In particular, modules are merely first-order namespaces, without mechanism for nesting them or linking them in a recursive fashion. Naturally programmers chafe under this module system and call for more flexibility.

At the same time, the theory of contracts assumes fixed and statically known boundaries between contract parties. Contract implementations combine compilers that can determine the parties to each contract from the source text with a run-time checking system that exploits this knowledge for blaming violators.

In this paper, we relax these restrictions and show how to add arbitrary contract boundaries to the PLT Scheme module system and how to implement

---

* This research was partially supported by the US Air Force Office of Scientific Research and the National Science Foundation.

M.T. Morazán and S.-B. Scholz (Eds.): IFL 2009, LNCS 6041, pp. 141–158, 2010.

contracts for its units, a higher-order, hierarchical, and dynamic component system [19, 20]. Sections 3 and 4 make up the core of the paper. Both use the same organization, explaining the nature of the contract boundary first and, based on that, its enforcement. In particular, the third section adds nested contract regions to PLT Scheme's module system, while the fourth section explains contracts for its unit system. In section 5 we revisit the design decisions concerning blame assignment with a side-by-side comparison of the two extensions. Finally, the last section compares this paper with a concurrent publication on a theoretical model of a structural (ML-like) module system [21]. The paper starts with a section that briefly describes the existing module system and its contracts.

2 Static Modules in PLT Scheme

PLT Scheme provides static modules that are neither nestable nor first-class. Figure 1 contains an example consisting of two modules. A module may export values via their names[1] through the use of the **provide** form. Another module makes use of these values via a **require** form. Modules may not require each other (or themselves) in a cyclic fashion.

server

```
#lang scheme
(define (sqrt n) ...)
... (sqrt 3) ... (sqrt 0) ...
(provide sqrt)
```

client

```
#lang scheme
(require server)
... (sqrt 3) ...
... (sqrt 0) ...
```

Fig. 1. Example modules

Findler and Felleisen's work on higher-order contracts [18] presents a model for adding contract checks to such a module system. The implementation of this model in the PLT Scheme module system operates via the **provide/contract** form, which specifies a sequence of names paired with contracts. The main idea behind this implementation is that module interfaces serve as natural *contract boundaries*. Values that flow across a contract boundary are checked for the specified properties, while values that stay on one side remain unchecked.

A contract boundary in PLT Scheme brings together two contract parties. One is the exporting server module; the other one is the importing client module in which the name is used. The contract monitoring system uses the module names to assign blame when it discovers and signals contract violations. In analogy to type theory, we call the name of the server module a *positive blame label* of a specific contract, and the name of the client module a *negative blame label*.

The design decision of not monitoring the uses of contracts within a module is due to both software engineering considerations and compilation issues. In particular, we consider the inside of a module a space where programmers should

---

[1] In PLT Scheme, modules can also export values for use at compile-time as well as run-time. Here we focus on run-time values.

trust their own instincts, even allowing temporary violations of contracts; the alternative poses severe challenges known as the callback problem [22]. Furthermore, monitoring the uses of contracts within a module would negatively affect opportunities for tail-call optimizations, an essential element of functional and object-oriented program design.

server

```
#lang scheme
(define (sqrt n) ...)
... (sqrt 3) ...  (sqrt −1)  ...
(provide/contract
  [sqrt (→ positive? positive?)])
```

client

```
#lang scheme
(require server)
...
... (sqrt 3) ...
...  (sqrt −1)  ...
```

Fig. 2. Modules with an example contract

Figure 2 displays contracted versions of the modules from figure 1. Specifically, the *server* module exports *sqrt* with a contract that demands positive numbers as inputs and promises the same for the results. The use of *sqrt* with −1 in *client*—see boxed code—triggers a contract violation error that blames *client* for applying *sqrt* to an inappropriate value. In contrast, the gray-shaded call to *sqrt* on −1 within *server* is not monitored and so does not signal a contract error; presumably *server* knows how to deal with complex numbers.

3   Nested Contract Regions

While programmers appreciate the rationale of not monitoring contracts within a module, they also commonly wish to isolate regions that they can protect with contracts, even within modules. This is especially true for debugging sessions or for modules that grow into large bodies of code. Unlike the static module system in section 2, one such region may be nested within another, or a module may contain several parallel regions. In response to this request, we introduce *contract regions*. The first subsection introduces the idea via a series of examples, which at the same time suggests design desiderata for this new feature. The second subsection describes our implementation.

3.1   The Pragmatics of Contract Regions

Consider the module fragment on the left-hand of figure 3. It displays the fragment of a module that contains the definition of the *serve* function, which implements a basic webserver, and two applications; the second one is faulty, applying *serve* to a low TCP port, that is, a TCP port with a numeric value less than 1024, for which the program does not have the necessary permissions.

To protect *serve* from such errors *within* the module, a programmer could create a separate static module that defines *serve* and exports it with an appropriate contract. Of course this strategy imposes a high overhead. Worse, it may

```
#lang scheme
(define (serve p)
  (let ([s (tcp-listen p)])
    (handle-request s)
    (serve p)))
...
(serve 8080)
...
(serve 80) ;; error, no superuser permissions
```

```
#lang scheme
(with-contract serve
  ([serve (→ high-tcp-port? void?)])
  (define (serve p)
    (let ([s (tcp-listen p)])
      (handle-request s)
      (serve p)))
...
(serve 80) ;; contract violation
```

Fig. 3. Modules and contract regions

not work if the to-be-separated parts are mutually referential, because the PLT Scheme module system does not support mutually recursive linking.

Instead we introduce the **with-contract** form. The right-hand side of figure 3 shows the simplest way to use the **with-contract** form. It consists of three pieces: a name, which is used to assign blame; a sequence of contracted variables; and a sequence of definitions. Every variable listed in the second part must have a definition in the third part, but there may be additional definitions in this third part that do not come with a contract.

Since the **with-contract** syntax is heavy-weight for single definitions, we introduce a convenience abbreviation named **define/contract**. The syntax of **define/contract** is similar to that of PLT Scheme's **define**, except for the addition of a contract before the body of the definition. With **define/contract**, the code in the above figure would look like this:

```
#lang scheme
(define/contract (serve n)
  (→ high-tcp-port? void?)
  (let ([s (tcp-listen p)]) (handle-request s) (serve p))))
...
```

The abbreviation is translated into a contract region that uses the name of the defined value as the blame label.

The **with-contract** form introduces a block of definitions. As such, it can be used in any syntactic position where definitions are allowed. It does *not* introduce a new lexical scope, meaning both contracted and uncontracted definitions are accessible in the surrounding lexical scope. Conversely, all internal definitions may access any external definitions at will.

Not surprisingly, the name of the contract region serves as the positive blame label for all contracts listed in the **with-contract** form. The question is what we should consider as the client of the region and what we should use as the negative blame label for the contracts. Obviously, if there is no other contract region in the module, the rest of the module is the client. If, however, a module contains several regions or regions are nested, we have a choice to make.

```
#lang scheme
(define/contract (encode key msg)
  (→ prime? string? string?)
  ...)
(define/contract (send-msg msg)
  (→ string? void?)
  ... (encode 20 m) ...) ;; contract error, blame: ???
```

Fig. 4. Two parallel contract regions

Consider the two regions in figure 4. It appears convenient to use *send-msg* as the most precise negative blame label for the use of *encode* here. Put differently, all parallel contract regions could be considered as clients of each other. Although this design choice is appealing, it is inappropriate. Instead we say that a contract region introduces a contract boundary between itself and its surrounding context. If this surrounding context allows the contracted value to flow into other contract regions, those regions are clients of the context not the original contract region. For our above example, this means that when *send-msg* is called, the enclosing module context is blamed for the misuse of *encode*. We revisit this choice at length in section 5.

```
#lang scheme
(with-contract serve
  ([serve (→ high-tcp-port? void?)])
  (define (serve p)
    (let ([s (tcp-listen p)]) (handle-request s) (serve p)))
  (define (serve-80) (with-su (serve 80)))) ;; ok
(serve 8080)
(serve 80) ;; contract error, module misused serve
```

Fig. 5. External vs. internal uses

Just as with module-based contracts, a contract region does not monitor internal uses of the contracted definitions. To illustrate this point, take a look at the *serve-80* function in figure 5, which correctly sets up the necessary permissions for accessing low TCP ports with the *with-su* form. The external uses of *serve* are checked according to the contract, and so the last call to *serve* still fails, but the internal use in the definition of *serve-80* is not restricted and succeeds.

The introduction of a distinction between internal and external uses of contracted variables naturally raises the question where the contract itself lives. In order to explain this issue, we use the example in figure 6. The contract region contains several functions to operate on record-like list values that represent student information. These records contain two fields: names, represented as strings, and nine-digit numbers used for unique identification. The predicates *id?* and *student?* are used within the contracts for the other operations. However, these predicates are also contracted, and thus we must decide whether the

```
#lang scheme
(with-contract student
    ([id? (→ any/c boolean?)] [make-student (→ string? id? student?)]
     [student-name (→ student? string?)] [student-id (→ student? id?)]
     [student? (→ any/c boolean?)])
    (define (id? n) (and (natural-number? n) (< n 1000000000)))
    (define (make-student s n) (list s n))
    (define (student-name s) (first s))
    (define (student-id s) (second s))
    (define (student? s)
        (and (list? s) (= (length s) 2) (string? (first s)) (id? (second s)))))
```

Fig. 6. Operations for student records

uses within those contracts must be checked. Since the contracts are a part of the **with-contract** form itself, we consider it reasonable to treat such uses as internal uses, meaning they are not protected.

```
#lang scheme
(define (salary? s) (or (natural-number? s) (eq? s #f)))
(define (make-employee s n) (list s n))
(define (employee? s)
    (and (list? s) (= (length s) 2) (string? (first s)) (salary? (second s))))
(define (employee-name e) (first e))
(define (employee-salary e) (second e))
;; test data
(define loe1 (list (make-employee "Bob" 45000) (make-employee "Stan" 50000)))
(define loe2 (list (make-employee "Ana" 50000) (make-employee "James"  #f)))
. . .
(define (get-salaries loe) (map employee-salary loe))
. . .
```

Fig. 7. An evolving payroll program

Protection Against Externally Defined Values. In contrast to modules, contract regions can exchange values in both directions, and this has serious implications for the contract system. In particular, the creator of a contract region may wish to protect it from values that flow in from its context. Thus, our **with-contract** construct supports this form of protection, too.

Consider the code snippets in figures 7 and 8, representing two stages in the evolution of an application. The application stores employee records, which are similar to the student records we saw earlier. Originally, employee salaries were always numbers, and the given definition for *get-salaries* sufficed. However, records are not removed immediately when the employee leaves the company. For now, an interim solution has been found in which the *salary* field is set to #f, but *get-salaries* has not been updated to report a salary of 0 for these cases.

```
...                                      ...
(define/contract (payroll loe)           (define/contract (payroll loe)
  (→ (listof employee?) number?)           (→ (listof employee?) number?)
  (foldl + 0 (get-salaries loe)))          #:freevars ([get-salaries
...                                                        (→ (listof employee?)
(payroll loe1)                                                (listof number?))])
...                                          (foldl + 0 (get-salaries loe)))
                                         ...
...                                      (payroll loe1)
(payroll loe2) ;; error                  ...
...                                      (payroll loe2) ;; contract error
...
```

Fig. 8. Payroll contracts

A new function *payroll* is added that retrieves the current payroll total for the company: see the left-hand side of figure 8. When the value #f used for James's salary flows into the payroll function, however, it causes an error. After all, the programmer of *payroll* expected *get-salaries* to return a list of numbers, but it doesn't always do so.

To express this kind of expectation and to pinpoint the contract violator, the **with-contract** and **define/contract** forms come with optional contracts on their free variables, which are introduced via the keyword #:freevars. These contracts affect all uses of the listed free variables within the contract region. With this feature, the programmer may add a contract for the *get-salaries* function as shown in the right-hand side of figure 8. This contract fails on the second use and appropriately blames *payroll* for providing a bad value for *get-salaries*.

3.2 Implementing Contract Regions

The addition of nested contract regions poses novel problems for the implementation of contract monitoring. Specifically, the revised contract monitor must be able to retrieve the blame label for the current contract region, replace uses of contracted definitions outside of the region with guarded versions, and replace uses of contracted free variables inside the region with guarded versions.

We describe the compilation of contract regions in terms of substitution. The macro-based compiler [23, 24] inspects the list of contracted names. For each contracted name, it chooses a fresh name and substitutes that name for uses of the original name within the body of the contract region. The compiler also replaces the original name where it is bound in its definition. These substitutions ensures that the definition of the contracted name is exchanged for a definition of the fresh name, and that all uses of the contracted name refer instead to the uncontracted, fresh name.

At this point, the compiler could create a new definition of the contracted name that wraps the value associated with the fresh name with a contract. This would, however, disassociate the value internal to the contract region, referred to by the fresh name, and the external value, referred to by the contracted name.

If either code internal or external to the contract region mutates their respective binding, that mutation is not reflected in the other portion of code.

To allow for checked mutation, our system binds the contracted name to a syntax transformer that expands each use to a guarded use of the fresh name. Doing so ensures that the use evaluates to the current value of the fresh name, and it also enforces that the contract system checks the current value for adherence to the contract. Furthermore, the syntax transformer also allows the compiler to track mutation of the contracted name. When this occurs, the compiler generates an expression that instead mutates the fresh name, guarding the new value with the contract. Here our system uses the context as the positive blame and the contract region as the negative blame, as the new value flows into the contract boundary during mutation.

To protect free variables with contracts, a similar set of substitutions is performed. The compiler produces a fresh name for each protected free variable, and creates a syntax transformation for that fresh name that expands references into guarded references and mutations into guarded assignments to the free variable.

The macros for contract regions need to access the blame label for the context. For this, we turn to *syntax parameters* [1], which provide a mechanism for temporarily setting compile-time values for the macro expansion of a specific region of code. Our system binds a syntax parameter to the appropriate blame label during the expansion of the body of a contract region; otherwise, the syntax parameter is instead set to the blame label for the current module.

4   Contracts for Nominally Linked Units

In addition to static first-order modules, PLT Scheme supports a separate component system, called units [19,20]. Units are analogous to ML's functor module system [25,26] and the mixins and traits of OO programming languages [27,28].

Roughly speaking, the unit system supports hierarchical programming with first-class components. Each unit is parameterized over its linking context; each unit also exports a set of names. The unit system supports two operations on units: linking and invoking. A number of units with matching signatures can be linked in a graph-based fashion; the result is a new unit with its own parameterization over its future contexts, which flow into its constituent units, and its own exports, which flow out of its constituent units. A unit whose parameterization is empty may be invoked, meaning the unit's body is evaluated sequentially. Units are first-class values and may even be loaded at run-time. They co-exist with modules and as such may flow across module boundaries.

Understanding unit signatures is key to understanding units as contract boundaries. The first subsection therefore describes signatures, which name collections of variables for import or export from a unit. It also introduces the addition of contracts for signatures. The second and third subsections then present examples of uncontracted and contracted units. The last subsection explains how to implement units as contract boundaries in PLT Scheme and how the addition of contracts affects our implementation.

```
#lang scheme
(define-signature worldˆ
  (key?
   key=?
   big-bang))


(define-signature clientˆ
  (world?
   tock
   clack))
...
```

```
#lang scheme
(define-signature world/cˆ
  ((contracted
     [key? (→ any/c boolean?)]
     [key=? (→ key? key? boolean?)]
     [big-bang (→ any/c void?)]))))

(define-signature client/cˆ
  ((contracted
     [world? (→ any/c boolean?)]
     [tock (→ world? world?)]
     [clack (→ world? any/c world?)]))))
...
```

Fig. 9. Signatures with contracts

4.1 Signatures and Contracts

A unit *signature* is a named collection of variables. Units use sequences of signatures to specify their imports and exports. An exported signature can satisfy an import requirement for another unit only if that unit imports the signature with the *same* name. In other words, the unit system uses nominal matching.

For our examples, we use the two signatures on the left side of figure 9.[2] These signatures describe interfaces that are useful for implementing interactive animations in a world-passing style [29]. The *worldˆ* signature contains three names: *key?*, which is a predicate that determines whether a value is a keyboard event; *key=?*, which is an equivalence predicate; and *big-bang*, which launches an animation when applied to a world (*world?*). The *clientˆ* signature also contains three names: *world?*, which is a predicate on worlds; *tock*, which is an event handler for clock ticks, mapping worlds to worlds; and *clack*, which is an event handler for keyboard events, from worlds and keyboard events to worlds.

Naturally, programmers wish to express such specifications as contracts in order to protect units. We have therefore extended the language of signatures with the **contracted** keyword, which combines signature variables with contracts. The right hand side of figure 9 shows the contracted versions of the signatures. Notice that signature contracts can involve elements of the same signature.

4.2 Units without Contracts

The import signatures of a unit introduce bindings for all their variables for the unit body; conversely, if a unit exports a signature, it must define all the variables listed in the signature. Figure 10 contains some sample units[3] that utilize the uncontracted signatures from the preceding subsection.

---

[2] The ˆ character at the end of signature names is merely a convention.
[3] As with ˆ, the use of @ is a naming convention for units.

```
. . .
;; get-last-key, a primitive, returns #f if no key was pressed
;; since the last call; otherwise it returns the pressed key
(define-unit world@ (import client^) (export world^)
  (define (key? k) (memq k (list "up" "down")))
  (define (key=? ke1 ke2) (string=? ke1 ke2))
  (define (big-bang w)
    (let ([ke (get-last-key)])
      (if ke (big-bang (clack w ke))
          (begin (sleep .1) (big-bang (tock w)))))))
;; Here a world is a number that represents the height of
;; a rocket on a 500 pixel high canvas (not shown here).
(define-unit client@ (import world^) (export client^)
  (define (world? n) (and (integer? n) (>= n 0) (<= n 500)))
  (define (tock n) (+ n 10))
  (define (clack n ke)
    (cond [(key=? ke "up") (+ n 10)]
          [(key=? ke "down") (- n 10)]))
  (big-bang 0))
. . .
```

Fig. 10. Example interactive animation units

When **compound-unit** is used to link a collection of units, the exported definitions from one unit are typically used to satisfy import requirements for one or more of the other units. Thus we can link *client@* and *world@* like this:

```
(define pgrm@
  (compound-unit/infer (import) (export) (link world@ client@)))
```

The "infer" suffix is a variant of **compound-unit** that infers how to wire up the exports and imports of the constituents.

In general, the result of linking is a unit that has its own list of imports and exports and whose body is a sequence of the constituent unit bodies in the order listed in the **link** clause. The exports of the compound unit are satisfied from the exports of the constituent units, and the imports of the compound unit may be used to satisfy imports of the constituents. In contrast to modules, units can thus be compounded hierarchically, and they may refer to each other's exports and imports in a mutually referential manner.

Finally, units with empty **import** signatures can be invoked, e.g.

```
(invoke-unit pgrm@)
```

The effect is to execute the body of *world@*, which consists entirely of definitions, and then to execute the body of *client@*, which calls *big-bang*.

4.3   Units with Contracts

The use of signatures with contracts turns units into contract regions and their boundaries into contract boundaries. In the following code, the definitions of *world@* and *client@* differ from the earlier definitions only in the import/export specification, and so we elide the bodies:

(**define-unit** *world@* (**import** *client/c ˆ*) (**export** *world/c ˆ*) ...)
(**define-unit** *client@* (**import** *world/c ˆ*) (**export** *client/c ˆ*) ...)

When we link *client@* and *world@* and invoke the result:

(**invoke-unit**
  (**compound-unit/infer** (**import**) (**export**) (**link** *world@ client@*)))

then *client@* is blamed if either *tock* or *clack* cause the world to become negative or increase beyond 500.

The signatures *world/c ˆ* and *client/c ˆ* illustrate that a contract in a signature may refer to other elements from the same signature. Thus, we must decide how these contracts interact with the linked units' contract boundaries. In particular, we must decide whether references to signature elements within contracts are guarded or not. For the purposes of this paper, we consider all signature contracts as occurring within the importing unit's contract boundary and therefore the compiler guards all uses of contracted signature elements inside those contracts. This ensures that exported variables are not misused by the contracts and concurs with our implementation strategy.[4]

4.4   Implementing Units as Contract Boundaries

Adding contracts to the unit system poses several challenges. First, units do not enter a contract with a known party; instead they specify via signature contracts what they expect from their context. Second, the same unit may be linked to several different units at run-time and may thus enter contracts with several different parties. Hence, the compiler cannot pass on enough knowledge about the contract parties to the run-time checks. Third, due to nominal linking, a compound unit may only link constituent units whose contracts are identical. Therefore blame labels can be exchanged as units are linked.

The first part of this section describes how units are implemented in PLT Scheme. The second part explains the addition of signature-based contracts to the existing implementation. The third part covers additional features of the unit system.

Units in PLT Scheme. The current unit system in PLT Scheme follows the model by Owens and Flatt [19] for first-class modules. In this model, signatures are matched nominally when units are linked. The implementation exploits this nominal matching to provide inference for linking.

---

[4] This design decision is overly conservative and deserves to be revisited once we have enough experience with our new contract system. Furthermore the current contract system does not permit programmers to use elements from one signature in a different signature for the specification of contracts. Extending the contract system in this direction may also force us to revisit the design decision on how to check contracted functions within contracts.

The compiler[5] translates a unit into a thunk that is hidden in a unique structure value. On application, the thunk returns two values:

- a mapping from exports to reference cells, and
- a function that implements the body of the unit. The function consumes a mapping from imports to reference cells; it returns the last value computed by the unit body.

In the unit's body, the compiler replaces uses of imports with accesses to the import mapping. To each definition of an exported item, the compiler adds an assignment to the appropriate reference cell. Once an export cell is set, its value never changes.

A unit invocation invokes the thunk to obtain an export mapping and a body function. The latter is then applied to an empty import mapping, which evaluates the unit body.

Since units are represented as thunks, the compiler translates a **compound-unit** form to a thunk, too. This thunk performs the following operations:

1. It applies the thunks for the constituent units and collects the resulting export mappings and body functions.
2. It constructs an export mapping for the compound unit from the collected export mappings.
3. It creates a body function that consumes the import mapping of the compound unit. For each linked unit in listed order, this new body function:
   (a) creates an import mapping from the compound unit's import mapping and the collected export mappings of the other units, and
   (b) applies that unit's body function to the created import mapping.
4. It returns the new export mapping and body function.

Contracts in Signatures. Since units must agree on their shared signatures *by name* and since we add contracts to signatures, linked units automatically agree on all of the contracts of the shared variables. That is, unlike a module that contains two parallel contract regions, a compound unit cannot possibly link two units whose contracts don't match, as in figure 11. Thus, it is impossible for the linker to assume any responsibility for contract errors. Put differently, there is no need for checking contracts within the compound unit and it need never be blamed. Put positively, our implementation limits blame to the exporting unit and the importing unit.

The key to our addition of contracts is to separate the translation of contracted signature variables from those of uncontracted ones. For contracted exports, the compiler generates code that sets the cell for the exported value to a structure with two fields:

---

[5] The unit system is actually implemented as a library based on the PLT macro system, though it is impossible for a programmer to discover this programmatically.

```
#lang scheme
(define-signature lexerˆ ((contracted [lex (→ string? (listof token?))])))
(define-signature lexer2ˆ ((contracted [lex (→ input-port? (listof token?))])))
(define-signature parserˆ ((contracted [parse (→ string? ast?)])))
(define-unit lexer@ (import) (export lexer2ˆ)
  (define (lex str) ...))
(define-unit parser@ (import lexerˆ) (export parserˆ)
  (define (parser str) (let ([tokens (lex str)]) ...)))
(compound-unit/infer (link lexer@ parser@))
```

Fig. 11. Mismatched signatures and contracts

– one for the value of the exported variable, and
– one that uniquely identifies the exporting unit, i.e., its blame label.

When the compiler encounters a contracted import, it deconstructs this kind of structure and retrieves the contract from the imported signature. From these two pieces, the compiler constructs an appropriate guard expression for the imported value. This contract-guard uses the export blame label for positive blame report and the importing blame label for negative blame reports.[6]

Structural Linking and a Contract Combinator. The unit system supports two more important linguistic constructs whose full descriptions are beyond the scope of this paper. One form, *unit/s*, provides a mechanism for linking units structurally. This provides backwards compatibility for use with an early implementation of units in PLT Scheme [20].

The *unit/s* form takes import and export specifications as well as a unit value and creates a new unit value. Its imports and exports must structurally match the imports and exports of the given unit value; the resulting unit value uses the given imports and exports and the given unit's body. Since this operation on units changes the import and export signatures, the contracts on the imported and exported values may be inappropriate for the original unit. Hence, the compiler must introduce contract checks into the result of *unit/s* that blames the new unit value when contract mismatches occur, instead of allowing either the original unit value or any unit with which it is linked to be blamed.

The other form, *unit/c*, is a new form of contract specification, since units are first-class values that also can cross contract boundaries. Technically, the contract combinator *unit/c* is used in contracts to express contracts on units. A contract on units is essentially a sequence of contracts for a unit's exports and imports. We implement this operation as a projection[6] on unit values, which means that it takes a unit value as input and returns a new unit value that monitors the flow of values across the unit boundary.

---
[6] Roughly speaking, it applies two projections to the value: one for its "elimination" (negative) and one for its "introduction" (positive). If something goes wrong with the negative position, the client is blamed; otherwise the server is blamed. For details on the general idea, see Findler and Blume's report [30].

Both of these forms require similar changes to the unit implementation, because both introduce structural notions of matching a unit's exports to another unit's imports. Structural units, in turn, are a central piece of related work, which we briefly compare to this work in section 6.

5   A Question of Blame

Now that we have described two new contract extensions—contract regions and unit contracts—we are in a good position to compare and contrast the blame story for the two. Examine the modules in figure 12. The module *regions* contains two contract regions: *server*, which provides the implementation of a webserver, and *client*, which (mis-)uses that implementation. Similarly, the module *units* contains two units, *server@* and *client@*, which are in a relationship that is analogous to that of *server* and *client*.

regions

```
#lang scheme
(with-contract server
   ([serve (→ high-tcp-port? void?)])
   ...)
...
...
...
...
...
(with-contract client
   ([...])
   ... (serve 80) ...)
```

units

```
#lang scheme
(define-signature web^
   ((contracted
      [serve (→ high-tcp-port? void?)])))
(define-unit server@
   (import) (export web^)
   ...)
(define-unit client@
   (import web^) (export)
   ... (serve 80) ...)
(invoke-unit
   (compound-unit/infer
      (link server@ client@)))
```

Fig. 12. A comparison between contract regions and units

When evaluated, both modules result in a contract violation. In *regions*, the module itself is blamed, since it is the context of the contract region *server*, whereas in *units*, *client@* is blamed. The inquisitive reader may be surprised that in the former case, the contract system did not blame *client* instead, which would be a more specific region. After all, the purpose of blame assignment is to assist programmers with debugging, calling for the most specific blame justifiable.

One reason for this design decision is that only parties that explicitly enter into a contract should be blamed for bad behavior. In the second module, the various units, via signatures, enter into contracts for both their imports and exports. That is, *server@* (respectively, *client@*) declares that the exported (respectively, imported) function *serve* is contracted through its use of the signature *web^*. Since both parties have agreed to the contract, the two units are the only sources of blame.

In the first module, only *server* declares a contract on the function *serve*. This agreement is with its context, i.e., the rest of the module *regions*. Thus only *server* or *regions* can be blamed if part of the contract is violated. If *client* had declared the same contract on *serve* via #:freevars, then it, too, would have agreed to the contract and could be blamed appropriately.

regions2

```
#lang scheme
(with-contract server
  ([serve (→ high-tcp-port? void?)])
  ...)
...
(with-contract client
  ([...])
  #:freevars ([serve (→ tcp-port? void?)])
  ... (serve 80) ...)
```

Fig. 13. Regions with differing contracts

Then again, *client* doesn't have to specify the same contract as *server*. Thus, in figure 13, neither contract region should be at fault, as both regions use the *serve* function according to their own contract. Instead, the fault lies with the context that ties the two regions together. It allows the value *serve* to flow from one region to another even though the two impose distinct requirements at their respective boundaries. This is analogous to the behavior of contracts for structurally linked units, which we briefly mentioned in conjunction with *unit/s* and which we discuss more extensively in the section on related work.

In fact, the first example can be seen as a special case of the second, if we treat all uncontracted free variables flowing into a contract region as if they had the implicit contract *any/c*, i.e., the most permissive contract. Thus, having the context of the contract region serve as the negative blame leads to a consistent handling of blame for contract regions.

6   Related Work

Our paper benefits from two pieces of related work. First, a parallel paper [21] explores the theory of contracts for the units described by Flatt and Felleisen [20], i.e., units with structural signature matching. Matching signatures structurally requires much deeper changes to the compiler and the run-time environment than PLT Scheme's unit system with nominal matching. Most importantly, it introduces a third party of potential blame—the compounding unit—and therefore demands contract machinery for linking.

Structural signature matching is closely related to the world of ML-like module systems based on functors and structures. As such, the parallel paper directly applies to this world. In contrast, the implementation presented here is much closer to the world of nominal interfaces from OO programming languages and should therefore carry over to contracts for mixins [27] and traits [28].

By inheritance, our paper extends the work by Findler and Felleisen [18] on higher-order contracts for static and global contract boundaries. Our implementation heavily relies on Findler's work with Blume [30], which is the current theoretical underpinning for contracts. It explains contracts as pairs of projections and is the model for the implementation of contracts in PLT Scheme.

Historically, the notion of contracts and modules is due to Parnas [31] though he did not coin the phrase "contract." Meyer's "design by contract" work introduces this terminology [13]; his work on Eiffel popularized the idea in the object-oriented community.

7 Conclusion

Software contracts enable programmers to protect collections of functions and methods with simple, executable descriptions of expected behavior. Contract monitoring ensures that all values that flow into and out of a protected region satisfy its stated boundary invariants. When the contract monitor discovers a contract violation, it must be able to pinpoint the guilty party and explain the nature of the violation. Doing so is critical for the debugging process.

Given the growing importance of contracts, our work provides the important generalization of introducing nested and dynamic contract boundaries. Technically, this paper introduces hierarchical contract regions for static modules and contract boundaries for a hierarchical and dynamic module system. We conjecture that future work on contract boundaries can benefit from either of those two or a mix of them. Our implementation is available with the current release of PLT Scheme (`http://www.plt-scheme.org/`).

Acknowledgments. We gratefully acknowledge comments and suggestions from Robby Findler and the anonymous reviewers for IFL on early drafts of this paper.

References

1. Flatt, M., et al.: PLT Scheme. Reference Manual PLT-TR2009-reference-v4.2.1., PLT Scheme Inc. (January 2009), `http://plt-scheme.org/techreports/`
2. Beugnard, A., Jézéquel, J.M., Plouzeau, N., Watkins, D.: Making components contract aware. IEEE Software, 38–45 (June 1999)
3. Carrillo-Castellon, M., Garcia-Molina, J., Pimentel, E., Repiso, I.: Design by contract in Smalltalk. Journal of Object-Oriented Programming 7(9), 23–28 (1996)
4. Duncan, A., Hölzle, U.: Adding contracts to Java with Handshake. Technical Report TRCS98-32, The University of California at Santa Barbara (December 1998)
5. Edwards, S., Shakir, G., Sitaraman, M., Weide, B., Hollingsworth, J.: A framework for detecting interface violations in component-based software. In: Proceedings of the Fifth International Conference on Software Reuse, pp. 46–55. IEEE, Los Alamitos (June 1998)

6. Helm, R., Holland, I.M., Gangopadhyay, D.: Contracts: specifying behaviorial compositions in object-oriented systems. In: Proceedings of Object-Oriented Programming, Systems, Languages, and Applications, pp. 169–180 (1990)
7. Kim, M., Kannan, S., Lee, I., Sokolsky, O., Viswanathan, M.: Java-MaC: a run-time assurance tool for Java. Electronic Notes in Theoretical Computer Science 55(2), 218–235 (2001)
8. Kramer, R.: iContract: the Java design by contract tool. In: Proceedings of Technology of Object-Oriented Languages and Systems, pp. 295–307 (August 1998)
9. Karaorman, M., Hölzle, U., Bruno, J.: jContractor: a reflective Java library to support design by contract. In: Cointe, P. (ed.) Reflection 1999. LNCS, vol. 1616, pp. 175–196. Springer, Heidelberg (1999)
10. Leavens, G.T., Leino, K.R.M., Poll, E., Ruby, C., Jacobs, B.: JML: notations and tools supporting detailed design in Java. In: Proceedings of Object-Oriented Programming, Systems, Languages, and Applications, Companion, pp. 105–106 (2000)
11. Luckham, D.C.: Programming with Specifications: An Introduction to Anna, a Language for Specifying ADA Programs. Springer, Heidelberg (1990)
12. Microsoft Corporation: Microsoft C# Language Specifications. Microsoft Press (2001)
13. Meyer, B.: Applying design by contract. IEEE Computer 25(10), 40–51 (1992)
14. Weck, W.: Inheritance using contracts and object composition. In: Proceedings of the Workshop on Components-Oriented Programming, pp. 384–388 (1997)
15. Gomes, B., Stoutamire, D., Vaysman, B., Klawitter, H.: A Language Manual for Sather 1.1 (August 1996)
16. Plösch, R., Pichler, J.: Contracts: from analysis to C++ implementation. In: Proceedings of Technology of Object-Oriented Languages and Systems, pp. 248–257 (August 1999)
17. Ruby, C., Leavens, G.T.: Safely creating correct subclasses without seeing superclass code. In: Proceedings of Object-Oriented Programming, Systems, Languages, and Applications, pp. 208–228 (October 2000)
18. Findler, R.B., Felleisen, M.: Contracts for higher-order functions. In: Proceedings of the International Conference on Functional Programming, pp. 48–59 (October 2002)
19. Owens, S., Flatt, M.: From structures and functors to modules and units. In: Proceedings of the International Conference on Functional Programming, pp. 87–98 (September 2006)
20. Flatt, M., Felleisen, M.: Units: Cool modules for HOT languages. In: Proceedings of Programming Language Design and Implementation, pp. 236–248 (June 1998)
21. Strickland, T.S., Felleisen, M.: Contracts for first-class modules. In: Proceedings of the Fifth Dynamic Languages Symposium, pp. 27–38 (October 2009)
22. Szyperski, C.: Component Software. Addison-Wesley, Reading (1997)
23. Flatt, M.: Composable and compilable macros: You want it when?. In: Proceedings of the International Conference on Functional Programming, pp. 72–83 (October 2002)
24. Culpepper, R., Tobin-Hochstadt, S., Flatt, M.: Advanced macrology and the implementation of Typed Scheme. In: Proceedings of the Scheme Workshop, Université Laval Technical Report DIUL-RT-0701, pp. 1–14 (September 2007)
25. Leroy, X.: Manifest types, modules, and separate compilation. In: Proceedings of Principles of Programming Languages, pp. 109–122 (January 1994)
26. Harper, R., Lillibridge, M.: A type-theoretic approach to higher-order modules with sharing. In: Proceedings of Principles of Programming Languages, pp. 123–137 (January 1994)

27. Flatt, M., Findler, R.B., Felleisen, M.: Scheme with classes, mixins, and traits. In: Proceedings of the Asian Symposium on Programming Languages and Systems, pp. 270–289 (November 2006)
28. Schärli, N., Ducasse, S., Nierstrasz, O., Black, A.: Traits: Composable units of behavior. In: Cardelli, L. (ed.) ECOOP 2003. LNCS, vol. 2743, pp. 248–274. Springer, Heidelberg (2003)
29. Felleisen, M., Findler, R.B., Flatt, M., Krishnamurthi, S.: A functional i/o system or, fun for freshman kids. In: Proceedings of the International Conference on Functional Programming, pp. 47–58 (October 2009)
30. Findler, R.B., Blume, M.: Contracts as pairs of projections. In: Hagiya, M., Wadler, P. (eds.) FLOPS 2006. LNCS, vol. 3945, pp. 226–241. Springer, Heidelberg (2006)
31. Parnas, D.L.: On the criteria to be used in decomposing systems into modules. Communications of the ACM 15, 1053–1058 (1972)

Pull-Ups, Push-Downs, and Passing It Around

Exercises in Functional Incrementalization

Sean Leather[1], Andres Löh[1], and Johan Jeuring[1,2]

[1] Utrecht University, Utrecht, The Netherlands
[2] Open Universiteit Nederland
{leather,andres,johanj}@cs.uu.nl

Abstract. Programs in languages such as Haskell are often datatype-centric and make extensive use of folds on that datatype. Incrementalization of such a program can significantly improve its performance by transforming monolithic atomic folds into incremental computations. Functional incrementalization separates the recursion from the application of the algebra in order to reduce redundant computations and reuse intermediate results. In this paper, we motivate incrementalization with a simple example and present a library for transforming programs using upwards, downwards, and circular incrementalization. Our benchmarks show that incrementalized computations using the library are nearly as fast as handwritten atomic functions.

1 Introduction

In functional programming languages with algebraic datatypes, many programs and libraries "revolve" around a collection of datatypes. Functions in such programs form the spokes connecting the datatypes in the center to a convenient application programming interface (API) or embedded domain-specific language (EDSL) at the circumference, facilitating the development cycle. These *datatype-centric* programs can take the form of games, web applications, GUIs, compilers, databases, etc. We can find examples in many common libraries: finite maps, sets, queues, parser combinators, and zippers. Datatype-generic libraries with a structure representation are also datatype-centric.

Programmers developing datatype-centric programs often define recursive functions that can be defined with primitive recursion. A popular form of recursion, the *fold* (a.k.a. catamorphism or reduce), is (categorically) the unique homomorphism (structure-preserving map) for an initial algebra. That is, an algebraic datatype T provides the starting point (the initial algebra) for a fold to map a value of T to a type S using an algebra $F\ S \to S$, all the while preserving the structure of the type T. Folds can be defined using an endofunctor F (another homomorphism), and an F-algebra. Given a transformation that takes a recursive datatype T to its base functor $F\ T$, we can define a fold that works for any type T. Before we get

M.T. Morazán and S.-B. Scholz (Eds.): IFL 2009, LNCS 6041, pp. 159–178, 2010.

too far outside the scope of this paper, however, let us put some concrete notation down in Haskell[1].

The base functor for a type t can be represented by a datatype family[1]:

```
data family F t :: * → *
```

A datatype family is a type-indexed datatype[2] that gives us a unique structure for each type t. The types t and F t should have the same structure (i.e. same alternatives and products) with the exception that the recursive points in t are replaced by type parameters in F (this being the reason for the kind $* \rightarrow *$). The isomorphism between t and F t is captured by the *InOut* type class.

```
class (Functor (F t)) ⇒ InOut t where
    inF   :: F t t → t
    outF :: t → F t t
```

An algebra for a functor f is defined as a function f s → s for some result type s. In the case of a fold, f is the base functor F t. We use the following type synonyms to identify algebras:

```
type Alg  f s = f s → s
type AlgF t s = Alg (F t) s
```

As mentioned above, the fold function is a structure-preserving map from a datatype to some value determined by an algebra. Using the above definitions and fmap from the *Functor* class, we implement fold as follows.

```
fold :: (InOut t) ⇒ AlgF t s → t → s
fold alg = alg ∘ fmap (fold alg) ∘ outF
```

A fold for a particular datatype T requires three instances: F T, *InOut* T, and *Functor* (F T). Here is the code for a binary tree.

```
data              Tree a   = Tip  | Bin  a (Tree a) (Tree a)
data instance F (Tree a) r = TipF | BinF a r        r
instance Functor (F (Tree a)) where
    fmap _ TipF          = TipF
    fmap f (BinF x rL rR) = BinF x (f rL) (f rR)
instance InOut (Tree a) where
    inF  TipF          = Tip
    inF  (BinF x tL tR) = Bin x tL tR
    outF Tip           = TipF
    outF (Bin x tL tR)  = BinF x tL tR
```

---

[1] We use Haskell 2010 along with the following necessary extensions: MultiParamTypeClasses, TypeFamilies, FlexibleContexts, KindSignatures, and Rank2Types.

One F-algebra for Tree is calculating the number of binary nodes in a value.

```
sizeAlg :: Alg_F (Tree a) Int
sizeAlg Tip_F        = 0
sizeAlg (Bin_F _ s_L s_R) = 1 + s_L + s_R
```

The simplicity of the above code[2] belies the power it provides: a programmer can define numerous recursive functions for Tree values using fold and an algebra instead of direct recursion. With that understanding, let us return to our story.

Folds are occasionally used in repetition, and this can negatively impact a program's performance. If we analyze the evaluation of such code, we might see the pattern in Figure 1. The variables x_i are values of some foldable datatype and the results y_i are used elsewhere. If the functions f_i change their values in a "small" way relative to the size of the value, then the second fold performs a large number of redundant computations. A fold is an *atomic computation*: it computes the results "all in one go." Even in a lazily evaluated language such as Haskell, there is no sharing between the computations of fold in this pattern.

In this article, we propose to solve the problem of repetitive folds by transforming repeated atomic computations into a single *incremental computation*. Incremental computations take advantage of small changes to an input to compute a new output. The key is to subdivide a computation into smaller parts and reuse previous results to compute the final output.

$$x_1 \leftarrow f_0 \; x_0$$
$$y_1 \leftarrow \text{fold alg } x_1$$
$$x_2 \leftarrow f_1 \; x_1$$
$$y_2 \leftarrow \text{fold alg } x_2$$
$$...$$

Fig. 1. Evaluation of repeated folds. The symbol $\leftarrow$ indicates that the right evaluates to the left.

Our focus is the *incrementalization*[4] of purely functional programs with folds and fold-like functions. To incrementalize a program with folds, we separate the application of the algebra from the recursion. We first merge the components of the F-algebra with the initial algebra (the constructors). We may optionally define smart constructors to simplify use of the transformed constructors. The recursion of the fold is then implicit, blending with the recursion of other functions.

We motivate our work in Section 2 by taking a well-known library, incrementalizing it, and looking at the improvement over the atomic version. In Section 3, we generalize this form of incrementalization—which we call "upwards"—into library form. Sections 4 and 5 develop two alternative forms of incrementalization, "downwards" and "circular." In Section 6, we discuss other aspects of incrementalization. We discuss related work in Section 7 and conclude in Section 8. All of the code presented in this paper is available online[3].

---

[2] As simple as they are, the F, *Functor*, and *InOut* instances may be time-consuming to write for large datatypes. Fortunately, this code can be generated with tools such as Template Haskell[3].

[3] http://people.cs.uu.nl/andres/Incrementalization/

2   Incrementalization in Action

We introduce the Set library as a basis for understanding incrementalization. Starting from a simple, naive implementation, we systematically transform it to a more efficient, incrementalized version.

The Set library has the following API.

```
empty    :: Set a                    insert   :: (Ord a) ⇒ a → Set a → Set a
singleton :: a → Set a               fromList :: (Ord a) ⇒ [a] → Set a
size      :: Set a → Int
```

The interface is comparable to the Data.Set library provided by the Haskell Platform.

One can think of a value of Set a as a container of a-type elements such that each element is unique. For the implementation, we use an ordered, binary search tree[5] with the datatype introduced in Section 1.

```
type Set = Tree
```

We have several options for constructing sets. Simple construction is performed with empty and singleton, which are trivially defined using Tree constructors. Sets can also be built from lists of elements.

```
fromList = foldl (flip insert) empty
```

The function fromList uses insert which builds a new set given an old set and an additional element. This is where the ordering aspect from the type class *Ord* is used.

```
insert x Tip           = singleton x
insert x (Bin y tL tR) = case compare x y of
                   LT → balance y (insert x tL) tR
                   GT → balance y tL          (insert x tR)
                   EQ → Bin     x tL          tR
```

We use the balance function to maintain the invariant that a look-up operation has logarithmic access time to any element.

```
balance :: a → Set a → Set a → Set a
balance x tL tR | sL + sR ≤ 1 = Bin x tL tR
                | sR ≥ 4 * sL  = rotateL x tL tR (size tRL) (size tRR)
                | sL ≥ 4 * sR  = rotateR x tL tR (size tLL) (size tLR)
                | otherwise    = Bin x tL tR
    where (sL, sR)      = (size tL, size tR)
          Bin _ tRL tRR = tR
          Bin _ tLL tLR = tL
```

Here, we use the size of each subtree to determine how to rotate nodes between subtrees. We omit the details[4] of balance but call attention to how often the

---
[4] It is not important for our purposes to understand how to balance a binary search tree. The details are available in the code of Data.Set and other resources[5].

size function is called. We implement size using fold with the algebra defined in Section 1.

size = fold sizeAlg

The astute reader will notice that the repeated use of the size in balance leads to the pattern of folds described in Figure 1. In this example, we are computing a fold over subtrees immediately after computing a fold over the parent. These are redundant computations, and the subresults should be reused. In fact, size is an atomic function that is ideal for incrementalization.

The key point to highlight is that we want to store results of computations with Tree values. We start by allocating space for storage.

data Tree^i a = Tip^i Int | Bin^i Int a (Tree^i a) (Tree^i a)

We need to preserve the result of a fold, and the logical location is each recursive point of the datatype. In other words, we annotate each constructor with an additional field to contain the size of that Tree^i value. This can be visualized as a Tree value with superscript annotations.

Bin^4 2 (Bin^1 1 Tip^0 Tip^0) (Bin^2 3 Tip^0 (Bin^1 4 Tip^0 Tip^0))

We then define the function size^i to extract the annotation without any recursion.

size^i (Tip^i i)   = i
size^i (Bin^i i _ _ _) = i

The next step is to implement the part of the fold that applies the algebra to a value. To avoid obfuscation, we create an API for Tree values by lifting the structural aspects (introduction and elimination) to a type class.

class Tree$_S$ t **where**
  type Elem t
  tip   :: t
  bin   :: Elem t → t → t → t
  caseTree :: r → (Elem t → t → t → r) → t → r

An instance of Tree$_S$ permits us to use the smart constructors tip and bin for introducing t values and the method caseTree (instead of **case**) for eliminating them. Since the element type depends on the instance type, we use the associated type Elem t to identify the values of the bin nodes. Applying this step to Tree^i, we arrive at the following instance.

instance Tree$_S$ (Tree^i a) **where**
  type Elem (Tree^i a) = a
  tip   = Tip^i 0
  bin x t$_L$ t$_R$ = Bin^i (1 + size^i t$_L$ + size^i t$_R$) x t$_L$ t$_R$
  caseTree t b n = **case** n **of** {Tip^i _ → t ; Bin^i _ x t$_L$ t$_R$ → b x t$_L$ t$_R$}

We have separated the components of sizeAlg and merged them with the constructors, in effect creating an initial algebra that computes the size.

For the finishing touches, we adapt the library to use the new datatype and *Tree*$_S$ instance. The refactoring is not difficult, and the types of all functions should be the same (of course, using Tree^i instead of Tree). Refer to the associated code for the refactored functions. We have one last check to verify that we achieved our objective: speed-up of the Set library.

To benchmark[5] our work, we compare two implementations of the fromList function. The first is given by the definition above. The second is from the aforementioned refactored Set library using the Tree^i type. For each run, we build a set from the words of a wordlist text file. The word counts increase with each input to give an idea how well fromList scales.

Figure 2 lists the results. To collect these times, we evaluate the values strictly to head normal form. Since Haskell is by default a lazily evaluated language, these times are not necessarily indicative of real-world use; however, they do give the worst case time, in which the entire set is needed.

It is clear (and no surprise) from the results that incrementalization has a significant effect. We have changed the time complexity of the size calculation from linear to constant, thus reducing the time of fromList by nearly 100% for all inputs.

In this section, we developed a library from a naive implementation with atomic folds into an incrementalized implementation. This particular work is by no means novel, and no one would use the naive approach; however, it does identify a design pattern that may improve the efficiency of other programs. In the remainder of this article, we capture that design pattern in a library and explore other variations on the theme.

3   Upwards Incrementalization

We take the design pattern from the previous section and create reusable components and techniques that can be applied to incrementalize another program. We call the approach used in this section *upwards incrementalization*, because we pull the results upward through the tree-like structure of an algebraic datatype.

The first step we took in Section 2 was to allocate space for storing intermediate results. As mentioned, the logical locations for storage are the recursive points of a datatype. That leads us to identify the fixed-point view as a natural representation.

```
newtype Fix f = In { out :: f (Fix f) }
```

The type Fix encapsulates the recursion of some functor type f and allows us access to each recursive point. We use another datatype to extend a functor with a new field.

```
data Ann s f r = Ann s (f r)
```

---

[5] All benchmarks were compiled with GHC 6.10.1 using the -02 flag and run on a MacBook with Mac OS X 10.5.8, a 2 GHz Intel Core 2 Duo, and 4 GB of RAM.

	5,911	16,523	26,234	*words*
Atomic	3.876	19.561	61.151	*seconds*
Incrementalized	**0.010**	**0.028**	**0.056**	

Fig. 2. Performance of the atomic and incrementalized fromList

The type Ann pairs an *annotation* with a functor. Combined, Fix and Ann give us an annotated fixed-point representation.

type Fix^a s f = Fix (Ann s f)

We supplement this type with its base functor (along with instances of *Functor* and *InOut*) and functions to introduce (in^a), eliminate (out^a), and extract the annotation (ann) from Fix^a values.

data instance F (Fix^a s f) r = In$_F^a$ s (f r)
in^a :: s → f (Fix^a s f) → Fix^a s f
out^a :: Fix^a s f → f (Fix^a s f)
ann :: Fix^a s f → s

Another function that will be useful later is foldMap^a.

foldMap^a :: (*Functor* f) ⇒ (r → s) → Fix^a r f → Fix^a s f
foldMap^a f = fold (λ(In$_F^a$ s x) → in^a (f s) x)

To continue with the example used in the Set library, we now represent the binary search tree using the base functor of Tree introduced in Section 1. We can define an alternative representation for Tree^i as Tree^U.

type Type^a s t = Fix^a s (F t)
type Tree^U a = Type^a Int (Tree a)

We can use this type with an instance of *Tree$_S$* in the same way as before; however, we must first define a general form of upwards incrementalization.

Recall that our objective is to separate a fold into its elements: the application of the algebra and the recursion. First, let us determine how to get an annotated fixed-point type from a Haskell type; then, we can dissect the fold. Upwards incrementalization is specified by upwards.

upwards :: (*InOut* t) ⇒ Alg$_F$ t s → t → Type^a s t
upwards = fold ∘ pullUp

pullUp :: (*Functor* f) ⇒ Alg f s → Alg f (Fix^a s f)
pullUp alg fs = in^a (alg (fmap ann fs)) fs

The function upwards is naturally defined with fold. The pullUp function transforms an algebra on a functor f with the result s to an algebra that results in the annotated fixed point Fix^a s f. It does this by mapping each annotated fixed point to its annotation in f. The in^a function (also an algebra) pairs the annotation with x. This value is built atomically (since upwards is a fold). To construct

the same value incrementally, we define introduction and elimination operations
under the $Tree_S$ instance.

```
instance Tree_S (Tree^U a) where
    type Elem (Tree^U a) = a
    tip          = pullUp sizeAlg Tip_F
    bin x t_L t_R = pullUp sizeAlg (Bin_F x t_L t_R)
    caseTree t b n = case out^a n of { Tip_F → t ; Bin_F x t_L t_R → b x t_L t_R }
```

The primary differences from the $Tree^i$ instance are that we use the base functor
constructors and that we wrap them with the algebra pullUp sizeAlg and unwrap
them with the coalgebra out^a.

The library defined in this section allows programmers to write programs
with upwards incrementalization. Given a datatype, the programmer defines
an algebra that they want incrementalized. Using pullUp and the base functor
of that datatype, the programmer can easily build incremental results. Smart
constructors or a structure type class such as $Tree_S$ are not required, but they
can simplify the programming by hiding the complexities of incrementalization.

We now compare the performance of our generalized upwards incrementalization against the specialized incrementalization presented in Section 2. Since the
incrementalized Set library was refactored to use the $Tree_S$ class, we can use the
same code for the generalized implementation but with the type $Tree^U$ instead
of $Tree^i$. We used the same benchmarking methodology as before to collect the
results in Figure 3.

Surprisingly, the generalized fromList performs better, running 15 to 17%
faster than the specialized version. It is not clear precisely why this is, though we
speculate that it is due to the structure of the explicit fixed point and annotation
datatypes.

An alternative benchmark is the time taken to build large values of each
datatype. This is independent of any library and reflects clearly the impact of
the incrementalization on construction. We compare the evaluation of building
three isomorphic tree values: construction of the Tree datatype with "built-in"
Haskell syntax, construction of the incrementalized $Tree^U$ type, and $Tree^U$ values
transformed from constructed Tree values.

We arrive at the results shown in Figure 4 using QuickCheck[6] to reproducibly
generate each arbitrary value with the approximate size shown. Each time is the
average over three different random seeds. As with previous comparisons, we
evaluate to head normal form. To be consistent with later comparisons, the
element type of the trees is Float.

The times of the comparison are virtually indistinguishable. This provides
good indication that upwards incrementalization does not impact the performance of constructing values. Again, note that due to lazy evaluation, this only
predicts the worst case time, not the expected time for incremental updates.

In the next two sections, we look at other variations of incrementalization. It
could be said that upwards is the most "obvious" adaptation of folds; however,
it is also limiting in the functions that can be written. Algebraic datatypes
are tree-structured and constructed inductively; therefore, it is naturally that
information flows upward from the leaves to the root. It is also possible to pass

	5,911	16,523	26,234	*words*
Specialized	10.0	28.4	56.1	*milliseconds*
Generalized	**8.3**	**24.1**	**46.8**	

Fig. 3. Performance of the specialized and generalized fromList

	1,000	10,000	100,000	*nodes*
Tree	7.4	39.7	137.3	*milliseconds*
Incrementalized with pullUp	**7.4**	**39.5**	**136.5**	
Transformed with upwards	7.4	39.6	137.4	

Fig. 4. Performance of constructing trees with upwards incrementalization using the size algebra

information downward from the root to the leaves as well as both up and down simultaneously. We venture into this territory next.

4   Downwards Incrementalization

There are other directions that incrementalization can take. We have demonstrated upwards incrementalization, and in this section, we discuss its dual: *downwards incrementalization*. In this direction, we accumulate the result of calculations using information from the ancestors of a node. As with its upwards sibling, the result of downwards computations is stored as an annotation on a fixed-point value. To distinguish between the two, we borrow vocabulary from attribute grammars[7]: a downwards annotation is *inherited* by the children while an upwards annotation is *synthesized* for the parent.

Let us establish a specification of a fixed-point value with inherited annotations. To do this, we start with Gibbons' accumulations[8], in particular downwards accumulations. Accumulation is similar to incrementalization in the sense that information flows up or down the structure of the datatype. Accumulations collect this information in the polymorphic elements (e.g. the a in Tree a) while incrementalization collects it at the recursive points. Gibbons modeled downwards accumulation using paths, and we borrow this concept for downwards incrementalization.

A *path* is a route from a constructor in a value to the root of that value (i.e. the sequence of ancestors). The type of a path is characteristic of the datatype whose path we want, so we define Path as a type-indexed datatype. The Path instance for the Tree type helps clarify the structure a path.

data family Path t

data instance Path (Tree a)
    = PRoot | PBin$_L$ a (Path (Tree a)) | PBin$_R$ a (Path (Tree a))

    data instance F (Path (Tree a)) r = PRoot$_F$ | PBin$_{LF}$ a r | PBin$_{RF}$ a r

In downward accumulations, every element is replaced with the path from that constructor. Then, a fold is applied to each path to determine the result that is stored in the element. In downwards incrementalization, we annotate every constructor with its path. The primitives for this operation are defined by the *Paths* class and exemplified by the Tree instance.

```
class (InOut t, InOut (Path t), ZipWith (F t)) ⇒ Paths t where
  proot  :: Path t
  pnode  :: F t r → F t (Path t → Path t)
instance Paths (Tree t) where
  proot                = PRoot
  pnode TipF           = TipF
  pnode (BinF x _ _)   = BinF x (PBinL x) (PBinR x)
```

The methods proot and pnode are used to link the constructors of Path t to the constructors of the type t. The mapping is quite straightforward: there is always one root constructor, and the remaining constructors match recursive nodes. The function paths uses the methods of *Paths* to annotate every recursive point with its path.

```
paths :: (Paths t) ⇒ t → Typeᵃ (Path t) t
paths = appᵃ proot ∘ fold (inᵃ id ∘ zipApp compᵃ pnode)
appᵃ x      = foldMapᵃ ($x)
compᵃ f     = foldMapᵃ (∘f)
zipApp f g x = zipWith f (g x) x
```

In paths, we are folding over the type t with an algebra that again folds over the annotated value to push the latest known constructor to the bottom of each child path using function composition. We follow up with a second fold to apply the composed functions to proot. We use an instance of the class *ZipWith* to merge the recursive path nodes (that contain functions applying the constructor) with the original base function.

```
class ZipWith f where
  zipWith :: (a → b → c) → f a → f b → f c
```

The instances of *ZipWith* are trivial. Alternatively, we might have used a datatype-generic programming library to zip functors together. To get an intuition of how paths works, refer to the following example.

$$\text{Bin}^{\text{PRoot}} \; 2 \; \text{Tip}^{\text{PBin}_L \; 2 \; \text{PRoot}}$$
$$(\text{Bin}^{\text{PBin}_R \; 2 \; \text{PRoot}} \; 1 \; \text{Tip}^{\text{PBin}_L \; 1 \; (\text{PBin}_R \; 2 \; \text{PRoot})} \; \text{Tip}^{\text{PBin}_R \; 1 \; (\text{PBin}_R \; 2 \; \text{PRoot})})$$

Each constructor is initially annotated with the with id. As the outer fold works upwards, the inner fold composes the current path constructor (e.g. PBin_L or PBin_R) with the results. Finally, the function annotation for every node is applied to the root PRoot.

We can now give a specification for inherited annotations.

```
downwards :: (Paths t) ⇒ AlgF (Path t) s → t → Typeᵃ s t
downwards alg = foldMapᵃ (fold alg) ∘ paths
```

We use paths to annotate all recursive points with their paths, and we fold over the annotated result with an algebra that contains a fold over a path. The path algebra is provided by the programmer. For example, suppose we want to calculate the depth of a constructor:

$$\text{depthAlg}^D \; p = \textbf{case } p \textbf{ of } \{\, \text{PRoot}_F \rightarrow 1 \,;\, \text{PBin}_{LF} \_ \, i \rightarrow \text{succ } i \,;\, \text{PBin}_{RF} \_ \, i \rightarrow \text{succ } i \,\}$$

Applying the depth algebra with a fold draws the information up from the bottom, but in the case of a path, the "bottom" is the root of the tree. In this way, inheritance is flipped head-over-heels.

Given the number of folds and redundant traversals of the fixed-point value and paths, the definition of downwards is clearly inefficient. We may, of course, improve its performance with manual optimizations, but in the end, it will still be a fold. Instead, we deviate from this in our approach for downwards incrementalization. The primary difference lies with the algebraic structure.

$$\textbf{type } \text{Alg}^D \; f \; i = \textbf{forall } s.i \rightarrow f \; s \rightarrow f \; i$$
$$\textbf{type } \text{Alg}^D_F \; t \; i = \text{Alg}^D \; (F \; t) \; i$$

This algebra gives us the point of view of a constructor in a recursive datatype. We no longer fold over a path, but rather inherit an i-type annotation, which would have been the result of a fold on the path, from the parent. The type $f \; s \rightarrow f \; i$ indicates that this algebra changes the elements of a functor f using the inherited value, and the explicit quantification over s (producing rank-2 polymorphism below) preserves the downward direction of data flow. We used a similar device in the type of pnode. Also similar to pnode, an Alg^D algebra must preserve the structure of the input.

We perform downwards incrementalization with an algebra transformation similar to pullUp. The function pushDown demonstrates some similarities with paths.

$$\text{pushDown} :: (\textit{ZipWith } f) \Rightarrow i \rightarrow \text{Alg}^D \; f \; i \rightarrow \text{Alg} \; f \; (\text{Fix}^a \; i \; f)$$
$$\text{pushDown init alg} = \text{in}^a \; \text{init} \circ \text{zipApp push (alg init)}$$
$$\textbf{where } \text{push } i = \text{pushDown } i \; \text{alg} \circ \text{out}^a$$

We use zipApp to merge altered and unaltered functor values. The altered values come by applying the initialized algebra. (In paths, we alter with pnode.) We have removed most folds in pushDown, but we cannot remove recursion completely. Finite values are constructed inductively (i.e. upward), yet we are pushing inherited annotations down to the children. If we construct a new Bin 1 x y value from two Bin values x and y, we must (in a sense) ensure that x and y receive their inheritance from their new parent.

The function pushDown takes a different algebra from downwards, but the difference between the algebra on paths and Alg^D requires manageable changes. The PRoot_F case is replaced by an initial inherited value, and the left and right Bin paths are replaced by a single Bin_F case. We rewrite depthAlg^D as the following:

$$\text{depthInit} \quad = 1$$
$$\text{depthAlg } i \; t = \textbf{case } t \textbf{ of } \{\, \text{Tip}_F \rightarrow \text{Tip}_F \,;\, \text{Bin}_F \; x \_ \_ \rightarrow \text{Bin}_F \; x \; (\text{succ } i) \; (\text{succ } i) \,\}$$

We can then use pushDown depthInit depthAlg to define the smart constructors—in an instance of $Tree_S$, perhaps—for downwards incrementalization.

Evaluating downwards incrementalization would ideally be done with a program that made use of it. We have observed, however, that it is not clear how useful downwards incrementalization is. We reuse the depth algebra from Gibbons[8] in our example, but we have found very few interesting algebras. As a matter of opinion, the incrementalization found in the next section appears much more useful. Indeed, perhaps downwards incrementalization serves better to introduce some concepts, in a simpler setting, that reappear in the next section. At the very least, this section serves to make the discussion of incrementalization more complete.

To evaluate the performance of downwards incrementalization, we benchmark the construction of tree values annotated with depth. We look at the same comparison for downwards as we did for upwards. The details are given in Figure 5.

Downwards incrementalization is clearly less efficient than upwards incrementalization and constructing Tree values: 12 to 21% slower. The recursive downward push accounts for the extra time. On the other hand, it is encouraging to see that, at the worst case, downwards depth incrementalization is not too much slower. In general, the evaluation time of downwards incrementalization can vary greatly depending on the depth of the values and especially the algebra used. As an algebra, depth is perhaps detrimental to efficiency since every new node on top of the tree results in updates to every node down to the leaves. Lastly, note that the downwards transformation is 8 to 11% slower in evaluation. This difference indicates the time spent folding over the paths and the repetitive folds over the tree.

The downwards direction puts an interesting twist on purely functional incrementalization. The development of a Path and its use in downwards allows us to understand inherited annotations while the incrementalizing function pushDown provides a more efficient approach. In the next section, we look at the merger of upwards and downwards incrementalization.

5   Circular Incrementalization

Combining upwards and downwards incrementalization leads us to another form: *circular incrementalization*. Circular incrementalization merges the functionality of both to allow for much more interesting algebras. Information flows both from the descendants to the ancestors and vice versa. Circularity is achieved by introducing feedback at the leaves and the root such that the result of one direction of flow may influence the other. Fittingly, we annotate recursive points with both synthesized and inherited annotations. The following functions serve to access the annotations:

```
inh :: Fixᵃ (i, s) f → i
syn :: Fixᵃ (i, s) f → s
```

We illustrate circular annotations with a specification similar to upwards and downwards. Every annotation combines both synthesized data from the *subtree*

	1,000	10,000	100,000	nodes
Tree	7.4	39.7	137.3	milliseconds
Incrementalized with pushDown	**8.3**	**46.6**	**167.1**	
Transformed with downwards	9.0	51.7	185.4	

Fig. 5. Performance of constructing trees with downwards incrementalization using the depth algebra

(whose root is the annotated node) and inherited data from the *context* (the entire tree-like value inverted, with a path from the current node to the root: the same concept used in zippers[9]). At each node, we can use the algebra to pass results either up or down or both. In our model, we build both subtrees and contexts for each node and compute each annotation with a fold. In order to create circularity, we use algebras whose results are functions that take the other annotation as an argument. We first describe contexts, and then we extend an annotated value with subtrees.

A context is an expansion of a path, and it can be defined in much the same way. We use the type-indexed datatype Context and the type class *Contexts* to give the structure of a datatype's context and the primitives for building it, respectively.

```
data family Context t
data instance Context (Tree a)
    = CRoot | CBinL a (Context (Tree a)) (Tree a) | CBinR a (Tree a) (Context (Tree a))
data instance F (Context (Tree a)) r
    = CRootF | CBinLF a r (Tree a) | CBinRF a (Tree a) r
class (InOut t, InOut (Context t), ZipWith (F t)) ⇒ Contexts t where
    croot  :: Context t
    cnode :: F t t → F t (Context t → Context t)

instance Contexts (Tree a) where
    croot              = CRoot
    cnode TipF         = TipF
    cnode (BinF x tL tR) = BinF x (λc → CBinL x c tR) (CBinR x tL)
```

Note the differences from paths. A context traces a path to the root, but a Context value, unlike a Path, contains a node's sibling recursive values. To annotate all nodes with contexts, we use the following function:

```
contexts :: (Contexts t) ⇒ t → Typeᵃ (Context t) t
contexts = appᵃ croot ∘ fold (inᵃ id ∘ zipApp compᵃ (cnode ∘ fmap rmᵃ))
rmᵃ :: (InOut t) ⇒ Typeᵃ s t → t
rmᵃ = fold (inF ∘ outᶠᵃ)
```

The only difference from **paths** is the need to fold the fixed point into its built-in representation for context nodes. This is in accordance with the fact that the only difference Context has from Path is the inclusion of sibling values represented with the Haskell type. Here is an example of a context-annotated value.

$\text{Bin}^{\text{CRoot}}\ 2\ \text{Tip}^{\text{CBin}_L}\ 2\ \text{CRoot (Bin 1 Tip Tip)}$

$(\text{Bin}^{\text{CBin}_R\ 2\ \text{Tip CRoot}}\ 1\ \text{Tip}^{\text{CBin}_L}\ 1\ (\text{CBin}_R\ 2\ \text{Tip CRoot})\ \text{Tip}\ \text{Tip}^{\text{CBin}_R\ 1\ \text{Tip}\ (\text{CBin}_R\ 2\ \text{Tip CRoot})})$

Given a value with contexts, we pair each annotation with its subtree via a fold over a fixed-point value.

subtrees :: $(InOut\ t) \Rightarrow \text{Type}^a\ c\ t \rightarrow \text{Type}^a\ (c, t)\ t$
subtrees = fold $(\lambda(\text{In}_F^a\ c\ x) \rightarrow \text{in}^a\ (c, \text{in}_F\ (\text{fmap rm}^a\ x))\ x)$

With subtree and context annotations, we can define circular annotations. Circular annotations can be constructed with the following function:

circular :: $(Contexts\ t)$
        $\Rightarrow \text{Alg}_F\ (\text{Context}\ t)\ (s \rightarrow i) \rightarrow \text{Alg}_F\ t\ (i \rightarrow s) \rightarrow t \rightarrow \text{Type}^a\ (i, s)\ t$
circular $\text{alg}^D\ \text{alg}^U$ = foldMap^a cycle ∘ subtrees ∘ contexts
    where cycle (ct, st) = **let** (i, s) = (fold alg^D ct s, fold alg^U st i) **in** (i, s)

Two algebras are necessary: one for each context and one for each subtree. The result of each algebra is a function that is the inverse of the other. Subsequently, each fold is applied to the result of the other, using a technique called *circular programming*[10]. A circular program uses lazy evaluation to avoid multiple explicit traversals, and this is key to circular incrementalization. It allows us to define algebras that rely on as-yet-unknown inputs. Feedback occurs when the upwards algebra alg^U takes input from the downwards algebra alg^D, and vice versa. It is possible to create multiple passes by defining multiple such dependencies. Of course, it is also possible to create non-terminating cycles, but we accept that chance in order to support expressive algebras.

Examples of problems that can be solved by circular incrementalization include the "repmin" problem from Bird[10] and the "diff" problem from Swierstra[11]. The latter is used to show why attribute grammars matter. Circular incrementalization shares some similarities with attribute grammar systems, so it is worth exploring this in more detail.

The naive implementation of Swierstra's problem is a function that, given a list of numbers, calculates the difference of each number from the average of the whole list and returns the results in a list.

diff :: $[\text{Float}] \rightarrow [\text{Float}]$
diff xs = **let** avg = sum xs / genericLength xs **in** map (subtract avg) xs

Swierstra demonstrates two more efficient implementations: one is manually developed and significantly more complex, and the other is generated from a simpler attribute grammar specification using the UUAG system. We add to this an implementation using circular incrementalization, though our definition works on Tree values instead of lists.

The following types serve as specification for the annotations.

newtype Diff^i = DI $\{\text{avg}^i :: \text{Float}\}$
data Diff^s = DS $\{\text{sum}^s :: \text{Float}, \text{size}^s :: \text{Float}, \text{diff}^s :: \text{Float}\}$

In the inherited annotation Diff^i, we have the only inherited value, the average. In the synthesized annotation Diff^s, we have the sum of all element values, the size or count of elements (genericLength for lists), and the resulting difference.

The algebra for subtrees establishes the synthesized annotation.

```
diffAlg^U :: Alg_F (Tree Float) (Diff^i → Diff^s)
diffAlg^U Tip_F       _ = DS {sum^s = 0, size^s = 0, diff^s = 0}
diffAlg^U (Bin_F x s_L s_R) i = dbin^s x (s_L i) (s_R i) i

dbin^s :: Float → Diff^s → Diff^s → Diff^i → Diff^s
dbin^s x s_L s_R i = DS {sum^s  = x + sum^s s_L + sum^s s_R
                      , size^s = 1 + size^s s_L + size^s s_R
                      , diff^s = x − avg^i i}
```

In the Tip component, the values are initialized to zero. In the Bin component, we perform the operations: summing the elements, counting the number of elements, and computing the difference from the average. Since the elements of the algebra are functions, we apply s_L and s_R to the inherited value i, ultimately used in diff^s.

The algebra for contexts establishes the inherited annotation.

```
diffAlg^D :: Alg_F (Context (Tree Float)) (Diff^s → Diff^i)
diffAlg^D CRoot_F        s  = DI {avg^i = sum^s s / size^s s}
diffAlg^D (CBin_LF x i t_R) s_L = let j = i $ dbin^s x s_L (fold diffAlg^U t_R j) j in j
diffAlg^D (CBin_RF x t_L i) s_R = let j = i $ dbin^s x (fold diffAlg^U t_L j) s_R j in j
```

The CRoot_F case holds the calculation of the average because the sum and size have been determined for the entire tree. The CBin_{LF} and CBin_{RF} cases determine the synthesized annotations with folds of the trees not included in the subtree. In these cases, we must also apply the upwards algebra effectively in reverse: the result is used by the algebra's function element i and passed onwards. Note that we must be sure to always use the final inherited annotation (j in these cases) in, for instance, fold diffAlg^U t_R j. Otherwise, the average value does not arrive correctly at every node. Using j instead of i leads to more circular programming, but it does not lead to cycles since there is no other feedback route from diffAlg^D into diffAlg^U.

Here is an example of a value annotated with the diff algebra.

$$\text{Bin}^{DI\ 1.5, DS\ 3\ 2\ 0.5}\ 2\ \text{Tip}^{DI\ 1.5, DS\ 0\ 0\ 0}$$
$$(\text{Bin}^{DI\ 1.5, DS\ 1\ 1\ (−0.5)}\ 1\ \text{Tip}^{DI\ 1.5, DS\ 0\ 0\ 0}\ \text{Tip}^{DI\ 1.5, DS\ 0\ 0\ 0})$$

The same average value has been inherited by every node. In the synthesized annotations, the Bin constructors have the appropriate sum, size, and difference annotations, and the Tip constructors have zeroes.

The specification of circular incrementalization above is clear but (of course) not efficient. To define an efficient version, as with the downwards approach, we use a different algebraic structure.

```
type Alg^C f i s = i → f s → (s, f i)
type Alg_F^C t i s = Alg^C (F t) i s
```

The Alg^C type expands upon Alg^D such that the synthesized annotations are available for use as well as passed on to the parent. Put another way, we marry the Alg and Alg^D types and bear Alg^C. The circular algebra is used in the following algebra transformation.

```
passAround :: (Functor f, ZipWith f) ⇒ (s → i) → AlgC f i s → Alg f (Fixᵃ (i, s) f)
passAround fun alg fis = inᵃ (i, s) (zipWith pass fi fis)
  where i      = fun s
        (s, fi) = alg i (fmap syn fis)
        pass j = passAround (const j) alg ∘ outᵃ
```

The function passAround borrows some aspects from pullUp and pushDown. From the former, we take the upwards algebra applied to the mapped synthesized results. As with the latter, we push the inherited annotations downward by zipping the structures together and recursing. But unlike either previous form, passAround also has circular dependencies on the annotations. The circularity of i and s works in the same way as circular: by enabling the algebra to implicitly traverse the structure and pass around annotations.

The attentive reader will notice that passAround supports restricted capabilities compared to circular. In passAround, we only have feedback from synthesized to inherited annotations at the top level, using the fun parameter. In the internal nodes, the fun argument is const j, meaning we simply pass the inherited value downwards. Since the definition of circular uses algebras with function results, feedback can happen at any node. This means that circular is more expressive; however, it also means that algebras for passAround are simpler to define. At this point, we do not see the need for the increased expressiveness of circular, but we do appreciate the simplified algebra of passAround.

We can solve the diff problem using the parameters of passAround. First, we define the top-level feedback function.

```
diffFunC :: Diffˢ → Diffⁱ
diffFunC s = DI {avgⁱ = sumˢ s / sizeˢ s}
```

This is nothing more than the calculation of the inherited annotation. The circular algebra is also quite simple.

```
diffAlgC :: AlgℱC (Tree Float) Diffⁱ Diffˢ
diffAlgC _ Tip_F           = (DS {sumˢ = 0, sizeˢ = 0, diffˢ = 0}, Tip_F)
diffAlgC i (Bin_F x s_L s_R) = (dbinˢ x s_L s_R i, Bin_F x i i)
```

Unlike with diffAlg^D, we are not concerned with deciding which inherited annotation to pass on, and we do not need any (additional) circularity. We may complete the circular incrementalization for Tree by defining a straightforward Tree_S instance using passAround diffFun^C diffAlg^C for the smart constructors.

We benchmark circular incrementalization in the same way as downwards with one addition. We manually define a fast, accumulating diff function (type Tree Float → Tree Float) that replaces each element with its difference. This function provides a basis for comparison with more typical atomic implementation. See Figure 6 for results.

	1,000	10,000	100,000	*nodes*
Tree	7.4	39.7	137.3	*milliseconds*
Accumulating diff	7.7	41.3	142.9	
Incrementalized with passAround	**9.2**	**53.4**	**210.5**	
Transformed with circular	30.6	737.1	17,233.4	

Fig. 6. Performance of constructing trees with circular incrementalization using the diff algebra

Circular incrementalization is 12 to 26% slower than downwards incremental-ization. It also is 20 to 47% slower than the accumulation. The accumulation is, of course, an atomic function and would incur costs when used again while the time for incrementalization would be amortized over repeated computations. The circular transformation is radically less efficient and would not be useful in practice.

This concludes our look at the various forms of incrementalization. In the following sections, we discuss aspects of incrementalization and related work.

6 Discussion

Several aspects of incrementalization deserve further discussion.

6.1 Combining Algebras

To simplify the presentation of incrementalization, we have ignored a potential issue. Suppose we have the function union for incrementalized trees. If we define the function for the Set library, the solution is the same as without incremen-talization. On the other hand, we may define it more generally with the type Type^a s t $\to$ Type^a s t $\to$ Type^a s t. But with the approach described in this paper, there is no guarantee that the annotation types in each parameter match the same algebra. For example, we might have a type Int for size and a type Int for sum. How do we merge these when we combine values from each parameter?

One option is to allow for different algebras and to use an additional algebra for pairing the annotations together. At every node, we compute the annotations for the algebras of each input. For union, this would result in a type Type^a r t $\to$ Type^a s t $\to$ Type^a (r, s) t. However, for some applications (such as the Set library) this may not be desirable, since it changes the annotation types.

An alternative option is to ensure that an algebra is unique for the entire program. We can do this by creating a multiparameter type class for annotations that attach a type s to a type t: *Annot* s t. We then define union to have the type (*Annot* s t) $\Rightarrow$ Type^a s t $\to$ Type^a s t $\to$ Type^a s t. There can be only one instance of *Annot* for this pair of types, so the type system prevents an inconsistency between the parameters.

6.2 Optimization

One possibility for speeding up incrementalization is the use of *memoization* or storing the results of a function application in order to reuse them if the function is applied to the same argument. Typically, this technique involves a table mapping arguments to results. In both downwards and circular incrementalization, pushing the inherited annotation down leads to recursion through the subtree structure, and this is a large time factor in the these techniques. To memoize the downwards function (push in pushDown and pass in passAround), we must create a memo table for the inherited annotation.

There are several options for memoization from which we might choose. GHC supports a rough form of global memoization using stable name primitives[12]. Generic tries may be used for purely functional memo tables[13] in lazy languages.

In general, the best choice for memoization is strongly determined by the algebra used, but the options above present potential problems when used with incrementalization. Creating a memo table for every node in a tree can lead to an undesirable space explosion. For example, suppose the memo table at every node in the downwards depth example contains two entries. The size of the incrementalized value is already triple the size of an unincrementalized one.

To avoid space issues, we use a memo table size of one with an equality check. The function push is easily modified (as is pass, using inh instead of ann)

```
push i x | i == ann x = x
         | otherwise = pushDown i alg (outᵃ x)
```

In our experiments, unfortunately, memoization did not have a significant effect. The memoized pushDown was up to 1% slower with the depth algebra, and the memoized passAround was up to 1% faster with the diff algebra.

We leave it to future work to explore other forms of optimization.

6.3   Going Datatype-Generic

We have described incrementalization as a library with type classes for a programmer to instantiate. It can also serve as part of a datatype-generic programming library.

For example, for datatypes that are represented using *pattern functors* or structural functor types with explicit recursive points, we can define generic functions such as folds and zips to use with all such types. Such a library is described for rewriting[14] and mutually recursive datatypes[15]. Both *Functor* and *ZipWith* can be instantiated with such a library, so by extension, we can use the above definitions for pullUp, pushDown, and passAround. More details are available in a technical report[16].

6.4   Applications of Incrementalization

We continue to search for particular uses of incrementalization outside of the Set library, but one particular application appears very attractive: a generic incremental *zipper*. The zipper[9] is a technique for navigating and editing values of algebraic datatypes. By incrementalizing a zipper, annotations may be computed incrementally as we navigate and change a value. Examples where this would be useful include (partial) evaluation of an abstract syntax tree and online formatting of structured documents or code. We have outlined an implementation of a generic incremental zipper elsewhere[16].

7   Related Work

As we have mentioned, incrementalization is quite similar to attribute grammars[7]. In addition, Fokkinga, et al[17] prove that attribute grammars can be translated to folds. An annotation on a node in incrementalization is the result of computing an attribute on a production.

Saraiva, et al[18] demonstrate incremental attribute evaluation for a purely functional implementation of attribute grammars. They transform syntax trees to improve the performance of incremental computation. Our approach is considerably more "lightweight" since we write our programs directly in the target language (i.e. Haskell) instead of using a grammar or code generation. On the other hand, we cannot easily boost performance by rewriting.

Viera, et al[19] describe first-class attribute grammars in Haskell. Their approach ensures the well-formedness of the grammar and allows for combining attributes in a type-safe fashion. Our approach to combining annotations is more ad-hoc and we do not ensure well-formedness; however, we believe our approach is simpler to understand and implement. We also show that our technique can improve the performance of a library.

Our initial interest in incremental computing was inspired by Jeuring's work on incremental algorithms for lists[20]. This work shows that incremental algorithms can also be defined not just on lists but on algebraic datatypes in general.

Carlsson[21] translates an imperative ML library supporting high-level incremental computations[22] into a monadic library for Haskell. His approach relies on references to store intermediate results and requires explicit specification of the incremental components. In contrast, our approach is purely functional and uses the structure of the datatype to determine where annotations are placed. We can also hide the incrementalization using type classes such as $Tree_S$. Incrementalization, however, is limited to computations that can be defined as folds, while Carlsson's work is more free-form.

Bernardy[23] defines a lazy, incremental, zipper-based parser for the text editor Yi. His implementation is rather specific to its purpose and lacks an apparent generalization to other datatypes. Further study is required to determine whether Yi can take advantage of incrementalization.

8   Conclusion

We have presented a number of exercises in purely functional incrementalization. Incrementalizing programs decouples recursion from computation and storing intermediate results. Thus, we remove redundant computation and improve the performance of some programs. By utilizing the fixed-point structure of algebraic datatypes, we demonstrate a library that captures all the elements of incrementalization for folds.

Acknowledgments. We thank Edward Kmett for an insightful blog entry and Stefan Holdermans and the anonymous reviewers for suggestions that contributed to significant improvements. This work has been partially funded by the

Netherlands Organization for Scientific Research through the project on "Real-Life Datatype-Generic Programming" (612.063.613).

References

1. Chakravarty, M.M.T., Keller, G., Peyton Jones, S.L., Marlow, S.: Associated Types with Class. In: POPL, pp. 1–13 (2005)
2. Hinze, R., Jeuring, J., Löh, A.: Type-indexed data types. Science of Computer Programming 51(1-2), 117–151 (2004)
3. Sheard, T., Peyton Jones, S.L.: Template Meta-programming for Haskell. In: Haskell, pp. 1–16 (2002)
4. Liu, Y.A.: Efficiency by Incrementalization: An Introduction. Higher-Order and Symbolic Computation 13(4), 289–313 (2000)
5. Adams, S.: Functional Pearls: Efficient sets – a balancing act. J. of Functional Programming 3(04), 553–561 (1993)
6. Claessen, K., Hughes, J.: QuickCheck: A Lightweight Tool for Random Testing of Haskell Programs. In: ICFP, pp. 268–279 (2000)
7. Knuth, D.E.: Semantics of context-free languages. Theory of Computing Systems 2(2), 127–145 (1968)
8. Gibbons, J.: Upwards and downwards accumulations on trees. In: Bird, R.S., Woodcock, J.C.P., Morgan, C.C. (eds.) MPC 1992. LNCS, vol. 669, pp. 122–138. Springer, Heidelberg (1993)
9. Huet, G.: The Zipper. J. of Functional Programming 7(05), 549–554 (1997)
10. Bird, R.S.: Using Circular Programs to Eliminate Multiple Traversals of Data. Acta Informatica 21(3), 239–250 (1984)
11. Swierstra, W.: Why Attribute Grammars Matter. The Monad .Reader 4 (2005)
12. Peyton Jones, S.L., Marlow, S., Elliott, C.: Stretching the storage manager: weak pointers and stable names in Haskell. In: Mohnen, M., Koopman, P. (eds.) IFL 2000. LNCS, vol. 2011, pp. 37–58. Springer, Heidelberg (2001)
13. Hinze, R.: Memo functions, polytypically! In: Jeuring, J. (ed.) WGP (2000)
14. van Noort, T., Rodriguez Yakushev, A., Holdermans, S., Jeuring, J., Heeren, B.: A lightweight approach to datatype-generic rewriting. In: WGP, pp. 13–24 (2008)
15. Rodriguez Yakushev, A., Holdermans, S., Löh, A., Jeuring, J.: Generic Programming with Fixed Points for Mutually Recursive Datatypes. In: ICFP, pp. 233–244 (2009)
16. Leather, S., Löh, A., Jeuring, J.: Pull-Ups, Push-Downs, and Passing It Around: Exercises in Functional Incrementalization. Technical Report UU-CS-2009-024, Dept. of Information and Computing Sciences, Utrecht University (November 2009)
17. Fokkinga, M.M., Jeuring, J., Meertens, L., Meijer, E.: A Translation from Attribute Grammars to Catamorphisms. The Squiggolist 2(1), 20–26 (1991)
18. Saraiva, J., Swierstra, S.D., Kuiper, M.: Functional Incremental Attribute Evaluation. In: Watt, D.A. (ed.) CC 2000. LNCS, vol. 1781, pp. 279–294. Springer, Heidelberg (2000)
19. Viera, M., Swierstra, S.D., Swierstra, W.: Attribute Grammars Fly First-Class: How to do Aspect Oriented Programming in Haskell. In: ICFP, pp. 245–256 (2009)
20. Jeuring, J.: Incremental algorithms on lists. In: van Leeuwen, J. (ed.) SION Conference on Computer Science in the Netherlands, pp. 315–335 (1991)
21. Carlsson, M.: Monads for incremental computing. In: ICFP, pp. 26–35 (2002)
22. Acar, U.A., Blelloch, G.E., Harper, R.: Adaptive functional programming. In: POPL, pp. 247–259 (2002)
23. Bernardy, J.P.: Lazy Functional Incremental Parsing. In: Haskell, pp. 49–60 (2009)

A Typical Synergy
Dynamic Types and Generalised Algebraic Datatypes

Thomas van Noort, Peter Achten, and Rinus Plasmeijer

Institute for Computing and Information Sciences
Radboud University Nijmegen
P.O. Box 9010, 6500 GL Nijmegen, The Netherlands
{thomas,p.achten,rinus}@cs.ru.nl

Abstract. We present a typical synergy between dynamic types (dynamics) and generalised algebraic datatypes (GADTs). The former provides a clean approach to integrating dynamic typing in a statically typed language. It allows values to be wrapped together with their type in a uniform package, deferring type unification until run time using a pattern match annotated with the desired type. The latter allows for the explicit specification of constructor types, as to enforce their structural validity. In contrast to ADTs, GADTs are heterogeneous structures since each constructor type is implicitly universally quantified. Unfortunately, pattern matching only enforces structural validity and does not provide instantiation information on polymorphic types. Consequently, functions that manipulate such values, such as a type-safe update function, are cumbersome due to boilerplate type representation administration. In this paper we focus on improving such functions by providing a new GADT annotation via a natural synergy with dynamics. We formally define the semantics of the annotation and touch on novel other applications of this technique such as type dispatching and enforcing type equality invariants on GADT values.

1   Introduction

In this paper we discuss a typical synergy between two concepts: dynamic types (dynamics) and generalised algebraic datatypes (GADTs).

Types play an important role in strongly typed functional programming languages such as Clean and Haskell. Using static type checking, erroneous behaviour at run time is prevented. Moreover, more efficient code can be generated using the knowledge provided by the types at compile time. However, in dynamic systems that deal with user input, some types will only be known at run time. Using dynamics, monomorphic [1] and polymorphic [2] values can be wrapped together with their type in a black box. The dynamic is unwrapped by pattern matching on the required type in a function definition, instead of specifying the type explicitly in its signature. This approach defers part of the type checking process until run time, exactly when the final required type information is made available. Fortunately, this does not take place at the cost of the advantage of

M.T. Morazán and S.-B. Scholz (Eds.): IFL 2009, LNCS 6041, pp. 179–197, 2010.
© Springer-Verlag Berlin Heidelberg 2010

static typing since the type system guarantees that when pattern matching succeeds, the unwrapped dynamic can be used safely as dictated by the specified type. Of course, pattern matching can fail and cause a run-time error, but this is not different from conventional pattern matching.

Algebraic datatypes (ADTs) in functional languages allow us to inductively define structures. Unfortunately, it does not allow us to enforce structural validity at compile time. With the arrival of generalised algebraic datatypes (GADTs) [6,10,14], this restriction is relieved by allowing constructors to explicitly dictate their types. On the one hand, this prevents us from constructing ill-structured (i.e., ill-typed) values, and on the other hand this ensures structural validity once a GADT value is pattern matched. In contrast to ADTs, GADTs are heterogeneous structures since each constructor occurrence is implicitly universally quantified. Pattern matching such a value only introduces information regarding the structure of the constructor types, leaving the type variables polymorphic. However, more information on their instantiation is often required, typically in functions that manipulate such values. Conventional approaches to this problem are cumbersome, due to boilerplate type representation administration.

The main contribution of this paper is to define a type-safe update function on GADT values via an annotation, achieved by a natural synergy between dynamics and GADTs.

Overview

This paper is organised as follows. First, we elaborate on both dynamics and GADTs (Section 2). We motivate the need for the synergy by defining an update function on λ-terms (Section 3). Then, we formally define a semantics for the new annotation via a synergy between dynamics and GADTs (Section 4). We conclude with related work (Section 5) and a discussion on future work and other applications of this technique (Section 6). In this paper we use Clean's dynamics and Haskell's GADTs. For the sake of presentation, our examples use Haskell syntax, augmented with Clean's notation for dynamics.

2   Preliminaries

We start by introducing dynamics (Section 2.1) and GADTs (Section 2.2).

2.1   Dynamic Types

The advantage of statically typed languages is that types are verified at compile time, preventing erroneous behaviour at run time due to ill-typed values. However, static typing sometimes does not suffice since a type might only be known at run time. Using dynamic types, values are wrapped in a black box, not exposing the type of the contents to the outside world. But unlike existential types [9], both the value and its type are unwrapped by pattern matching the black box, thereby obtaining a value of the matched content type.

In Clean, the keyword **dynamic** provides the mechanism to wrap values together with their type in a dynamic [13], obtaining a value of type *Dynamic*:

$$wrapInt :: Int \rightarrow Dynamic$$
$$wrapInt\ x = \mathbf{dynamic}\ x$$

Unwrapping the integer value is achieved by pattern matching on the dynamic value using the :: annotation, thereby providing a required type:

$$unwrapInt :: Dynamic \rightarrow Int$$
$$unwrapInt\ (x :: Int)\quad = x$$
$$unwrapInt\ (x :: String) = stringToInt\ x$$
$$unwrapInt\ \_\qquad\quad = 0$$

The first arm of the function pattern matches on a value x of type *Int* in the dynamic. If this is the case, the value is returned unchanged. However, the value in the dynamic is possibly a string and has to be converted to an integer first. Due to run-time type unification, the dynamic pattern match can fail in case the wrapped value is not of the type *Int* or *String*. It is our responsibility to provide a catch-all arm which either returns a default value or a run-time error message.

Instead of defining a function for each value type that is turned into a dynamic, we define a single function:

$$wrap :: TC\ \alpha \Rightarrow \alpha \rightarrow Dynamic$$
$$wrap\ x = \mathbf{dynamic}\ x$$

Since this function is polymorphic in the argument type, we require the context to provide the type code (i.e., the value representation of the type) of α which is stored together with the value x, using Clean's built-in *TC* class constraint. A type code also contains the definition of the type it describes, because dynamics can be (de)serialised across modules and verifying name equivalence in a dynamic pattern match does not suffice. Consequently, *TC* instances are only available for nonabstract types.

Unlike Haskell, Clean supports type-dependent dynamics [11], which allows us to use pattern variables in the type of a dynamic pattern match:

$$unwrap :: TC\ \alpha \Rightarrow Dynamic \rightarrow \alpha$$
$$unwrap\ (x :: \alpha^{\wedge}) = x$$
$$unwrap\ \_\qquad\quad = error\ \texttt{"unwrap: incorrect type"}$$

We require x to be of type α and refer to the same variable in the result type of *unwrap* using the $^{\wedge}$ annotation. This causes both types to be coerced automatically at run time. Therefore, a type code is required for α such that it can be compared with the type code obtained from the dynamic pattern match. The context in which this function is used determines which type code is provided.

Pattern variables can also be used to enforce type equality, for example, to define function application of dynamics:

$$apply :: TC\ \alpha \Rightarrow Dynamic \rightarrow Dynamic \rightarrow Maybe\ \alpha$$
$$apply\ (f :: \beta \rightarrow \alpha^\wedge)\ (x :: \beta) = Just\ (f\ x)$$
$$apply\ \_ \qquad\qquad \_ \qquad = Nothing$$

The dynamic pattern matches in the first arm share the same scope. Therefore, they only succeed once the argument type of the function matches the type of the argument. Because the result type of the function in the first dynamic pattern match refers to α in the result type of *apply*, a type code is required for this type. As an example, consider the following expressions:

$$apply\ (\textbf{dynamic}\ fst)\ (\textbf{dynamic}\ (1, \texttt{"2"}))\quad \leadsto\quad Just\ 1$$
$$apply\ (\textbf{dynamic}\ fst)\ (\textbf{dynamic}\ 1)\qquad\qquad \leadsto\quad Nothing$$

While the first expression succeeds, the second expression fails since the argument is not a pair. Finally, dynamics preserve lazy behaviour of functional programs:

$$apply\ (\textbf{dynamic}\ fst)\ (\textbf{dynamic}\ (1, \bot))\quad \leadsto\quad Just\ 1$$

Although the value $\bot$ is part of the tuple that is wrapped in a dynamic, it is not evaluated when (un)wrapped.

2.2   Generalised Algebraic Datatypes

Algebraic datatypes are an oft-used abstraction in functional languages since they provide an inductive approach to defining complex structures by enumerating the alternatives of a type and the associated fields. For example, in Haskell, an ADT representing λ-terms could be defined as follows:

$$\textbf{data}\ Lam = Undef$$
$$\qquad\qquad |\ Const\ Value$$
$$\qquad\qquad |\ App\ Lam\ Lam$$

The *Undef* constructor has no fields, while the *Const* constructor has a single field for a value. The *App* constructor has two fields, which both can be any term. The values are enumerated by another ADT:

$$\textbf{data}\ Value = VInt\ Int$$
$$\qquad\qquad\quad |\ VFun\ (Value \rightarrow Value)$$

Next, we define an evaluation function:

$$eval :: Lam \rightarrow Value$$
$$eval\ Undef\quad = \bot$$
$$eval\ (Const\ x) = x$$
$$eval\ (App\ f\ x) = \textbf{case}\ eval\ f\ \textbf{of}$$
$$\qquad\qquad\qquad\qquad VFun\ f \rightarrow f\ (eval\ x)$$
$$\qquad\qquad\qquad\qquad \_ \qquad\quad \rightarrow error\ \texttt{"eval: not a function"}$$

The arms for *Undef* and *Const* are straightforward. However, since nothing prevents us from constructing ill-typed terms, the arm for *App* has to ensure that its first field actually evaluates to a function.

With the arrival of generalised abstract datatypes, we are able to enforce structural validity by providing an explicit type signature to each constructor. Consequently, a GADT imposes a heterogeneous structure since all constructors are implicitly universally quantified. We illustrate the use of GADTs by defining the *Lam* type again, this time describing typed λ-terms:

data *Lam* :: $\star \to \star$ **where**
  Undef :: *Lam* α
  Const :: $\alpha \to Lam\ \alpha$
  App   :: *Lam* $(\beta \to \alpha) \to Lam\ \beta \to Lam\ \alpha$

The *Lam* type is parameterised by the result type of the term once it is evaluated. With each constructor, we explicitly specify its result type. The *Undef* constructor represents an undefined value. Since its result type α is free and not bound by any fields, it can be unified with any other type. The *Const* constructor lifts any value to the *Lam* type. The *App* constructor is more explicit about the types of its two field. The argument type of the function term must match the type of the argument term. Then, its result type is the result type of the function term. The explicit constructor types prevent us from constructing ill-typed terms. Consider the following examples:

$\bot\ 1$ $\equiv$ *App Undef* (*Const* 1)

Since the return type of the *Undef* constructor can be anything, it is instantiated to a function as *App* requires, thereby returning a value of type *Lam* α. When we provide a term that does not return a function, the term becomes ill typed:

0 1 $\equiv$ *App* (*Const* 0) (*Const* 1)

A more useful example actually applies a function. Consider the absolute value of an integer:

abs 1 $\equiv$ *App* (*Const abs*) (*Const* 1)

This term is well typed and returns a value of type *Lam Int*.

Type information described in the type of the constructors is also employed when the constructors are pattern matched in a function definition. Since only well-typed terms can be constructed, we can now safely and concisely define the evaluation function:

eval :: *Lam* $\alpha \to \alpha$
eval Undef $= \bot$
eval (*Const x*) $= x$
eval (*App f x*) $= eval\ f\ (eval\ x)$

The result type of the function depends on the term that is evaluated. Each constructor dictates the type of its fields as well as the result type. For example, evaluating the first field of the *App* constructors returns a function, which can safely be applied to its evaluated second field. However, be aware that the exact types of these fields are not known since we are dealing with a heterogeneous structure.

3   Motivation

In this section, we motivate the need for the typical synergy between dynamics and GADTs in the context of update functions on GADTs (Section 3.1). Next, we discuss why the conventional approach is not suited to this problem (Section 3.2) and how the synergy elegantly improves on these issues using a new GADT annotation (Section 3.3).

3.1   Setting the Scene

We use as the running example the definition from Section 2.2 that represents λ-terms. Our goal is to define an update function that takes such a term, and updates a field of a constructor at a specified position with a new value. Then, the desired type of the update function becomes:

$$update :: Lam\ \alpha \rightarrow Path \rightarrow \beta \rightarrow Lam\ \alpha$$

The argument and result type of the function are the same since we only consider updates that do not affect the top-level type of the term. However, an update can change the structure. The path depicts the location of the update in the heterogeneous structure:

type $Path = [Int]$

The path is represented as a list of integers. The length of the list indicates the recursive level (where the empty list is the root) of the target and each value the field (where 0 is the first field) that must be considered. Since the path possibly dictates an update anywhere in the heterogeneous structure, the type of the new value is unrestricted. Hence, the challenge we face lies in only allowing type-safe updates.

3.2   Conventional Approach

The conventional approach to this problem makes extensive use of equality types [3,5]. By comparing the value representations of the type of the old and new value, a proof of type equality can be obtained to ensure only type-safe updates.

First, we modify our original *Lam* definition from Section 2.2 to the following:

data $Lam_R :: \star \to \star$ **where**
$\quad Undef_R :: Lam_R\ \alpha$
$\quad Const_R :: RepOf\ \alpha \to Lam_R\ \alpha$
$\quad App_R \quad :: RepOf\ (Lam_R\ (\beta \to \alpha)) \to RepOf\ (Lam_R\ \beta) \to Lam_R\ \alpha$

The difference is that the types of the constructor fields now include a type representation:

type $RepOf\ \alpha = (\alpha,\ Rep\ \alpha)$

The *Rep* type enumerates the possible types, including the integer type, the function type, and the Lam_R type:

data $Rep :: \star \to \star$ **where**
$\quad RInt \quad :: Rep\ Int$
$\quad RFun \quad :: Rep\ \alpha \to Rep\ \beta \to Rep\ (\alpha \to \beta)$
$\quad RLam_R :: Rep\ \alpha \to Rep\ (Lam_R\ \alpha)$

The *Rep* type is only a witness of a type, for example, the type $Lam_R\ (Int \to Int)$ is witnessed by the value $RLam_R\ (RFun\ RInt\ RInt)$. For the sake of brevity, this representation type only reflects monomorphic types. Given such witnesses, we are able to construct the actual proof that the types of such *Rep* values are the same. Such a proof is constructed by the following GADT:

data $Equal :: \star \to \star \to \star$ **where**
$\quad Refl :: Equal\ \alpha\ \alpha$

The *Equal* type consists of a single constructor *Refl*, one that proves that both of the type arguments are the same. Then, we define a type equality function that performs a point-wise comparison of type representations, using Haskell's **do** notation:

$eq_R :: Rep\ \alpha \to Rep\ \beta \to Maybe\ (Equal\ \alpha\ \beta)$
$eq_R\ RInt \qquad\qquad RInt \qquad\qquad -\ Just\ Refl$
$eq_R\ (RFun\ x_1\ x_2)\ (RFun\ y_1\ y_2) = \textbf{do}\ Refl \leftarrow eq_R\ x_1\ y_1$
$\qquad\qquad\qquad\qquad\qquad\qquad\qquad Refl \leftarrow eq_R\ x_2\ y_2$
$\qquad\qquad\qquad\qquad\qquad\qquad\qquad return\ Refl$
$eq_R\ (RLam_R\ x) \quad (RLam_R\ y) \quad = \textbf{do}\ Refl \leftarrow eq_R\ x\ y$
$\qquad\qquad\qquad\qquad\qquad\qquad\qquad return\ Refl$
$eq_R\ - \qquad\qquad\quad - \qquad\qquad\quad = Nothing$

Given two *Rep* values, this function either returns *Just Refl* if the type representations are the same, thereby implicitly indicating that the types α and β are the same as well, or *Nothing*. In the arms for *RFun* and $RLam_R$ we have to explicitly pattern match the result of the recursion as to obtain its type equality proof. Finally, we define a catch-all arm which returns *Nothing* for *Rep* values that are not equal.

Then, using the modified *Lam* definition and a type representation added to the new value, we are finally able to define our update function:

$$update_R :: Lam_R\ \alpha \rightarrow Path \rightarrow RepOf\ \beta \rightarrow Lam_R\ \alpha$$

$$
\begin{array}{lll}
update_R\ Undef_R & [\,] \quad \_ & = Undef_R \\
update_R\ (Const_R\ (x, rx))\ [0] & (y, ry) & = \textbf{case}\ eq_R\ rx\ ry\ \textbf{of} \\
& & \quad Just\ Refl \rightarrow Const_R\ (y, ry) \\
& & \quad Nothing \ \rightarrow Const_R\ (x, rx) \\
update_R\ (App_R\ (f, rf)\ x)\ [0] & (y, ry) & = \textbf{case}\ eq_R\ rf\ ry\ \textbf{of} \\
& & \quad Just\ Refl \rightarrow App_R\ (y, ry)\ x \\
& & \quad Nothing \ \rightarrow App_R\ (f, rf)\ x \\
update_R\ (App_R\ f\ (x, rx))\ [1] & (y, ry) & = \textbf{case}\ eq_R\ rx\ ry\ \textbf{of} \\
& & \quad Just\ Refl \rightarrow App_R\ f\ (y, ry) \\
& & \quad Nothing \ \rightarrow App_R\ f\ (x, rx) \\
update_R\ (App_R\ (f, rf)\ x)\ (0:p)\ y & & = App_R\ (update_R\ f\ p\ y, rf)\ x \\
update_R\ (App_R\ f\ (x, rx))\ (1:p)\ y & & = App_R\ f\ (update_R\ x\ p\ y, rx) \\
update_R\ x & \_ \quad \_ & = x \\
\end{array}
$$

In the arm for $Undef_R$ there is nothing left to do, we only have to make sure that the path is fully consumed. The $Const_R$ is the first interesting case, since we have to verify that the types match by testing the equality of the *Rep* values. Once these values are the same, we provide a proof that α and β are equal types by pattern matching on the *Refl* constructor. Then, in the arms for App_R we use the same approach and either replace its first or second field, or dispatch on the head of the path and continue to recurse in either of its fields. Finally, a catch-all arm is included to return the original term once the provided path is incorrect. Whenever the function is applied, all the type representations need to be provided explicitly:

$$update_R\ (Const_R\ (abs, RFun\ RInt\ RInt))\ [0]\ (neg, RFun\ RInt\ RInt)$$

$$\rightsquigarrow$$

$$Const_R\ (neg, RFun\ RInt\ RInt)$$

Although this approach guarantees type-safe updates, it is not a very elegant definition. First of all, the invasive inclusion of *Rep* values in the datatype clutters the update function with type equality witnesses and manual proofs. Moreover, the types of the values that are updated have to be known beforehand since these are enumerated in the *Rep* type and traversed in the type equality function. Above all, this approach does not scale up to more complex structures and update functions.

3.3 The Synergy

The conventional approach requires us to carry around type representations that are used to convince the type checker of type equality. When we look back at Section 2.1, we notice that this is actually what Clean's *TC* type class provides. We propose to adapt the original *Lam* definition from Section 2.2 again:

data $Lam_T :: \star \to \star$ **where**
$$Undef_T ::\qquad\qquad\qquad Lam_T\ \alpha$$
$$Const_T :: TC\ \alpha \qquad\qquad \Rightarrow \alpha \to Lam_T\ \alpha$$
$$App_T \quad :: (TC\ \beta, TC\ \alpha) \Rightarrow Lam_T\ (\beta \to \alpha) \to Lam_T\ \beta \to Lam_T\ \alpha$$

Instead of including Rep values, we include TC class constraints with the constructors that can be updated. Then, we define the update function using the new $::^{\mathcal{G}}$ annotation on the field of a GADT constructor:

$$update_T :: TC\ \beta \Rightarrow Lam_T\ \alpha \to Path \to \beta \to Lam_T\ \alpha$$
$$update_T\ Undef_T \qquad\qquad [\,] \qquad \_ = Undef_T$$
$$update_T\ (Const_T\ (x ::^{\mathcal{G}} \beta^{\wedge}))\ [0] \qquad y = Const_T\ y$$
$$update_T\ (App_T\ (f ::^{\mathcal{G}} \beta^{\wedge})\ x)\ [0] \qquad y = App_T\ y\ x$$
$$update_T\ (App_T\ f\ (x ::^{\mathcal{G}} \beta^{\wedge}))\ [1] \qquad y = App_T\ f\ y$$
$$update_T\ (App_T\ f\ x) \qquad\qquad (0 : p)\ y = App_T\ (update_T\ f\ p\ y)\ x$$
$$update_T\ (App_T\ f\ x) \qquad\qquad (1 : p)\ y = App_T\ f\ (update_T\ x\ p\ y)$$
$$update_T\ x \qquad\qquad\qquad \_ \qquad \_ = x$$

Let us take a look at the differences between this update function and the conventional definition $update_R$ from Section 3.2. First of all, this function operates on the Lam_T type that is decorated with TC constraints, and its type contains a TC constraint to obtain a type code for the new value of type β. Although the update function was intended to be polymorphic at first, this constraint only forbids abstract types to occur as new values, as discussed earlier in Section 2.1. Another difference is that the function is no longer cluttered with verbose type equality witnesses and manual proofs. Instead, the fields of the constructors are annotated using the $::^{\mathcal{G}}$ annotation, accessing the instantiated polymorphic type information. For example, in the arm for $Const_T$, the annotation denotes that x is of type β, or even more specific, the type of the new value as determined by the context in which this function is used. Note that the catch-all arm now also takes care of any failing tests for type equality. Comparing the use of this update function to the conventional approach emphasises the elegance of our approach:

$$update_T\ (Const_T\ abs)\ [0]\ neg \quad \rightsquigarrow \quad Const_T\ neg$$

Instead of explicitly providing type representations and equality proofs, it is now the context that implicitly determines which fields are eligible for an update.

4   Semantics

In this section we present the formal semantics of the synergy. We formally define a core functional language and the GADT annotation extension (Section 4.1). Then, we describe the idea behind the translation from the extended language to the core language by means of an example (Section 4.2), followed by a formal approach (Section 4.3).

$$
\begin{array}{lll}
(program) & \pi ::= \overline{\delta}\ \overline{\phi} \\[6pt]
(datatype\ declaration) & \delta ::= \mathbf{type}\ T\ \overline{\alpha} = \tau \\
& \quad |\ \mathbf{data}\ T\ \overline{\alpha} = \overline{C\ \tau} \\
& \quad |\ \mathbf{data}\ T :: \kappa\ \mathbf{where}\ \overline{C :: \sigma} \\[6pt]
(qualified\ type) & \sigma ::= \overline{TC\ \alpha} \Rightarrow \tau \\
(base\ type) & \tau ::= \alpha\ |\ Int\ |\ T \\
& \quad |\ \tau_1\ \tau_2\ |\ \tau_1 \rightarrow \tau_2 \\
& \quad |\ Dynamic \\
(annotation\ type) & \omega ::= \alpha\ |\ \alpha^{\wedge}\ |\ Int\ |\ T \\
& \quad |\ \omega_1\ \omega_2\ |\ \omega_1 \rightarrow \omega_2 \\
& \quad |\ Dynamic \\
(kind) & \kappa ::= \star\ |\ \kappa_1 \rightarrow \kappa_2 \\[6pt]
(function\ declaration) & \phi ::= \mathbf{fix}\ f :: \sigma = \epsilon \\
(expression) & \epsilon ::= \bot\ |\ i\ |\ x\ |\ C \\
& \quad |\ \epsilon_1\ \epsilon_2\ |\ \lambda x \rightarrow \epsilon\ |\ \mathbf{case}\ \epsilon_s\ \mathbf{of}\ \overline{\rho \rightarrow \epsilon} \\
& \quad |\ \mathbf{dynamic}\ e :: \omega \\
(nested\ pattern) & \rho ::= \varrho\ |\ C\ \overline{\rho} \\
(base\ pattern) & \varrho ::= \_\ |\ i\ |\ x \\
& \quad |\ x :: \omega
\end{array}
$$

Fig. 1. The core language FC

4.1 Formal Language

The functional core language FC, which forms the basis of our semantics, is depicted in Fig. 1. It is a common subset of Clean and Haskell, extended with Clean's dynamics and Haskell's GADTs. An FC program consists of zero or more datatype declarations and function declarations. A datatype is either a type synonym, an ADT, or a GADT. A type comes in three flavours: a qualified type, a base type, and an annotation type. A qualified type only includes the TC constraint, as to facilitate dynamics, where we write τ as a shorthand for the qualified type $\cdot \Rightarrow \tau$ with no constraints. Second, a base type comprises the polymorphic types. Very much like a base type, we define a separate annotation type, but one that also allows the use of the $\wedge$ annotation. A named function is defined by its type and body. Amongst the well-known expressions, our language supports the case construct to pattern match values, typically the arguments of a function, and dynamic values. In the language of patterns we distinguish a nested pattern from a base pattern, as to prepare for the language extension. Finally, we do not explicitly include lists and tuples of arbitrary arity in the language of expressions, patterns and types, since these can easily be realized through predefined ADTs. We do not provide operational semantics and typing for the core language since these have been studied in-depth elsewhere [2,4,6].

$$(expression) \quad \epsilon ::= \cdots$$
$$| \quad \cdots \mid \mathbf{case}\ \epsilon_s\ \mathbf{of}\ \overline{\theta \to \epsilon}$$
$$| \quad \cdots$$
$$(pattern) \qquad \theta ::= \varrho \mid C\ \overline{\vartheta}$$
$$(field\ pattern)\ \vartheta ::= \rho \mid x ::^{\mathcal{G}} \omega$$

Fig. 2. The extended language FC$^+$

Next, we define the extended language FC$^+$ that allows us to use the GADT annotation, as shown in Fig. 2. For the sake of simplicity, we only allow the new annotation to occur on the top level of a constructor field pattern. However, nested patterns can be easily achieved by nesting case expressions. We redefine patterns in FC case expressions to be either a base pattern or a constructor with field patterns. Then, a pattern in a constructor field is either an original nested pattern, or an identifier annotated with a type.

As an example, we define the $update_T$ function from Section 3.3 in the FC$^+$ language:

$$\mathbf{fix}\ update_T :: TC\ \beta \Rightarrow Lam_T\ \alpha \to Path \to \beta \to Lam_T\ \alpha =$$
$$\lambda x \to \lambda p \to \lambda y \to \mathbf{case}\ (x, p)\ \mathbf{of}$$

$$(Undef_T\quad,[\,]) \qquad \to\ Undef_T$$
$$(x \qquad\quad, (0:[\,])) \to \mathbf{case}\ x\ \mathbf{of}$$
$$\qquad\qquad\qquad Const_T\ (x ::^{\mathcal{G}} \beta^{\wedge}) \to Const_T\ y$$
$$\qquad\qquad\qquad App_T\ (f ::^{\mathcal{G}} \beta^{\wedge})\ x \to App_T\ y\ x$$
$$\qquad\qquad\qquad \_ \qquad\qquad\qquad\quad \to x$$
$$(x \qquad\quad, (1:[\,])) \to \mathbf{case}\ x\ \mathbf{of}$$
$$\qquad\qquad\qquad App_T\ f\ (x ::^{\mathcal{G}} \beta^{\wedge}) \to App_T\ f\ y$$
$$\qquad\qquad\qquad \_ \qquad\qquad\qquad\quad \to x$$
$$(App_T\ f\ x, (0:p)) \to App_T\ (update_T\ f\ p\ y)\ x$$
$$(App_T\ f\ x, (1:p)) \to App_T\ f\ (update_T\ x\ p\ y)$$
$$\_ \qquad\qquad\qquad \to x$$

While being slightly more verbose than the original definition, a translation from a Clean or Haskell definition is easily made. Note that the definitions of the *Path* and Lam_T type from Section 3.1 and Section 3.3 respectively do not change in the formal model.

4.2 Intuition

The general idea behind the translation is to take each GADT and translate it to an extended parallel definition in which only constructor fields that are annotated in the program are decorated with additional type information. A conversion function inserts type information in the original definition and the $::^{\mathcal{G}}$ annotations are translated accessesing this information.

For example, the Lam_T type from Section 3.3 translates to the following:

data $Lam_T^\circ :: \star \to \star$ **where**
$\quad Undef_T^\circ ::$ $\qquad\qquad\qquad Lam_T^\circ \alpha$
$\quad Const_T^\circ :: TC\ \alpha$ $\qquad \Rightarrow TypeOf\ \alpha \to Lam_T^\circ \alpha$
$\quad App_T^\circ \quad :: (TC\ \beta, TC\ \alpha) \Rightarrow TypeOf\ (Lam_T\ (\beta \to \alpha)) \to TypeOf\ (Lam_T\ \beta)$
$\qquad\qquad\qquad\qquad\qquad\qquad\qquad \to Lam_T^\circ \alpha$

The extended definition, as well as its constructors, is given a new name. Since all
fields of the constructors are annotated in the update function from Section 3.3,
all fields of the $Const_T^\circ$ and App_T° constructor now contain a typed value. Note
that in order to only have to translate patterns instead of complete functions
later on, the addition of type information is nonrecursive:

type $TypeOf\ \alpha = (\alpha, Dynamic)$

A typed value is simply the original value paired with its type stored in a dynamic. As a $Dynamic$ can contain a value of any type, not necessarily the type
α, we use the following function to obtain correctness by construction:

fix $typeOf :: TC\ \alpha \Rightarrow \alpha \to TypeOf\ \alpha =$
$\quad \lambda x \to (x, \textbf{dynamic } \bot :: \alpha^\wedge)$

Since we only need the type of a value, it suffices to wrap $\bot$ instead of an actual
value. As described in Section 2.1, the $^\wedge$ annotation refers to context-dependent
type information. The context in which $typeOf$ is used determines the type that
is stored in the dynamic. Note that constructors can contain GADT values,
like App_T°, which requires such types to be stored in a dynamic. Unfortunately,
type code facilities are yet to be defined for GADTs. Although GADTs greatly
complicate the type inference process [10,12], we hypothesize that storing such
values in dynamics is not different from ADT values since it does not affect the
unification of type codes that describe a GADT.

Then, the conversion from the original to the extended definition injects the
type information in constant time using the function $typeOf$:

fix $toLam_T^\circ :: Lam_T\ \alpha \to Lam_T^\circ \alpha =$
$\quad \lambda x \to \textbf{case } x \textbf{ of}$
$\qquad Undef_T \quad \to Undef_T^\circ$
$\qquad Const_T\ x \to Const_T^\circ\ (typeOf\ x)$
$\qquad App_T\ f\ x \to App_T^\circ\ (typeOf\ f)\ (typeOf\ x)$

The conversion only renames the $Undef_T$ constructor since it has no fields.
The fields of the $Const_T$ and App_T constructor are extended with their types.
As the function $typeOf$ dictates, this requires a type code for the field types.
The translation relies critically on this assumption, which is enforced by only
considering a FC$^+$ program well typed if and only if each constructor has TC
constraints on every type variable occurring in its annotated fields. Fortunately,
as mentioned before in Section 2.1, the TC constraint is easily discharged for

$$\boxed{[\![\pi_{\mathsf{FC}+}]\!] \equiv \pi_{\mathsf{FC}}}$$

$$\frac{[\![\delta]\!] \equiv \overline{\delta'}\ \phi^\circ \qquad [\![\phi]\!] \equiv \overline{\phi'}}{[\![\overline{\delta}\ \overline{\phi}]\!] \equiv \overline{\delta'}\ \phi^\circ\ \overline{\phi'}}\ (\text{T-PROG})$$

Fig. 3. Translation of programs

any nonabstract type, which only forbids the use of the GADT annotation in combination with abstract types.

Finally, we define the translation of the actual $::^{\mathcal{G}}$ annotation, accessing the inserted type information. For example, the FC$^+$ function $update_T$, as defined in Section 4.1, is translated to FC:

fix $update_T :: TC\ \beta \Rightarrow Lam_T\ \alpha \rightarrow Path \rightarrow \beta \rightarrow Lam_T\ \alpha =$
$\lambda x \rightarrow \lambda p \rightarrow \lambda y \rightarrow$ **case** (x, p) **of**
$\quad \cdots$
$\quad (x, (0 : [\,])) \rightarrow$ **case** $toLam_T^\circ\ x$ **of**
$\qquad\qquad\qquad Const_T^\circ\ (x, \_ :: \beta^\wedge) \quad\ \rightarrow Const_T\ y$
$\qquad\qquad\qquad App_T^\circ\ (f, \_ :: \beta^\wedge)\ (x, \_) \rightarrow App_T\ y\ x$
$\qquad\qquad\qquad \_ \qquad\qquad\qquad\qquad\quad \rightarrow x$
$\quad (x, (1 : [\,])) \rightarrow$ **case** $toLam_T^\circ\ x$ **of**
$\qquad\qquad\qquad App_T^\circ\ (f, \_)\ (x, \_ :: \beta^\wedge) \rightarrow App_T\ f\ y$
$\qquad\qquad\qquad \_ \qquad\qquad\qquad\qquad\quad \rightarrow x$
$\quad \cdots$

The conversion from the original to the extended GADT is applied to the scrutinee of the case expression. This provides type information in the pattern match, allowing it to interact naturally like a conventional dynamic, in this case with the type of the function using the $^\wedge$ annotation. Note that since the conversion function is specific to a program, and not to each case expression, the fields that do not use the annotation must discard the inserted type information as in the case for App_T°.

4.3   Formal Translation

We continue by defining the formal translation from the extended language FC$^+$ to the core language FC. We conjecture that the translation is sound, every well-typed FC$^+$ program is translated to a well-typed FC program.

Let us begin by translating programs, as depicted by Rule T-PROG in Fig. 3. A program in the FC$^+$ language is translated to the FC language by translating both the datatype declarations and the function declarations.

In Fig. 4 we define the translation of datatype declarations. Type synonyms and ADTs are left unchanged, as defined by Rules T-DATA-TSYN and T-DATA-ADT. We distinguish GADTs by using the metafunction annotated(T) to test if it is

$$\boxed{[\![\delta_{\mathsf{FC}+}]\!] \equiv \overline{\delta}_{\mathsf{FC}}; \phi_{\mathsf{FC}}}$$

$$\frac{}{[\![\mathbf{type}\ T\ \overline{\alpha} = \tau]\!] \equiv \mathbf{type}\ T\ \overline{\alpha} = \tau; \cdot}\ (\text{T-DATA-TSYN})$$

$$\frac{}{[\![\mathbf{data}\ T\ \overline{\alpha} = \overline{C\ \tau}]\!] \equiv \mathbf{data}\ T\ \overline{\alpha} = \overline{C\ \tau}; \cdot}\ (\text{T-DATA-ADT})$$

$$\frac{\neg\ \mathsf{annotated}(T)}{[\![\mathbf{data}\ T :: \kappa\ \mathbf{where}\ \overline{C :: \sigma}]\!] \equiv \mathbf{data}\ T :: \kappa\ \mathbf{where}\ \overline{C :: \sigma}; \cdot}\ (\text{T-DATA-GADT-1})$$

$$\frac{\begin{array}{c}\mathsf{annotated}(T)\\[2pt] [\![\sigma]\!]_C \equiv \overline{\sigma^\circ; \overline{x}; \overline{\epsilon^\circ}} \qquad \delta^\circ \equiv \mathbf{data}\ T^\circ :: \kappa\ \mathbf{where}\ \overline{C^\circ :: \sigma^\circ}\\[2pt] \phi^\circ \equiv \mathbf{fix}\ to T^\circ :: T\ \overline{\alpha} \to T^\circ\ \overline{\alpha} =\\[2pt] \mathsf{tarity}(T) \equiv \overline{\alpha} \qquad \lambda x \to \mathbf{case}\ x\ \mathbf{of}\\[2pt] \overline{C\ \overline{x} \to C^\circ\ \overline{\epsilon^\circ}}\end{array}}{[\![\mathbf{data}\ T :: \kappa\ \mathbf{where}\ \overline{C :: \sigma}]\!] \equiv \mathbf{data}\ T :: \kappa\ \mathbf{where}\ \overline{C :: \sigma}\ \delta^\circ; \phi^\circ}\ (\text{T-DATA-GADT-2})$$

Fig. 4. Translation of datatypes

$$\boxed{[\![\sigma_{\mathsf{FC}+}]\!]_C \equiv \sigma_{\mathsf{FC}}; \overline{x}; \overline{\epsilon}_{\mathsf{FC}}}$$

$$\frac{[\![\tau]\!]_{C;0} \equiv \tau^\circ; \overline{x}; \overline{\epsilon^\circ}}{[\![\overline{TC\ \alpha} \Rightarrow \tau]\!] \equiv \overline{TC\ \alpha} \Rightarrow \tau^\circ; \overline{x}; \overline{\epsilon^\circ}}\ (\text{T-QTYPE})$$

Fig. 5. Translation of qualified types

pattern matched somewhere in the program using the GADT annotation (e.g., $\mathsf{annotated}(Lam^\circ) \equiv True$). If not, the original definition is returned without any modifications, as defined by Rule T-DATA-GADT-1. However, an annotated GADT requires some effort. In Rule T-DATA-GADT-2, the translation results in the original definition, an extended definition δ°, and a conversion function ϕ°. By translating the types of the constructors parameterized by the respective constructor name, we obtain extended types together with corresponding pattern variables and expressions that extend these variables. The former is used to define the constructor types of the extended definition, the latter two to define the corresponding conversion function. The metafunction $\mathsf{tarity}(T)$ provides zero or more fresh type variables, determined by the arity of the type T (e.g., $\mathsf{tarity}(Lam_T) \equiv \alpha$).

The translation of qualified types, parameterised by a constructor name, is shown in Fig. 5. A qualified type propagates the translation to its base type, adding a parameter which represents the index of the constructor field type under translation.

In Fig. 6 we define the parameterised translation of such types, resulting in an extended type, pattern variables, and expressions that extends these

$$\boxed{[\![\tau_{\mathsf{FC+}}]\!]_{C;n} \equiv \tau_{\mathsf{FC}}; \overline{x}; \overline{\epsilon}_{\mathsf{FC}}}$$

$$\frac{}{[\![T]\!]_{C;n} \equiv T; \cdot; \cdot} \text{ (T-TYPE-DATA)} \qquad \frac{}{[\![\tau_1\ \tau_2]\!]_{C;n} \equiv \tau_1\ \tau_2; \cdot; \cdot} \text{ (T-TYPE-APP)}$$

$$\frac{\neg\ \mathsf{annotated}(C, n) \qquad [\![\tau_2]\!]_{C;n+1} \equiv \tau_2^\circ; \overline{x_2}; \overline{\epsilon_2^\circ}}{[\![\tau_1 \to \tau_2]\!]_{C;n} \equiv \tau_1 \to \tau_2^\circ; x_1\ \overline{x_2}; x_1\ \overline{\epsilon_2^\circ}} \text{ (T-TYPE-FUN-1)}$$

$$\frac{\mathsf{annotated}(C, n) \qquad [\![\tau_2]\!]_{C;n+1} \equiv \tau_2^\circ; \overline{x_2}; \overline{\epsilon_2^\circ}}{[\![\tau_1 \to \tau_2]\!]_{C;n} \equiv TypeOf\ \tau_1 \to \tau_2^\circ; x_1\ \overline{x_2}; (typeOf\ x_1)\ \overline{\epsilon_2^\circ}} \text{ (T-TYPE-FUN-2)}$$

Fig. 6. Translation of base types

$$\boxed{[\![\phi_{\mathsf{FC+}}]\!] \equiv \phi_{\mathsf{FC}}}$$

$$\frac{[\![\epsilon]\!] \equiv \epsilon'}{[\![\mathbf{fix}\ f :: \sigma = \epsilon]\!] \equiv \mathbf{fix}\ f :: \sigma = \epsilon'} \text{ (T-FUN)}$$

Fig. 7. Translation of functions

variables. Since we are only interested in the fields of a constructor type, and the type of an empty constructor is either a type constructor or a type application, Rules T-TYPE-DATA and T-TYPE-APP result in an unchanged type and no pattern variables or expressions. The function type is the interesting case. If a constructor field is not annotated in the program, as shown in Rule T-TYPE-FUN-1, it is returned unchanged together with a fresh pattern variable and expression that corresponds to the identity. Otherwise, the translation in Rule T-TYPE-FUN-2 extends the type of the constructor field with additional type information and ensures that the fresh pattern variable is extended as well. In both cases we recurse in the translation by incrementing the second parameter to denote the next constructor field.

Next, we define the translation of functions by Rule T-FUN in Fig. 7. A function is translated by translating its body expression, which localises the conversion and thus does not change the type of a function.

The translation of expressions is shown in Fig. 8. The basic building blocks of expressions: bottom, integers, identifiers, and constructors, are left unchanged, as can be seen in Rules T-EXP-BOT, T-EXP-INT, T-EXP-ID, and T-EXP-CON respectively. Translation of an application is defined by Rule T-EXP-APP as translating both of its expressions. Rule T-EXP-ABS defines the translation of an abstraction by translating the body expression. For case expressions, we define two separate rules, testing if one of its patterns uses the GADT annotation. If not, it suffices to only translate the scrutinee and the expression of each pattern, as defined by Rule T-EXP-CASE-1. Otherwise, Rule T-EXP-CASE-2 defines that the conversion function must be applied

$$\boxed{[\![\epsilon_{\mathsf{FC+}}]\!] \equiv \epsilon_{\mathsf{FC}}}$$

$$\frac{}{[\![\bot]\!] \equiv \bot} \; (\text{T-EXP-BOT}) \qquad\qquad \frac{}{[\![i]\!] \equiv i} \; (\text{T-EXP-INT})$$

$$\frac{}{[\![x]\!] \equiv x} \; (\text{T-EXP-ID}) \qquad\qquad \frac{}{[\![C]\!] \equiv C} \; (\text{T-EXP-CON})$$

$$\frac{[\![\epsilon_1]\!] \equiv \epsilon'_1 \qquad [\![\epsilon_2]\!] \equiv \epsilon'_2}{[\![\epsilon_1 \; \epsilon_2]\!] \equiv \epsilon'_1 \; \epsilon'_2} \; (\text{T-EXP-APP}) \qquad\qquad \frac{[\![\epsilon]\!] \equiv \epsilon'}{[\![\lambda x \to \epsilon]\!] \equiv \lambda x \to \epsilon'} \; (\text{T-EXP-ABS})$$

$$\frac{x ::^{\mathcal{G}} \alpha \notin \overline{\theta} \qquad \overline{\theta} \equiv \overline{\rho} \qquad \overline{[\![\epsilon]\!] \equiv \epsilon'}}{[\![\mathbf{case}\ \epsilon_s\ \mathbf{of}\ \overline{\theta \to \epsilon}]\!] \equiv \mathbf{case}\ \epsilon'_s\ \mathbf{of}\ \overline{\rho \to \epsilon'}} \; (\text{T-EXP-CASE-1})$$

$$\frac{x ::^{\mathcal{G}} \alpha \in \overline{\theta} \qquad \mathsf{btype}(\epsilon_s) \equiv T}{[\![\mathbf{case}\ \epsilon_s\ \mathbf{of}\ \overline{\theta \to \epsilon}]\!] \equiv \mathbf{case}\ to\,T^{\circ}\ \epsilon'_s\ \mathbf{of}\ \overline{\rho \to \epsilon'}} \; (\text{T-EXP-CASE-2})$$

$$\frac{[\![\epsilon]\!] \equiv \epsilon'}{[\![\mathbf{dynamic}\ \epsilon :: \omega]\!] \equiv \mathbf{dynamic}\ \epsilon' :: \omega} \; (\text{T-EXP-DYN})$$

Fig. 8. Translation of expressions

$$\boxed{[\![\theta_{\mathsf{FC+}}]\!] \equiv \rho_{\mathsf{FC}}}$$

$$\frac{}{[\![\varrho]\!] \equiv \varrho} \; (\text{T-PAT-BASE}) \qquad\qquad \frac{\overline{[\![\vartheta]\!]}_{C;\mathsf{index}} \equiv \overline{\rho}}{[\![C\ \overline{\vartheta}]\!] \equiv C^{\circ}\,\overline{\rho}} \; (\text{T-PAT-CON})$$

Fig. 9. Translation of patterns

to the translated scrutinee. The name of this function is determined by the meta-function $\mathsf{btype}(\epsilon_s)$ which determines the base name of the type of the scrutinee ϵ_s (e.g., $\mathsf{btype}(Const_T\ 1) \equiv Lam_T$). Furthermore, each pattern is translated so that the actual use of the annotation is translated. As we will see in a moment, the translation of patterns takes care of renaming the constructors, which is required since the scrutinee is converted to the extended type. Finally, Rule T-EXP-DYN defines the translation of a dynamic, simply translating its expression.

Patterns possibly provide access to the inserted type information, their translation is shown in Fig. 9. A base pattern is left untouched, as depicted in Rule T-PAT-BASE. In Rule T-PAT-CON, the constructor in a constructor pattern is renamed and its fields are all translated, parameterised by the name of the original constructor and a metavalue index that provides the index of each constructor field.

$$\boxed{[\![\vartheta_{\mathsf{FC^+}}]\!]_{C;n} \equiv \rho_{\mathsf{FC}}}$$

$$\frac{\neg\,\mathsf{annotated}(C, n)}{[\![\rho]\!]_{C;n} \equiv \rho}\ (\text{T-FPAT-PAT-1}) \qquad\qquad \frac{\mathsf{annotated}(C, n)}{[\![\rho]\!]_{C;n} \equiv (\rho, \_)}\ (\text{T-FPAT-PAT-2})$$

$$\frac{}{[\![x ::^{\mathcal{G}}\omega]\!]_{C;n} \equiv (x, \_ :: \omega)}\ (\text{T-FPAT-ANN})$$

Fig. 10. Translation of field patterns

In Fig. 10 we conclude the translation from $\mathsf{FC^+}$ to FC by defining the translation of field patterns, being the language extension itself. Since the conversion function that inserts type information is specific to a program, we have to verify if the current field pattern is annotated somewhere in the program. Rule T-FPAT-PAT-1 states that if a field is never annotated, then it does not need to be translated. Otherwise, the additional information is discarded, as defined by Rule T-FPAT-PAT-2. The core of the translation is captured by Rule T-FPAT-ANN. A GADT annotation is erased by translating it to a dynamic type annotation, yielding a pair that matches the original value and the type that is stored in the dynamic.

5   Related Work

The foundations of structured programming on GADTs [7] provide an elegant approach to defining algebras on GADTs. While such algebras provide an abstraction mechanism to define an update function, explicit type representations and equality types [3,5] are still required. In Section 3.2, we discussed the disadvantages of such an approach. In our work, type representations and type equality proofs are implicitly provided by dynamics, which significantly improves the elegancy of the function definitions.

Another approach to heterogeneous structures reflects the structure of a value directly in its type [8]. For example, the type of a heterogeneous list is basically a structure of nested tuples. Then, functions are defined on such structures using the type class mechanism, dispatching on the type structure. To enforce type-safe updates, yet another type class is defined to reflect type equality. Consequently, this approach results in rather verbose definitions since all action takes place on the level of type classes. Since the structure of the types are available, direct manipulation enables type-changing functions. Looking at the type of the update function in Section 3.3, our approach seems to forbid any type-changing updates. However, subterms can be replaced by arbitrary complex terms, thereby changing the underlying type structure.

6   Conclusion

We have presented the typical synergy between dynamics and GADTs to elegantly define functions that manipulate GADTs, requiring instantiation information on polymorphic types. Our approach comprises a new GADT annotation and improves upon boilerplate type representation administration in conventional approaches, since the functions are no longer cluttered with type equality witnesses and manual proofs. Also, by using dynamics, the need to maintain a closed enumeration of the used types is eliminated. Above all, our approach scales up to more complex structures and functions due to its simplicity. We have shown that the language extension is easily translated to a functional core that supports both dynamics and GADTs.

One of the major limitations in our approach is that the use of type codes limits the use of the GADT annotation to non-abstract types. It remains as future work to define type codes for such types, as well as investigating if dynamics can be implemented without type codes as class constraints. This would improve our approach considerably since it will not require us to decorate GADTs beforehand with type code constraints. Also, we plan to verify our hypothesis that storing GADTs in dynamics is no different from conventional ADTs.

Despite these limitations, the translation to dynamics provides novel opportunities, such as type dispatching and enforcing type equality invariants on GADTs. These opportunities require a more intricate translation than described in this paper, since this class of functions projects values instead of manipulating the values as such.

Acknowledgements

The authors would like to thank the anonymous reviewers for their helpful comments and suggestions. This work has been funded by the Technology Foundation STW through its project on "Demand Driven Workflow Systems" (07729).

References

1. Abadi, M., Cardelli, L., Pierce, B., Plotkin, G.: Dynamic typing in a statically typed language. ACM Transactions on Programming Languages and Systems 13(2), 237–268 (1991)
2. Abadi, M., Cardelli, L., Pierce, B., Rémy, D., Taylor, R.: Dynamic typing in polymorphic languages. Journal of Functional Programming 5(1), 81–110 (1994)
3. Baars, A., Swierstra, D.: Typing dynamic typing. In: Peyton Jones, S. (ed.) Proceedings of the 7th International Conference on Functional Programming, ICFP 2002, Pittsburgh, PA, USA, pp. 157–166. ACM, New York (2002)
4. Cartwright, R., Donahue, J.: The semantics of lazy (and industrious) evaluation. In: Proceedings of the 2nd Symposium on LISP and Functional Programming, LFP 1982, Pittsburgh, PA, USA, pp. 253–264. ACM, New York (1982)
5. Cheney, J., Hinze, R.: A lightweight implementation of generics and dynamics. In: Chakravarty, M. (ed.) Proceedings of the 6th Haskell Workshop, Haskell '02, Pittsburgh, PA, USA, pp. 90–104. ACM, New York (2002)

6. Cheney, J., Hinze, R.: First-class phantom types. Technical Report TR2003-1901, Cornell University (2003)
7. Johann, P., Ghani, N.: Foundations for structured programming with GADTs. In: Necula, G., Wadler, P. (eds.) Proceedings of the 35th Symposium on Principles of Programming Languages, POPL 2008, San Francisco, CA, USA, pp. 297–308. ACM, New York (2008)
8. Kiselyov, O., Lämmel, R., Schupke, K.: Strongly typed heterogeneous collections. In: Nilsson, H. (ed.) Proceedings of the 8th Haskell Workshop, Haskell 2004, Snowbird, UT, USA, pp. 96–107. ACM, New York (2004)
9. Läufer, K., Odersky, M.: Polymorphic type inference and abstract data types. ACM Transactions on Programming Languages and Systems 16(5), 1411–1430 (1994)
10. Peyton Jones, S.L., Vytiniotis, D., Weirich, S., Washburn, G.: Simple unification-based type inference for GADTs. In: Lawall, J. (ed.) Proceedings of the 11th International Conference on Functional Programming, ICFP 2006, Portland, Oregon, USA, pp. 50–61. ACM, New York (2006)
11. Pil, M.: Dynamic types and type dependent functions. In: Koopman, P., Clack, C. (eds.) IFL 1999. LNCS, vol. 1868, pp. 169–185. Springer, Heidelberg (2000)
12. Schrijvers, T., Peyton Jones, S., Sulzmann, M., Vytiniotis, D.: Complete and decidable type inference for GADTs. In: Hutton, G., Tolmach, A. (eds.) Proceedings of the 14th International Conference on Functional Programming, ICFP 2009, Edinburgh, Scotland, pp. 341–352. ACM, New York (2009)
13. Vervoort, M., Plasmeijer, R.: Lazy dynamic input/output in the lazy functional language Clean. In: Trinder, P., Michaelson, G.J., Peña, R. (eds.) IFL 2003. LNCS, vol. 3145, pp. 101–117. Springer, Heidelberg (2004)
14. Xi, H., Chen, C., Chen, G.: Guarded recursive datatype constructors. In: Morrisett, G., Aiken, A. (eds.) Proceedings of the 30th Symposium on Principles of Programming Languages, POPL 2003, New Orleans, LA, USA, pp. 224–235. ACM, New York (2003)

The Very Lazy λ-Calculus and the STEC Machine

Jan Rochel*

Universiteit Utrecht, The Netherlands
Department of Computer Science
rochel@cs.uu.nl

Abstract. Current implementations of non-strict functional languages rely on call-by-name reduction to implement the λ-calculus. An interesting alternative is *head occurrence reduction*, a reduction strategy specifically designed for the implementation of non-strict, purely functional languages. This work introduces the *very lazy λ-calculus*, which allows a systematic description of this approach. It is not based on regular β-reduction but a generalised rewriting rule called *γ-reduction* that requires fewer reductions to obtain useful results from a term. It therefore promises more efficient program execution than conventional execution models. To demonstrate the applicability of the approach, an adaptation of the Pointer Abstract Machine (PAM) is specified that implements the very lazy λ-calculus and constitutes a foundation for a new class of efficient functional language implementations.

1 Introduction

The λ-calculus is the foundation for the semantics of functional programming languages. Decades of research on the compilation and execution of non-strict functional languages has resulted in a number of different abstract machines such as in [Fairbairn 1987] [Peyton Jones 1987] [Burn 1988] [Peyton Jones 1992] [Holyer 1998] [Leijen 2005] [Krivine 2007]. They implement the λ-calculus by applying non-strict (or *lazy*) reduction strategies, such as *call-by-name* reduction.

A promising alternative is the Pointer Abstract Machine [Danos 2004], which is based on a reduction strategy that is lazier than *call-by-name* reduction in a certain sense. The Pointer Abstract Machine (PAM) is derived from a generalised version of the λ-calculus and then extended to support the range of features required for the implementation of a full-fledged functional programming language. The result is the STEC machine, a concrete, implementation-oriented manifestation of the PAM.

After giving a brief recapitulation of the λ-calculus and lazy evaluation we introduce the *very lazy λ-calculus*, which forms the basis of the approach. It

---

* Many thanks to Carsten Sinz, Patrik Jansson, and Daniel P. Friedman whose kind support was indispensable for the publication of this work, and also to Vincent van Oostrom and Laurent Regnier for their helpful comments.

M.T. Morazán and S.-B. Scholz (Eds.): IFL 2009, LNCS 6041, pp. 198–217, 2010.

relies on a generalisation of β-reduction that leads to a new reduction strategy, called *head occurrence reduction*. We systematically develop the STEC machine, an abstract machine for the very lazy λ-calculus. It has unique characteristics that promises high-performance program execution. In the last section we discuss opportunities for further research in order to create a new kind of efficient functional language implementation.

2 Basics

2.1 The λ-Calculus

The pure, untyped λ-calculus [Barendregt 1984] is a term rewriting system that operates on terms called λ-*expressions*. For a given set of variables V they are defined by:

$$E ::= \lambda V.E \qquad (abstraction)$$
$$| \quad (E\,E) \qquad (application) \qquad\qquad (\lambda\text{-}expression)$$
$$| \quad V \qquad\qquad (variable)$$

We henceforth assume that $x, y, z \in V$ and $e, e_1, e_2 \in E$ and also that for each $v \in V$, abstractions of the form $\lambda v.E$ occur at most once in a term. This simplification conforms to the handling of the name-capture problem in the context of programming language implementation where at compile-time variables are resolved to an unambiguous representation.

Three rewrite rules are defined for the evaluation of such expressions: α-, β-, and η-*conversion*. For the implementation of functional programming languages, α- and η-conversion are of minor importance and are not discussed here, leaving β-*conversion* as the central evaluation mechanism of the λ-calculus.

As long as the substitution variable x occurs at most once beneath the reduced λ-abstraction, β-conversion reduces the size of the expression, therefore it is more often than not called *β-reduction* and is defined by:

$$(\lambda x.e_1)\, e_2 \longrightarrow_{\beta_{\omega}} e_1[x := e_2] \qquad\qquad (\beta\text{-}reduction)$$

A term is called a *reducible* expression (*redex*) if it has the form $(\lambda x.e_1)\, e_2$. A term in which no redexes occur is in *normal form* (NF).

2.2 Lazy Evaluation

In the implementation of programming languages the evaluation of an expression yields the result of a computation. The analogy of a result in the λ-calculus is however not fully obvious. While a term in NF can be considered a result (as it can no longer be reduced) in functional languages it turns out to be overkill to reduce any given term to NF. Instead, other forms that may still contain redexes are targeted, like *weak normal form* (WNF), *head normal form* (HNF), or *weak head normal form* (WHNF), specified as follows, where $A\,B^* ::= A \mid (A\,B)\,B^*$.

$$
\begin{aligned}
E_{\mathrm{NF}} &::= \lambda V.E_{\mathrm{NF}} \mid V\, E_{\mathrm{NF}}^* && (\textit{normal form})\\
E_{\mathrm{WNF}} &::= \lambda V.E \mid V\, E_{\mathrm{WNF}}^* && (\textit{weak normal form})\\
E_{\mathrm{HNF}} &::= \lambda V.E_{\mathrm{HNF}} \mid V\, E^* && (\textit{head normal form})\\
E_{\mathrm{WHNF}} &::= \lambda V.E_{\mathrm{WHNF}} \mid V\, E^* && (\textit{weak head normal form})
\end{aligned}
$$

If such a form semantically relates to a meaningful concept of a result, by evaluating to this form instead of NF, redundant reductions can be avoided. To ensure no effort is squandered due to such redundant reductions, a practical implementation of the λ-calculus requires a well-defined scheme (*reduction strategy*) to select for each β-reduction step a non-redundant abstraction. Well-established examples are: *normal order* reduction to NF, *hybrid normal order* reduction to NF, *applicative order* reduction to NF, *hybrid applicative order* reduction to NF, *call-by-value* reduction to WNF, *head spine* reduction to HNF, *call-by-name* reduction to WHNF [Sestoft 2002].

Generally, non-strict languages imply the use of one of the last two strategies, which never reduces redexes that occur within an argument. Moreover call-by-name never reduces redexes beneath a λ-abstraction.

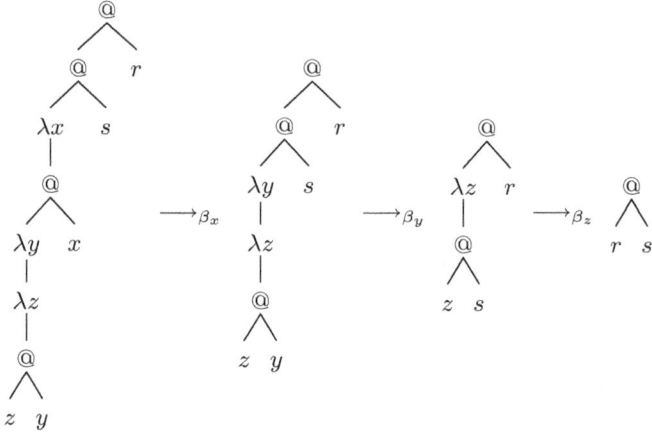

Fig. 1. Call-by-name reduction to WHNF

3   The Very Lazy λ-Calculus

To motivate the derivation of a new calculus it is helpful to relate to the properties specific to the targeted class of programming languages. Therefore we refer to language elements like constructors and case discrimination without explicitly introducing them (as a part of the calculus). Constructors can be thought of as free variables.

For the implemention of a non-strict language, it is in general desirable to increase the degree of laziness by using a normal form that requires fewer reductions. But then such a form is useless if it does not reflect the result of a computation in a sensible manner. Both WHNF and HNF fail to accomplish this with adequate precision in regard to the specifics of non-strict functional languages.

Operationally both forms of lazy evaluation (head spine reduction and call-by-name reduction) proceed by walking down the spine, reducing any occurring abstraction/application pairs on the way until the tip of the spine is reached. Further action then depends on the quality of this value.

Let us assume that an expression $e = ((\lambda x.y)\, e_1)\, e_2$ is the scrutinee in a case discrimination. The selection of the case alternative then solely depends on the constructor at the head position of its normal form $e_{NF} = y\, e_2$. However if y is a constructor, e already is in a form that at the tip of its spine without the need for any reductions reveals the value required to select the appropriate case alternative. Then why should all satisfied abstractions above y be reduced before effecting the case discrimination? After all such reductions may never affect a free variable at the tip of the spine.

Thus, we attempt to specify a calculus with a normal form that accurately captures this formulation of non-strict semantics, and a reduction strategy that efficiently reduces to this normal form. Both concepts relate to the variable at the tip of the spine, which we refer to as the *head occurrence* (hoc) [Danos 2004] of an expression:

$$
\begin{aligned}
hoc(\lambda x.e) &= hoc(e) \\
hoc(e_1\, e_2) &= hoc(e_1) \qquad\qquad\qquad (\textit{head occurrence}) \\
hoc(x) &= x
\end{aligned}
$$

3.1 The Quasi Head Normal Form

The normal form of the very lazy λ-calculus is called *quasi head normal form* (QHNF) [Danos 2004]. We give a definition that is more straightforward than the original one by relating to the hoc of the NF:

$$
E_{\text{QHNF}} := \{e \in E \mid hoc(e) = hoc(e_{NF})\} \qquad (\textit{quasi head normal form})
$$

An optimal reduction strategy that evaluates to QHNF in a minimum number of steps must not perform unneeded reductions. The most direct approach for such a strategy is to repeatedly substitute the variable l at the tip of the spine (hoc) by reducing the corresponding abstraction λt until QHNF is obtained. This is generally not possible with β-reduction, however. The term $e = ((\lambda x.(\lambda y.y))\, e_1)\, e_2$ for instance is not in QHNF, yet the λ-calculus does not allow substituting for y, as λy occurs directly beneath another abstraction λx and therefore cannot be β-reduced before λx.

Considering this restriction of the β-reduction as an unnecessary shortcoming of the λ-calculus, we now attempt to generalise β-reduction in order to make it more powerful.

3.2 The γ-Reduction

The very lazy λ-calculus evaluates λ-expressions by applying the *γ-reduction* rule, which allows reductions of abstraction/application pairs along the spine that are not adjacent to each other. We write $e_1 \longrightarrow_{\gamma_x} e_2$ to denote a γ-reduction $e_1 \longrightarrow_\gamma e_2$ that uses x as a substitution variable:

$$\frac{p_0(e_1) = x}{e_1\, e_2 \longrightarrow_{\gamma_x} e_1[\lambda x.e := e[x := e_2]]} \qquad (\gamma\text{-reduction})$$

Thereby p_0 is a function that implements a simple parentheses-matching algorithm treating applications as left and abstractions as right parentheses. The idea is to identify abstraction/application pairs along the spine that would be β-reduced in the course of head spine reduction to HNF. Subsequently, any of these pairs can be reduced individually even if the abstraction node is not directly adjacent to the application node.

$$
\begin{aligned}
&p_0(\lambda x.e) = x \\
&p_i(\lambda x.e) = p_{i-1}(e) \quad (i > 0) \qquad (abstraction/application\ matching) \\
&p_i(e_1\, e_2) = p_{i+1}(e_1)
\end{aligned}
$$

In the definition of γ-reduction above, $p_0(e_1)$ walks down the spine to locate the abstraction that matches the argument e_2. This permits γ-reduction to skip over abstraction and application nodes that occur in-between λx and e_2 that would have been reduced by conventional non-strict reduction strategies. For an example see *Fig. 4*.

A proof of the consistency of γ-reduction with the semantics of the λ-calculus is not given here, but much as in [Kamareddine 2001] β-equivalence is easily deduced by decomposing γ-reduction into a β-reduction embedded in a sequence of β-equivalent rearrangements of the spine. Moreover γ-reduction is a generalisation of β-reduction:

$$
\begin{aligned}
e_1 = \lambda x.e \implies\ &p_0(e_1) = p_0(\lambda x.e) = x \\
\implies\ e_1\, e_2 \longrightarrow_{\gamma_x}\ &e_1[\lambda x.e := e[x := e_2]] = e[x := e_2]
\end{aligned}
$$

We notice that indeed the β-irreducible expression e from above is γ-reducible:

$$((\lambda x.(\lambda y.y))\, e_1)\, e_2 \longrightarrow_{\gamma_y} (\lambda x.e_2)\, e_1$$

3.3   Quasi Head Normal Form, Revisited

Based on γ-reduction, QHNF can alternatively be redefined as

$$E_{\mathrm{QHNF}} ::= \lambda V.E_{\mathrm{QHNF}} \mid E_{\mathrm{QHNF}}\, E^* \mid i \qquad (quasi\ head\ normal\ form)$$

where i is a variable not substitutable by a γ-reduction. This is the case if either the hoc i is free (e.g. a constructor), or if the corresponding abstraction λi is *unsatisfied* (i.e. there is no matching application).

To see that both definitions of QHNF match, we show that for some term e the $hoc(e)$ is γ-irreducible if and only if $hoc(e) = hoc(e_{NF})$. This follows from the robustness of the parentheses-matching algorithm in respect to γ-reductions,

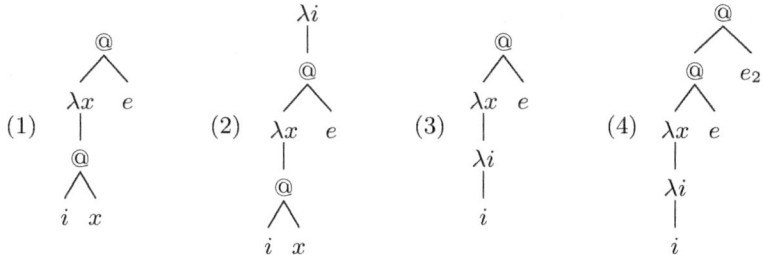

Fig. 2. Terms (1-3) are in QHNF, (4) is not as i is γ-reducible

which only ever reduce *matching* abstraction/application pairs from the spine. Because the γ-irreducible $hoc(e)$ cannot be substituted, it follows by induction that $hoc(e)$ remains at the tip of the spine during the entire γ-reduction to normal form and therefore $hoc(e) = hoc(e_{NF})$.

Conversely if $hoc(e) = hoc(e_{NF})$, γ-reduction may never substitute $hoc(e)$ since otherwise it would not be β-equivalent.

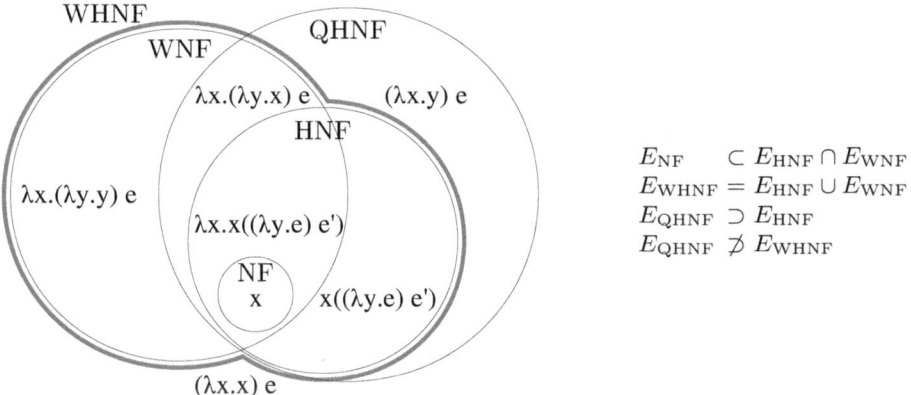

$$E_{\mathrm{NF}} \quad \subset E_{\mathrm{HNF}} \cap E_{\mathrm{WNF}}$$
$$E_{\mathrm{WHNF}} = E_{\mathrm{HNF}} \cup E_{\mathrm{WNF}}$$
$$E_{\mathrm{QHNF}} \supset E_{\mathrm{HNF}}$$
$$E_{\mathrm{QHNF}} \not\supset E_{\mathrm{WHNF}}$$

Fig. 3. Set relations between various normal forms

3.4   Head Occurrence Reduction

Based on this definition we can define an optimal reduction strategy to QHNF. γ-reductions that substitute the hoc are clearly sufficient and are always needed. We call the reduction strategy that in each step substitutes the hoc of the term using a γ-reduction *head occurrence reduction*:

$$\frac{e \longrightarrow_{\gamma_t} e' \quad t = hoc(e)}{e \longrightarrow e'} \qquad v \longrightarrow v \qquad \frac{e \longrightarrow e'}{\lambda x.e \longrightarrow \lambda x.e'} \qquad \frac{e_1 \longrightarrow e_1'}{e_1\, e_2 \longrightarrow e_1'\, e_2}$$

The evaluation of a term according to head occurrence reduction in each step needs to identify three nodes affected by the reduction of the graph: $t = hoc(e)$

at the tip of the spine, the corresponding abstraction node λt, which is located further up the spine, and the matching application node with the right-hand side e_2 even further up the spine.

Head occurrence reduction is lazier than conventional lazy reduction strategies in the sense that it reduces to a normal form that expresses the semantics of non-strict functional languages more accurately than WHNF. Thus reductions are avoided that deal with arguments of the result prematurely.

3.5   Examples

To compare our reduction strategy to conventional lazy evaluation, consider the term $((\lambda x.(\lambda y.\lambda z.z\,y)\,x)\,s)\,r$. Three β-reductions are required for call-by-need reduction to WHNF (*Fig. 1*). For the same term, head occurrence reduction requires only one γ-reduction to reduce to QHNF (*Fig. 4*). Furthermore β-reduction can not produce the depicted transition. Pathological cases can be constructed, such as $(\lambda x_1 \ldots \lambda x_n.\lambda y.y)\,e_1 \ldots e_n$ or $(\lambda y(\lambda x_1 \ldots \lambda x_n.y)\,e_1 \ldots e_n)\,e$ that require n additional reductions to obtain WHNF.

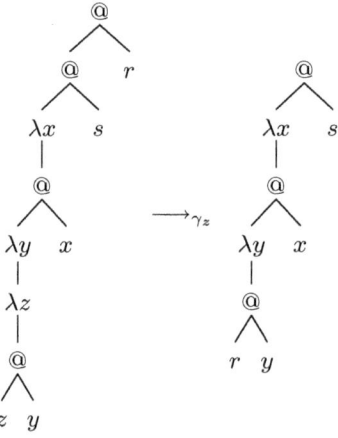

Fig. 4. Head occurrence reduction to QHNF

4   The STEC-Machine

We now derive an abstract machine that implements the very lazy λ-calculus exploiting its particular properties for improved efficiency. It is an adaptation of the PAM enriched by language elements like case discrimination and primitive functions to support practical functional languages.

A dominant issue in the design of such an abstract machine is that terms representing nontrivial programs are graphs with directed cycles rather than trees. This is due to functions that are used at different sites in the program definition, and may involve (mutual) recursion. So we cannot statically unfold the graph, since the resulting tree would be of infinite size. Therefore the graph needs to be expanded incrementally during evaluation. There are various solutions to this, from simple approaches like copying parts of the graph as needed, to more sophisticated techniques like super-combinator compilation [Hughes 1982].

Here however, we explore a new direction where the abstract machine's main run-time data structures remain unmodified once instantiated. While this seems contrary to the notion of graph rewriting, the approach combines well with the very lazy λ-calculus. Let us first take a glance at the untyped language interpreted by the abstract machine.

4.1 Abstract Machine Language, Pure Version

The term to be evaluated is given as a program definition comprising a set of function definitions of the form:

$$f = \lambda x_1 \ldots x_m.a_0 \ldots a_n \qquad m, n \geq 0$$

The *arity* of a function f denotes the number of parameters, here $arity(f) = m$. On its right-hand side it specifies a non-empty list of arguments $args(f) = a_0 \ldots a_n$ that can be individually addressed by index: $args_i(f) = a_i$. Note that only $a_1 \ldots a_n$ represent application nodes. Consequently a_0 is not included in the argument count $|args(f)| = n$.

The language interpreted by the STEC-machine is a simple, untyped, functional language with a flat structure, i.e. all arguments of a function f are atomic, such that each of f's arguments $args(f)$ is a variable, either addressing a function or a parameter. Non-atomic expressions in the source language occur through the placement of parentheses or other language constructs that lead to the nesting of expressions. The atomicity property is easily enforced at compile-time by factoring each non-atomic argument into a separate function definition. This atomicity of the function arguments induces a certain kind of linearity that characterises the evaluation procedure to a large extent.

It is understood that in a compiled setting, numeric rather than symbolic values are used to reference functions and parameters. Functions are referenced by the address of the memory location of their definition. It is straightforward to reference parameters by their index as they occur in the function's parameter list. However, the scope of a function f extends beyond its own parameter list. On the right-hand side of f not only f's own parameters may be referenced but also parameter variables that occur free in f. Therefore to unambiguously address a specific parameter not only its index but also the associated function must be specified.[1] We use P_i^f to denote f's ith parameter. This may be thought of as a form of reversed de-Bruijn index [De Bruijn 1972] with a pivot.

Another technique employed by today's functional language implementations to cope with free variables is λ-*lifting*, however this transformation is just the opposite of what we want to accomplish. Rather its reverse transformation called λ-*dropping* [Danvy 2000] might integrate well with our execution model.

---

[1] Instead of naming f explicitly, also the *nesting distance* between f and the referencing argument could be used, which is however less descriptive.

$$program\text{-}definition ::= function\text{-}definition^+$$
$$function\text{-}definition ::= function\text{-}id_{arity}\ argument^+$$
$$arity\qquad\qquad ::= \mathbb{N}^0$$
$$argument\qquad\quad ::= function\text{-}id\ |\ \mathbf{P}_{\mathbb{N}+}^{function\text{-}id}$$

Fig. 5. Abstract syntax of the STEC machine language

In the absence of named parameters, we do not need to maintain parameter lists. Instead we merely need to specify the arity of each function. We thus obtain a specification of the abstract machine language that represents as a function definition a term of the pure λ-calculus as a spine-sequence of abstraction nodes followed by application nodes (*Fig. 5*). Each function definition can be addressed by a unique function ID, which can be regarded as a function name. However, in compiled form is conveniently the memory address of the function definition.

What follows is a description of the dynamic behaviour of the STEC-machine and its data structures created at run-time. During the evaluation, the program definition is accessed only through the *arity-* and the *args-*functions. It is purely static data, i.e. it is generated at compile-time and no rewriting takes place on the original function definitions.

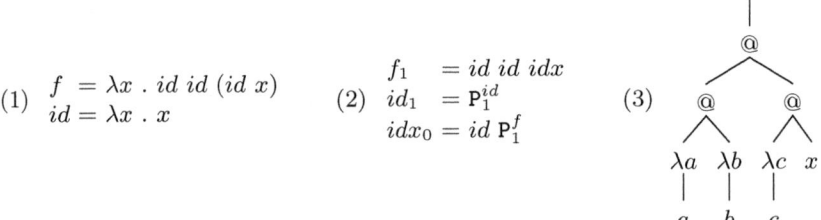

$$(1)\quad \begin{aligned} f &= \lambda x\ .\ id\ id\ (id\ x)\\ id &= \lambda x\ .\ x \end{aligned} \qquad (2)\quad \begin{aligned} f_1 &= id\ id\ idx\\ id_1 &= \mathbf{P}_1^{id}\\ idx_0 &= id\ \mathbf{P}_1^{f} \end{aligned} \qquad (3)$$

Fig. 6. Term given as (1) a λ-expression, (2) STEC machine code, (3) a fully-expanded graph

4.2   Graph Expansion

In each step of the evaluation, head occurrence reduction performs γ-reductions that substitute the variable at the tip of the spine (hoc). Therefore not only the appropriate abstraction/application pair must be located, also the hoc is usually not immediately at hand due to the fragmentation of the graph into function definitions. Thus walking down the spine to reach its tip often requires a series of graph expansions.

The root of the term to be evaluated is specified by a designated function f, whose definition directly represents the topmost fragment of the term.[2] If the hoc is not immediately visible, that is if the leftmost argument $args_0(f)$ references

---

[2] Generally this function is named `main` or similarly.

a function g rather than a parameter, then the graph has to be unfolded by instantiating g in order to locate the hoc of the spine within g's definition.

While this at first might seem like a description of regular non-strict function calls, those in the course of the instantiation also immediately pass the arguments supplied by its caller to the callee. There are two possibilities that perform such function calls, the *push/enter* and the *eval/apply* method [Marlow 2006]. Ultimately this is where β-reductions take place in conventional functional language implementations.

The very lazy λ-calculus however allows the β-reduction to be omitted, thus no arguments are passed to g. Therefore, according to head occurrence reduction, γ-reductions cannot take place before the tip of the spine is revealed. Until then the abstract machine simply proceeds to build the graph while walking down the spine.

As the graph is only expanded along its spine, it has a linear structure in the form of a series of functions that have been stuck together, which is easily represented using a stack. Instead of explicitly maintaining abstraction and application nodes (replicated from the function definitions), for efficiency, we use entire functions as the unit of the run-time data structure.

4.3   The Evaluation Stack

These functions are represented by function *instances*, which hold a pointer to the corresponding function definition and act as a copy of the function. Thus the primary run-time data structure of the STEC-machine is a stack of instances, the *evaluation stack*. It grows from right to left and unlike a usual stack, read accesses *within* the evaluation stack are permitted. Instances are addressed according to their stack position. The notation for an evaluation stack containing n instances:

$$E ::= I_n\ I_{n-1}\ \ldots\ I_1 \qquad\qquad (evaluation\ stack)$$

Besides the evaluation stack, the state of the abstract machine comprises a *status register* S that specifies the action that is to be taken next, and a *target register* T that points to the *stack address* targeted by the action:

$$STE ::= (S, T, E) \qquad\qquad (configuration)$$

Summarising, the evaluation stack encodes the current term as a sequence of function instances, each of them representing a segment of the term's spine. The graph is expanded along its spine as long as the leftmost instance t references another function in its 0th argument, namely if $args_0(f) - g$, assuming t is an instance of f. We say that an *argument request* A_0 is issued in order to examine the 0th argument of f. A graph expansion takes place by pushing another instance (in this case of g) on the stack.

4.4   Locating an Abstraction

At some point the tip of the spine (hoc) is reached, which is indicated by the 0th argument of the leftmost instance being a parameter P_i^f rather than

a function reference. In order to effect a γ-reduction, the corresponding abstrac-
tion/application pair must be located. The abstraction will occur somewhere
further up the spine within an instance of f. However, there might be multiple
f-instances on the evaluation stack, but we want only the one that corresponds
to the appropriate abstraction.

To determine the correct scope of an instance t it suffices to identify the
instance s that created t. We call s the *parent* of t. This corresponds to the
edge from an argument node of s to its right-hand side in the term graph. This
relationship is expressed by *parent edges* in the evaluation stack that connect each
function instance with another instance further right in the stack. So besides
the reference to the function definition it represents, a function instance also
maintains a pointer to its parent. How parent pointers are established is covered
later. An instance of a function f with a parent edge to the instance at stack
address a is denoted by f^a.

$$I ::= F^A \qquad\qquad\qquad \text{(function instance)}$$

If the argument P_i^f occurs in a function g, then for each instance of g, the
corresponding instance of f is connected by a chain of one or more parent edges.[3]
When an argument of this form is encountered, the status register is set to
$S = \mathsf{P}_i^f$, indicating a *parameter request*. Thereby the search for the abstraction
is conducted by following parent edges, which we call *backtracing*. Backtracing
is completed once the dynamic pivot (an instance of f) is located.[4] The sought-
after abstraction is the ith parameter of the located function instance:

$$
\begin{aligned}
&\text{Parameter-Request: } (\mathsf{P}_i^f, a, ...g_a^p...) \\
&\to (\mathsf{P}_i^f, p, ...g_a^p...) && f \neq g && \text{(Backtrace)} \\
&\to (\mathsf{A}_i, a - 1, ...g_a^p...) && f = g && \text{(Request argument)}
\end{aligned}
$$

4.5 Locating the Application

The application node that matches this abstraction is further up the spine, and
in the majority of cases (i.e. when the function application is perfectly saturated)
within the function instance just to the right of f, called f's *predecessor*.[5] This
is where the search for the application node begins ($T = a - 1$). Thereby $i - 1$
abstractions (parameters of f) have already been skipped, therefore the next
$i - 1$ abstraction nodes that occur further up the spine cannot belong to the
abstraction that is to be γ-reduced.

To locate the corresponding application node, the spine has to be walked
upwards applying the parentheses-matching algorithm. $S = \mathsf{A}_i$ indicates that

---

[3] This corresponds to static links and static chains in the call stack of the run-time
system of imperative programming languages.

[4] Due to the scoping rules of functional languages it is always the first occurrence of
an f-instance that binds the requested parameter.

[5] Accordingly in conventional execution models parameters of a perfectly saturated
function call passed directly by the caller.

$i - 1$ unmatched abstraction nodes have been passed while walking upwards. Thus the next $i-1$ application nodes must be skipped. Keeping in mind that each function f represents a sequence of $arity(f)$ abstractions followed by $|args(f)|$ applications, the algorithm is implemented as follows by the abstract machine:

$$Argument\text{-}Request: (\mathtt{A}_i, a, ...f_a^- ...)$$
$$\to (\mathtt{A}_{i-|args(f)|+arity(f)}, a - 1, ...f_a^- ...) \quad |args(f)| < i \quad (Skip)$$
$$\to (args_i(f), a, ...f_a^- ...) \quad\quad\quad\quad\quad |args(f)| \geq i \quad (Serve)$$

Once the matching application node is found its value $args_i(f)$ is to substitute the tip of the spine in the subsequent γ-reduction. We say it is *served* (put into the S for examination).

4.6   Very Lazy Evaluation

Once the hoc is identified and the corresponding abstraction/application pair is located, according to the definition of γ-reduction the term is to be rewritten in multiple positions: First, each occurrence of the substitution variable is replaced by the argument's right-hand side, then the abstraction and application nodes are discarded. However, not one of these operations are performed by the abstract machine, which at first may be surprising. Then again it is natural that modifications of individual nodes cannot easily be mapped to a representation of the term where function instances capture only its macro-structure and do not reproduce the internal structure of the function definitions.

Consequently the abstract machine retains the abstraction/application pair, which is semantically correct in terms of β-equivalency. This simplifies γ-reduction considerably, as the de-Bruijn indexes remain valid so no α-conversion is necessary. Here we do not discuss sharing, so we do not address multiple occurrences of substitution variables. Thus nothing but the hoc itself must be substituted, which coincides with what is defined as *head linear reduction* [Danos 2004].

But also the substitution of the hoc can be omitted, if it does not interfere with subsequent evaluation. Indeed the 0th argument of an instance of a function f is examined only once, directly after it is pushed on the stack. Also it is not counted in $|args(f)|$ so it has no impact on the parentheses-matching algorithm. Therefore the abstract machine leaves the hoc in place leaving all function instances unmodified.

There are two cases for the value of the application node to distinguish for further action. An argument may reference either a function or a parameter. Let us first assume the former, thus $S = f$. Then f is instantiated and pushed on the evaluation stack. Thereby the function instance containing the scrutinised application node (the current value of the T-register) is registered as the parent of the new function instance. Then S is set to $\mathtt{A}_0$ and T to the address of the newly created function instance, such that again the 0th argument of the leftmost function instance is examined for the next γ-reduction step.

$$Instantiate: (f, a, ...)$$
$$\to (\mathtt{A}_0, n, f_n^a ...) \quad\quad (Push\ Instance)$$

If the argument is a parameter $(S = \mathbf{P}_i^f)$ according to γ-reduction, it would substitute the hoc by this value. But once again, no such substitution is performed by the abstract machine, which saves an α-conversion. Instead, without any intermediate rewriting the argument is treated directly as if it was the hoc, according to the inference rules for parameter handling specified above.

4.7   Wrapping It Up

Based on the presented mechanisms a specification of the abstract machine can be given that implements the very lazy λ-calculus. The operational semantics (*Fig. 8*) is specified in a rather unconventional but quite intuitive manner. Note that variables with no relevance to a specific rule (*don't-cares*) are denoted as '–', similarly for sequences, denoted as '...'.

$$
\begin{array}{lll}
STE & ::= (S, T, E) & \textit{(configuration)} \\
S & ::= F \mid \mathbf{P}_{\mathbb{N}}^F \mid \mathbf{A}_{\mathbb{N}} & \textit{(status register)} \\
T & ::= A & \textit{(target register)} \\
E & ::= I_n\, I_{n-1}\, ...\, I_1 & \textit{(evaluation stack)} \\
A & ::= \mathbb{N} & \textit{(stack address)} \\
I & ::= F^A & \textit{(function instance)} \\
F & ::= \mathbb{N} & \textit{(function address)}
\end{array}
$$

Fig. 7. Configuration grammar

Summarising, some interesting characteristics of the abstract machine can be observed:

- Arguments are fetched at the latest moment possible in contrast to conventional execution models where arguments are passed by the caller as soon as they are available rather than as soon as they are required, which is a form of strictness in the argument handling. Therefore it is in fact justified to consider our model lazier.
- On the evaluation stack a function instance is always directly preceded by its caller. This relation is modeled without the help of pointers. That structure is exploited by the abstract machine when fetching arguments.
- There is no need to maintain a constantly updated environment. The evaluation stack can be thought of as an incremental definition of the environment.
- Interestingly, the sequence of instances on the evaluation stack directly encodes the path from the root of the fully expanded, unreduced term to the tip of its spine.
- The term is in QHNF either if the hoc is a free variable (such as a constructor), or if the term is functional such that for a selected abstraction no matching application is found. The latter case manifests itself in an argument request attempting to cross the right boundary of the evaluation stack.

– Very lazy evaluation is linear in many aspects such as the manner in which functions are defined, the linearity of the reduction strategy, and the run-time data structure (the evaluation stack). This is possibile due to the technique of using parent pointers and because of refraining from any rewriting on the spine.

Initial State: $(\mathtt{main}, \bot, \epsilon)$

Instantiate: $(f, a, ...)$
$\rightarrow (\mathbf{A}_0, n, f_n^a ...)$ $\hspace{6cm}$ *(Push Instance)*

Argument-Request: $(\mathbf{A}_i, a, ... f_a^- ...)$
$\rightarrow (\mathbf{A}_{i-|args(f)|+arity(f)}, a-1, ... f_a^- ...)$ $\quad |args(f)| < i$ $\hspace{2cm}$ *(Skip)*
$\rightarrow (args_i(f), a, ... f_a^- ...)$ $\hspace{1.8cm} |args(f)| \geq i$ $\hspace{2.6cm}$ *(Serve)*

Parameter-Request: $(\mathbf{P}_i^f, a, ... g_a^p ...)$
$\rightarrow (\mathbf{P}_i^f, p, ... g_a^p ...)$ $\hspace{2.5cm} f \neq g$ $\hspace{2.7cm}$ *(Backtrace)*
$\rightarrow (\mathbf{A}_i, a-1, ... g_a^p ...)$ $\hspace{2cm} f = g$ $\hspace{1.8cm}$ *(Request argument)*

Fig. 8. Operational semantics

4.8   Example Evaluated

To depict the evaluation as performed by the STEC machine we regard the execution of the example program from *Fig. 6*. It was chosen to exemplify the operational semantics of the STEC machine rather than to reveal the advantages of head occurrence reduction.

To understand the abstract machine evaluation given below, it is helpful to identify each instance on the evaluation stack with the corresponding sequence of spine nodes in *Fig. 9*. Therefore the function definitions from *Fig. 6* need to be consulted. First we expand the term along the spine beginning from the root f to locate its hoc.

Initial State: $\hspace{2.5cm} (f, \bot, \epsilon)$
Push Instance: $\rightarrow \hspace{1.5cm} (\mathbf{A}_0, 1, f_1^\bot)$
Serve: $\hspace{1.5cm} \rightarrow \hspace{1.5cm} (id, 1, f_1^\bot)$
Push Instance: $\rightarrow (\mathbf{A}_0, 2, id_2^1 \, f_1^\bot)$

The hoc is a (in *Fig. 9*). The corresponding argument belongs to id's caller f.

Serve: $\hspace{1.5cm} \rightarrow \hspace{1.2cm} (\mathbf{P}_1^{id}, 2, id_2^1 \, f_1^\bot)$
Request argument: $\rightarrow \hspace{1.2cm} (\mathbf{A}_1, 1, id_2^1 \, f_1^\bot)$ $\hspace{0.3cm}\Big\} \, a$
Serve: $\hspace{1.5cm} \rightarrow \hspace{1.2cm} (id, 1, id_2^1 \, f_1^\bot)$
Push Instance: $\hspace{0.8cm} \rightarrow (\mathbf{A}_0, 3, id_3^1 \, id_2^1 \, f_1^\bot)$

For the next argument request in order to locate the appropriate application node, a function instance must to be skipped. In *Fig. 9* this corresponds to the

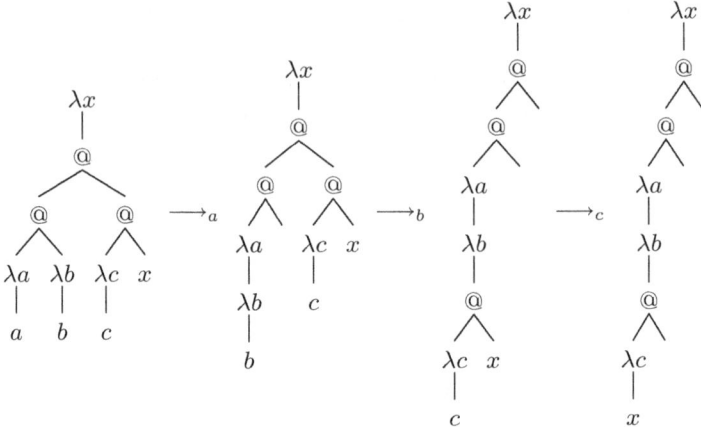

Fig. 9. Head linear reduction of the program graph of *Fig. 6*

abstraction node λa. The argument index is incremented by one such that the matching application node (the one above λa) is also skipped:

$$
\left.
\begin{array}{lcl}
\text{Serve:} & \to & (\mathsf{P}_1^{id}, 3, id_3^1\ id_2^1\ f_1^\perp) \\
\text{Request argument:} & \to & (\mathsf{A}_1, 2, id_3^1\ id_2^1\ f_1^\perp) \\
\text{Skip:} & \to & (\mathsf{A}_2, 1, id_3^1\ id_2^1\ f_1^\perp) \\
\text{Serve:} & \to & (idx, 1, id_3^1\ id_2^1\ f_1^\perp) \\
\text{Push Instance:} & \to & (\mathsf{A}_0, 4, idx_4^1\ id_3^1\ id_2^1\ f_1^\perp)
\end{array}
\right\} b
$$

The call of a known function id by idx is realised a spine expansion:

$$
\begin{array}{lcl}
\text{Serve:} & \to & (id, 4, idx_4^1\ id_3^1\ id_2^1\ f_1^\perp) \\
\text{Push Instance:} & \to & (\mathsf{A}_0, 5, id_5^4\ idx_4^1\ id_3^1\ id_2^1\ f_1^\perp)
\end{array}
$$

Here it can be seen that some γ-reductions may not even require an update of the evaluation stack.

$$
\left.
\begin{array}{lcl}
\text{Serve:} & \to & (\mathsf{P}_1^{id}, 5, id_5^4\ idx_4^1\ id_3^1\ id_2^1\ f_1^\perp) \\
\text{Request argument:} & \to & (\mathsf{A}_1, 4, id_5^4\ idx_4^1\ id_3^1\ id_2^1\ f_1^\perp)
\end{array}
\right\} c
$$

The request by idx for a parameter that was bound in a different function f requires a backtracing step to locate the abstraction that binds the current hoc.

$$
\left.
\begin{array}{lcl}
\text{Serve:} & \to & (\mathsf{P}_1^f, 4, id_5^4\ idx_4^1\ id_3^1\ id_2^1\ f_1^\perp) \\
\text{Backtrace:} & \to & (\mathsf{P}_1^f, 1, id_5^4\ idx_4^1\ id_3^1\ id_2^1\ f_1^\perp) \\
\text{Request argument:} & \to & (\mathsf{A}_1, \perp, id_5^4\ idx_4^1\ id_3^1\ id_2^1\ f_1^\perp)
\end{array}
\right\} x
$$

The evaluation terminates because a request attempts to cross the stack boundary. That means that no abstraction/application pair could be located within the spine, thus the term is in QHNF.

4.9   Case-Discrimination and Primitives

To implement functional programming languages, two more issues need attention: case discrimination and primitives operators. They cannot be modeled by
means of the pure λ-calculus, which has to be enriched for that purpose. Here,
this semantic extension is only realised on the abstract machine level, not as yet
another λ-calculus variant.

$$
\begin{aligned}
\textit{program-definition} &::= \textit{function-definition}^+ \\
\textit{function-definition} &::= \textit{function-id}_{arity}\ \textit{argument}^+\ \textit{alternative}^* \\
\textit{arity} &::= \mathbb{N}^0 \\
\textit{argument} &::= \textit{function-id}\ |\ \mathbf{P}^{function\text{-}id}_{\mathbb{N}+}\ |\ \mathbf{O}_{\mathbb{N}}\ |\ \textit{constant} \\
\textit{alternative} &::= \textit{integer function-id}\ |\ \mathbf{default}\ \textit{function-id} \\
\textit{constant} &::= \textit{integer}\ |\ \textit{float}\ |\ ...
\end{aligned}
$$

Fig. 10. Enriched abstract syntax of the STEC machine language

In the enriched abstract machine language, a case discrimination is specified
by attaching a non-empty, integer-indexed list of alternatives $alts(f)$ to a function definition f, its right-hand side $args(f)$ being the scrutinee. Constructors
are mapped to integers at compile-time unambiguously within the constructor set
of one data type. Constructor parameters can be accessed as the function parameters of the alternatives' right hand-side. No further measures are necessary
to model constructors, as they are adequately handled by the argument request
mechanism. A primitive operator ($\mathbf{O}_o$) addresses a platform-specific functionality
that is identified by a unique numeric identifier o.

The operational semantics needs to account for the strictness that these
language constructs imply. The scrutinee of a case discrimination reveals its constructor only in QHNF. Thus, to select the correct case alternative, a *continuation-*
mechanism is required to return to the case discrimination once the scrutinee is
evaluated. Likewise, primitive operators are generally strict in all of their arguments, so after the evaluation of each argument, the evaluation must return to its
call site, either to evaluate the next argument, or if it is saturated to apply the
operator.

Strict evaluation may nest, for instance, if the scrutinee of a case discrimination involves a further case discrimination. Therefore continuations are also
maintained in a stack, the *continuation stack* (C), thus we extend the abstract
machine configuration to:

$$
STEC ::= (S, T, E, C) \qquad\qquad (\textit{configuration})
$$

The continuation stack holds two types of tokens: case continuation tokens and
operator tokens, both of which specify the stack address that the continuation
returns to. Additionally an operator token needs to define the operator it represents as well as a list of previously evaluated operands.

$$C ::= K^* \qquad \text{(continuation stack)}$$
$$K ::= \mathsf{c}^A \mid \mathsf{0}_O^A[V^*] \qquad \text{(continuation)}$$
$$O ::= \mathbb{N} \qquad \text{(operator)}$$
$$V ::= integer \mid float \mid \ldots \qquad \text{(constant value)}$$

Continuations are pushed on the continuation stack when an operator or a function that defines a case discrimination is served. In the latter case the evaluation (besides pushing the continuation) proceeds as before by evaluating its right-hand side (the scrutinee). If an operator is served, its first operand is requested.

$$\text{Instantiate: } (f, a, \ldots)$$
$$\to (\mathsf{A}_0, n, f_n^a \cdots, \ldots) \qquad |alts(f)| = 0 \quad \textit{(Push Instance)}$$
$$\to (\mathsf{A}_0, n, f_n^a \cdots, \mathsf{c}^n \ldots) \qquad |alts(f)| > 0 \qquad \textit{(Scrutinise)}$$

$$\text{Operator: } (\mathsf{0}_{op}, -, t_n \cdots, \ldots)$$
$$\to (\mathsf{A}_1, n, t_n \cdots, \mathsf{0}_{op}^n[] \ldots) \qquad\qquad \textit{(First Operand)}$$

As soon as the subsequent computation yields a constant value c, indicated by $S = c$, the continuation on the top of the stack is examined. For a case continuation, the correct alternative is selected and served. For operator continuations, before applying the operator it must first be checked whether more arguments are required. Only when sufficient operands have been acquired, the operator is applied and the result of the primitive operation is propagated. This semantics is expressed in the last two groups of *Fig. 12*.

$$STEC ::= (S, T, E, C) \qquad \text{(configuration)}$$
$$S \qquad ::= F \mid \mathsf{P}_\mathbb{N}^F \mid \mathsf{A}_\mathbb{N} \mid \mathsf{0}_O \mid V \qquad \text{(status register)}$$
$$T \qquad ::= A \qquad \text{(target register)}$$
$$A \qquad ::= \mathbb{N} \qquad \text{(stack address)}$$
$$E \qquad ::= I_n\ I_{n-1}\ \ldots\ I_1 \qquad \text{(evaluation stack)}$$
$$C \qquad ::= K^* \qquad \text{(continuation stack)}$$
$$I \qquad ::= F^A \qquad \text{(function instance)}$$
$$F \qquad ::= \mathbb{N} \qquad \text{(function address)}$$
$$K \qquad ::= \mathsf{c}^A \mid \mathsf{0}_O^A[V^*] \qquad \text{(continuation)}$$
$$O \qquad ::= \mathbb{N} \qquad \text{(operator)}$$
$$V \qquad ::= integer \mid float \mid \ldots \qquad \text{(constant value)}$$

Fig. 11. Enriched configuration grammar

In this work we derived from the very lazy λ-calculus the STEC-machine, which is a concretisation of the PAM enriched by strict semantics to support case discriminations and operators. In [Danos 2004] different concepts of head linear reduction were mixed up in one definition. Here we clearly distinct between generalising β-reduction, defining a reduction strategy, and giving a concrete implementation that avoids rewriting. Furthermore we distinguish between program compilation and execution.

Initial State: $(\mathtt{main}, \bot, \epsilon, \epsilon)$

Instantiate: $(f, a, ..., ...)$
$\rightarrow (\mathtt{A}_0, n, f_n^a ..., ...)$ $\qquad$ $|alts(f)| = 0$ $\qquad$ *(Push Instance)*
$\rightarrow (\mathtt{A}_0, n, f_n^a ..., \mathtt{C}^n ...)$ $\qquad$ $|alts(f)| > 0$ $\qquad$ *(Scrutinise)*

Argument-Request: $(\mathtt{A}_i, a, ... f_a^- ..., ...)$
$\rightarrow (\mathtt{A}_{i-|args(f)|+arity(f)}, a - 1, ... f_a^- ..., ...)$ $\quad$ $|args(f)| < i$ $\quad$ *(Skip)*
$\rightarrow (args_i(f), a, ... f_a^- ..., ...)$ $\qquad$ $|args(f)| \geq i$ $\qquad$ *(Serve)*

Parameter-Request: $(\mathtt{P}_i^f, a, ... g_a^p ..., ...)$
$\rightarrow (\mathtt{P}_i^f, p, ... g_a^p ..., ...)$ $\qquad$ $f \neq g$ $\qquad$ *(Backtrace)*
$\rightarrow (\mathtt{A}_i, a - 1, ... g_a^p ..., ...)$ $\qquad$ $f = g$ $\qquad$ *(Request argument)*

Operator: $(\mathtt{0}_{op}, -, t_n ..., ...)$
$\rightarrow (\mathtt{A}_1, n, t_n ..., \mathtt{0}_{op}^n[] ...)$ $\qquad$ *(First Operand)*

Operand: $(v, -, ..., \mathtt{0}_{op}^a[v_1, ..., v_c] ...)$
$\rightarrow (apply_{op}(v_1, ..., v_c, v), -, ..., ...)$ $\qquad$ $arity(op) = c + 1$ $\qquad$ *(Apply Operator)*
$\rightarrow (\mathtt{A}_{c+2}, a, ..., \mathtt{0}_{op}^a[v_1, ..., v_c, v] ...)$ $\qquad$ $arity(op) > c + 1$ $\qquad$ *(Next Operand)*

Scrutinee: $(c, -, ... f_a^p ..., \mathtt{C}^a ...)$
$\rightarrow (alts_c(f), a, ... f_a^p ..., ...)$ $\qquad$ *(Serve alternative)*

Fig. 12. Enriched operational semantics

5 Perspectives

Even though the PAM has already been discovered years ago, it has not yet been investigated extensively. However, there is ample opportunity for further research, in particular it still remains a challenge to find efficient mechanisms for sharing as well as for garbage collection that take advantage of the abstract machine's prominent features.

While it is difficult to reason about the performance of the abstract machine compared to existing functional language implementations without taking these issues into account, there are aspects about our approach that hold much potential in this regard. Aside from the reduced amount of rewriting steps that are required by the very lazy λ-calculus, it is primarily the lean memory profile of the STEC-machine that is promising. The run-time data structures are compact, since per function instance only two pointers need to be allocated.[6] This results in a smaller memory footprint compared to conventional graph reduction models, which in each closure also maintain a set of parameters. Furthermore it is noticeable that no pointer updates are necessary resulting in very few write accesses. While partly compensated by additional read accesses (because of the

---

[6] A potential optimisation would be to allow variably-sized function instances, i.e. instances without a parent pointer for functions without free parameter variables.

need to locate abstraction/application pairs) still the advantage seems to predominate. This presumption however is yet to be validated in a comparison with a well-established execution model like the STG-machine [Peyton Jones 1992].

Implementations based on super-combinators usually compile the abstract-machine code into machine code of the target architecture that integrates the semantics of the abstract machine and therefore can be directly executed by a concrete machine. Due to the simplicity of the STEC-machine, a different compilation model, one that separates the abstract machine and the function definitions, seems to be adequate. The operational semantics can be implemented in a very small piece of executable machine code. Each function definition can be stored in a compact array as read-only data. Access to individual arguments of a function definition (as frequently performed by the STEC-machine) can be accomplished efficiently using an array lookup if a uniformly-sized representation for the arguments is chosen. This would hardly be the case when compiling the function definitions combined with the operational semantics to machine code, which would also lead to a considerable increase of the memory footprint.

Since the evaluation stack only grows, a garbage-collection mechanism is required to release memory occupied by function instances that are no longer required. In that sense the evaluation stack in fact is a heap. However, it would be short-sighted to neglect the fact that it is highly structured in comparison to a usual heap in which data is organised as memory blocks at arbitrary positions that refer to each other. Much is to be expected by a sophisticated garbage-collection mechanism that systematically exploits this structure for increased efficiency. Since the evaluation stack is an incremental definition of the environment, this would effectively be realised as a (linear) compaction of the evaluation stack.

Obviously this linearity cannot be sustained once sharing is introduced to the model, as sharing in a sense implies a non-linear structure. Still, the linearity of evaluation might offer new possibilities for integrating sharing-techniques that achieve a higher degree of sharing than full laziness by breaking the linear structure only at few, well-defined points. In particular the subject of optimal evaluation in the sense of [Lévy 1978] should be investigated in the light of very lazy evaluation.

Summarising, there is still much opportunity for completion and optimisation of the STEC-machine in order to obtain a new type of practical high-performance functional language implementation. In particular it is an interesting question which of the optimisations used by today's compilers can be applied to the STEC-machine and what new kind of possibilities for optimisations are opened up by the model.

References

[Fairbairn 1987]   Fairbairn, J., Wray, S.: Tim: A simple, lazy abstract machine to execute supercombinators. In: Kahn, G. (ed.) FPCA 1987. LNCS, vol. 274, pp. 34–45. Springer, Heidelberg (1987)

[Krivine 2007]   Krivine, J.-L.: A call-By-name lambda-calculus machine. Higher Order and Symbolic Computation 20(3), 199–207 (2007)

[Peyton Jones 1987]   Peyton Jones, S.L., Wadler, P., Hancock, P.: The implementation
                      of functional programming languages. Prentice Hall International,
                      Englewood Cliffs (1987)
[Burn 1988]   Burn, G.L., Peyton Jones, S.L., Robson, J.D.: The spineless G-
                      machine. In: Proceedings of the 1988 ACM conference on LISP and
                      functional programming, pp. 244–258. ACM, New York (1988)
[Peyton Jones 1992]   Peyton Jones, S.L.: Implementing lazy functional languages on
                      stock hardware: the Spineless Tagless G-machine - Version 2.5,
                      Department of Computing Science, University of Glasgow, July 9
                      (1992)
[Leijen 2005]   Leijen, D.: The lazy virtual machine specification, Institute of In-
                      formation and Computing Sciences, Utrecht University, August 22
                      (2005)
[Holyer 1998]   Holyer, I., Spiliopoulou, E.: The Brisk Machine: a simplified STG
                      machine, University of Bristol, Department of Computer Science
                      (March 1998)
[Barendregt 1984]   Barendregt, H.P.: The Lambda Calculus: Its syntax and semantics
                      (1984)
[Danos 2004]   Danos, V., Regnier, L.: Head linear reduction (unpublished),
                      http://iml.univ-mrs.fr/~regnier/articles.html (June 7,
                      2004)
[Danos 1996]   Danos, V., Herbelin, H., Regnier, L.: Game semantics and abstract
                      machines. In: Symposium on Logic in Computer Science, September
                      2, p. 394. IEEE Computer Society, Los Alamitos (1996)
[De Bruijn 1972]   De Bruijn, N.G.: Lambda Calculus Notation with Nameless Dum-
                      mies – a Tool for Automatic Formula Manipulation, with Applica-
                      tion to the Church-Rosser Theorem. Indagationes Mathematicae,
                      381–392 (1972)
[Hughes 1982]   Hughes, R.J.M.: Super-Combinators – a new implementation
                      method for applicative languages. In: Proceedings of the 1982
                      ACM symposium on LISP and functional programming, pp. 1–
                      10. ACM, New York (1982)
[Kamareddine 2001]   Kamareddine, F., Bloo, R., Nederpelt, R.: De Bruijn's syntax and
                      reductional equivalence of λ-terms. In: Proceedings of the 3rd ACM
                      SIGPLAN international conference on Principles and practice of
                      declarative programming, pp. 16–27. ACM, New York (2001)
[Danvy 2000]   Danvy, O., Schultz, U.P.: Lambda-dropping: transforming recursive
                      equations into programs with block structure. Partial evaluation and
                      semantics-based program manipulation 248(1-2), 243–287 (2000)
[Marlow 2006]   Marlow, S., Peyton Jones, S.: Making a fast curry: push/enter
                      vs. eval/apply for higher-order languages. Journal of Functional
                      Programming 16, 415–449 (2006)
[Sestoft 2002]   Sestoft, P.: Demonstrating lambda calculus reduction. In: Jones,
                      D., Mogensen, T.Æ., Schmidt, D.A., Sudborough, I.H. (eds.) The
                      Essence of Computation. LNCS, vol. 2566, pp. 420–435. Springer,
                      Heidelberg (2002)
[Lévy 1978]   Lévy, J.-J.: Optimal reductions in the lambda-calculus. In: Seldin,
                      J.P., Hindley, J.R. (eds.) To H.B. Curry: Essays on Combinatory
                      Logic, Lambda Calculus and Formalism, Academic Press, London
                      (1978)

Engineering Higher-Order Modules in SML/NJ

George Kuan and David MacQueen

University of Chicago

Abstract. SML/NJ and other Standard ML variants extend the ML module system with higher-order functors, elevating the module language to a full functional language. In this paper, we describe the implementation of higher-order modules in SML/NJ, which is unique in providing "true" higher-order static behavior. This implementation is based on three key ideas: unique internal variables (entity variables) for naming static entities, factorization of the static information in both basic modules and functors into signatures and realizations, and representing the static "effects" and type-level mapping performed by a functor using a static lambda calculus (the *entity calculus*). This design conforms to MacQueen-Tofte's re-elaboration semantics without having to re-elaborate functor bodies at functor applications.

1 Introduction

The ML module system has evolved considerably over the past 25 years. One of the Standard ML of New Jersey (SML/NJ) compiler's more significant extensions is support for higher-order functors, achieved by allowing structures, including functor parameters and results, to contain functors as components. MacQueen and Tofte [18] describe the original semantics for higher-order functors, which has a strong policy regarding how functors propagate type information through functor applications. We will refer to the MacQueen-Tofte higher-order functor semantics as *true higher-order behavior*. This model of higher-order functors was first implemented in SML/NJ Version 0.93 (1993), using techniques described in Crégut and MacQueen [2]. That implementation evolved from an earlier implementation of first-order functors, and its adaptation to handle higher-order functors was complex and *ad hoc*. Here we describe the second generation implementation used in current versions of SML/NJ, which is significantly simpler and more principled. We focus on the representations and processes used in the static elaboration phase of the compiler. The relatively straightforward elaboration of the dynamic semantics of the module system through abstract syntax is beyond the scope of this paper.

Due to space limitations, we can provide only a brief sketch of the context of this work in the design of Standard ML and the evolution of its module system. We assume the reader is familiar with Standard ML, including its module system [19]. Further background is available from the tutorial by Harper and Pierce [9]. An expanded version of this paper is available as a tech report [12], and extensive background discussion and rigorous formal semantics for the design

M.T. Morazán and S.-B. Scholz (Eds.): IFL 2009, LNCS 6041, pp. 218–235, 2010.

will be included in the first author's forthcoming PhD thesis [11]. Full source code for the implementation is available at www.smlnj.org.

1.1 SML 97 Module System

The ML module system provides a set of constructs for expressing large-scale program architecture, and is also the means for defining and enforcing abstractions. Basic modules, called *structures*, are collections of types, values, and hierarchically nested modules. *Signatures* express static interfaces of structures, functioning as types for structures. A signature comprises a collection of named type[1], value, and module specifications, specifying their kinds[2], types, and signatures, respectively. A *functor* is a module-level function formed by parameterizing a structure (the functor body) with respect to a structure variable constrained by a signature. Signatures and structures have a many-to-many relationship: multiple structures can match a single signature, and different signatures can be ascribed to a given structure. *Signature ascription* coerces a structure to conform to a signature. ML supports two kinds of signature ascription. *Transparent signature ascription* passes a type definition through to the coerced structure even when the ascribed signature only has an open type spec corresponding to that type. *Opaque signature ascription* (also called *sealing* ascription) generates a fresh abstract tycon for each open type specification, enforcing abstraction by hiding the original definition of the type name.

1.2 Higher-Order Functors

The need for higher-order functors arises naturally in a module system with functors. Just as a first-order functor is formed by abstracting with respect to an external structure name used in a structure expression, a higher-order functor should result from abstracting with respect to the name of an external functor. The module expression abstracted over could be either a basic structure or a functor. So, for orthogonality, we should be able to abstract with respect to both structure names and functor names over both structure and functor expressions. However, this obvious extension raises some significant issues for design, semantics, and implementation.

When abstracting over the name of either an imported structure or functor, the parameter is described by a signature, which expresses all the static interface information about the parameter that the client structure is allowed to know. In the case of first-order structures (with no functor components), the signature language is capable of expressing a fairly complete static description of a given structure using definitional specs and where clauses to pin down the type components. But when we abstract over an imported structure we normally use a looser, less exact signature for the parameter to allow the parameter types to vary

---

[1] Actually type constructors, but it is a common and convenient abuse of terminology to refer to *types* when we mean *type constructors* (abbreviated as *tycons*).

[2] *Open* type specs (e.g., **type** ('a,'b) t) specify only the kind or arity, while *definitional* type specs (**type** 'a u = 'a list) include definitions.

from one application to another. Signatures may be looser in two senses. First, for some of the parameter's tycons, we may use an open rather than definitional spec, leaving the definitions to be supplied later by the argument structures when the functor is applied. Second, the argument structure may contain excess components, which will be dropped during coercion, or value components whose types are more polymorphic than specified in the signature.

A functor can express complex static-level computations mapping its input tycons to its output tycons, and we call this mapping the *functor static action*, or simply the *functor action*. The defining characteristic of true higher-order static behavior in functors is the faithful propagation of functor actions through functor application. A functor action may involve the generation of fresh tycons (a *static effect*), introduced either by datatype declarations or by opaque signature ascriptions. However, functor signatures, which consist of only a named parameter signature and a result signature, are only capable of expressing very simple functor actions where the result tycons can be defined directly in terms of the parameter tycons, so functor signatures have a very limited ability to describe functor static actions. Hence a full description of the static content of a functor must include information beyond the functor signature, in all but the simplest cases.

When a functor G is a component of the parameter of a functor F, G is called a *formal functor*, and all we know about G is its functor signature. When elaborating the body of F we need to determine a functor action for the formal functor G, i.e., we need to synthesize a default functor action from a functor signature. When F is applied to an actual parameter A, then the action of A.G (suitably coerced) should be used in place of the approximation derived from G's specification in F. In other words, the static action of F should be properly parameterized with respect to the static action of G. This requirement is the essence of true higher-order behavior.[3]

The standard example illustrating this point is the Application functor:

```
signature SIG = sig type t end

functor F(functor G(Y: SIG): SIG
          structure A: SIG): SIG
  = G(A)

functor Id(X: SIG) = struct type t = X.t end
functor Const(X: SIG) = struct type t = int end
structure B: SIG = struct type t = bool end

structure R1 = F(Id, B)      (* R1.t = bool *)
structure R2 = F(Const, B)   (* R2.t = int *)
```

---

[3] A common alternative solution to this problem is applicative functor semantics [14]. However, such semantics cannot capture generative functor actions. Applicator functor semantics is also fragile in the presence of aliasing of structures.

Here the action of functor Id maps its argument tycon to itself ($\lambda t. t$), while the action of Const maps any argument tycon to int ($\lambda t.\text{int}$). Applications of F invoke F's action, which in turn invokes the functor actions of its parameters.

1.3   Overview

The following two sections describe the module elaboration in SML/NJ. Section 2 describes the internal static representations of types, signatures, structures, and functors. The main ideas are the use of internal entity variables and paths for relative references to tycons, the factorization of the static representations of modules into signatures and corresponding *realizations* of the signatures, and the *entity calculus*, a static lambda calculus of *entity expressions* that we used to represent the realization part of functors (their *functor actions*).

Section 3 covers the processes involved in the elaboration of modules, which create and utilize the representations in Section 2. These processes include the basic elaboration of signature, structure, and functor declarations, the static aspect of functor application, and signature matching. An important subsidiary process is *signature instantiation*, which is used in the elaboration of functors and the application of formal functors (e.g., G in the example above).

Section 4 covers related work, and we conclude in Section 5 with some justification of the success of the design.

2   Semantic Objects

In the core ML language, a tycon always has a fixed identity such as a primitive type or some specific user-defined type, e.g., **type** t = int. We call these tycons *nonvolatile*. As discussed in Section 1.2, a functor parameter signature may specify only the name and kind of a tycon without defining it. Such a tycon is *volatile* because its actual definition is supplied upon each functor application, and it can vary from one application to another. Tycons defined in terms of volatile tycons are also considered volatile. For example, in the signature **sig type** t **type** u = t list **end**, t and u are both volatile. Although volatile tycons bear some resemblance to abstract types, volatility is not the same as abstractness. The definition of a volatile tycon will be eventually determined, e.g., by the actual parameter passed to a functor, after which the tycon may become nonvolatile. However, a future definition of a volatile tycon cannot play a role while type checking the functor itself, because it is not yet available.

2.1   Entity Paths

Following Harper and Lillibridge [8], we use internal names, which we call *entity variables*, to provide a robust means to refer to tycons, structures, and functors in the presence of shadowing of symbolic names. The term *entity* refers to the internal representation of anything that may contain or produce static information in the form of tycons, namely tycons themselves, structures, and functors.

Entity variables are unique by construction and entity variable bindings cannot be shadowed. Sequences of entity variables called *entity paths* are used to refer to an entity that is located inside a hierarchy of nested structures.

Consider the example in Fig. 1. Assuming that e_A is an entity variable for A, and so on, type A.B.u can be referred to by the entity path e_A, e_B, e_u. The symbolic path and the corresponding entity path both designate an entity, but an entity path is robust, in that there will always be a valid entity path for any entity even when no corresponding symbolic path exists due to shadowing.

```
signature S =                        S_SEM =
sig                                  sig
  structure A :                        structure A (e_A) :
    sig                                  sig
      type t                               type t (e_t)
      structure B :                        structure B (e_B) :
        sig                                  sig
          type u                               type u (e_u)
          val x : t                            val x : [e_t]
        end                                  end
      val y : t * B.u                      val y : [e_t] * [e_B, e_u]
    end                                  end
end                                  end
```

Fig. 1. A syntactic signature and its semantic representation

---

2.2   Semantic Representations of Signatures

The semantic representation of a signature is a list of tuples consisting of a name, a specification, and, for static components, a unique entity variable. Hereafter, we use the term *signature* to refer to such semantic representations. We construct signature representations either by translating a syntactic signature expression or by inferring a signature from a basic structure expression. Using the entity variables in a signature, we can map a symbolic path for a static component to a corresponding entity path. In Fig. 1, S_SEM represents the translation of the syntactic signature S. We can traverse this signature following a symbolic path A.B.u, collecting the corresponding entity path e_A, e_B, e_u as we go.

We represent volatile tycon occurrences in value specifications by an entity path *relativized* to the scope of the occurrence. For example, the spec for value y has the relativized form $[e_t] * [e_B, e_u]$. Due to the presence of volatile tycons, a signature is only a partial representation of the static information in any structure that matches the signature. The representation of such a structure complements the signature with a *realization* that maps entity variables and paths for volatile tycons to actual tycons, thus defining them.

2.3   Structure Realization

A *structure realization* is a finite map from entity variables to entities. An entity variable for a tycon component is mapped to a tycon. An entity variable for a substructure is mapped to another structure realization. In the case of a functor component, its entity variable is mapped to a functor realization, which will be described in Section 2.5. Because structure realizations contain only static entities, value components are not represented. Because a structure realization may contain nested structure realizations, it can be thought of as a tree where the edges are labeled by entity variables, internal nodes are subtrees (structure realizations), and leaves are tycons or functor realizations. For example, Fig. 2 shows a structure M matching signature S and the corresponding structure realization r_M that complements S with entities from M.

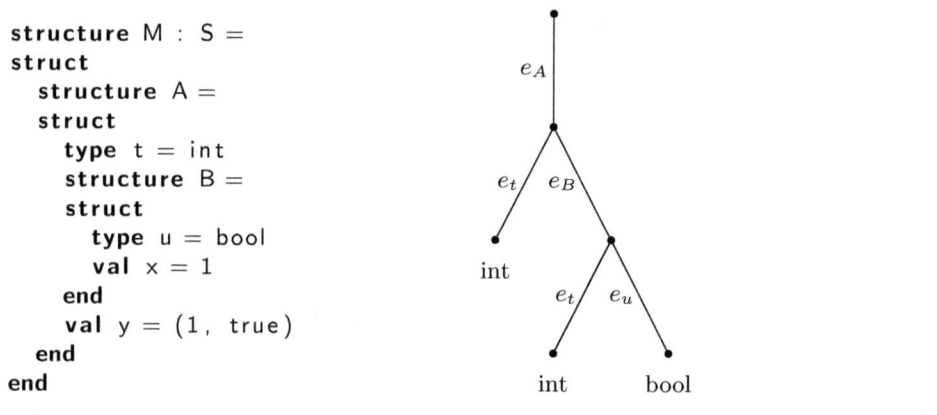

```
structure M : S =
struct
  structure A =
  struct
    type t = int
    structure B =
    struct
      type u = bool
      val x = 1
    end
    val y = (1, true)
  end
end
```

Fig. 2. A structure and structure realization matching signature S

The seemingly duplicate e_t edge under node B may look peculiar. Because substructures such as B may be selected out by later declarations such as structure B' = M.A.B, the structure realization of B must be able to stand on its own. Consequently, we need to close the structure realization for B by including the mapping for e_t, which is not a local component of B.

Looking up the type for value component M.A.y using S and this matching realization takes two steps. First, we fetch the signature for A and use its entity variable e_A to select from r_M the corresponding realization subtree r_A. Then we get the type specification $[e_t]$ * $[e_B, e_u]$ for y from A's signature spec and interpret its entity paths relative to r_A, yielding int * bool.

A generative type declaration such as datatype declaration produces a fresh tycon with a unique identifying *stamp*. Other type declarations define tycon components in terms of other tycons using a type expression or type function. All tycons components are located at leaf nodes in the structure's realization tree, accessed by entity paths that specify their position in the structure hierarchy.

2.4   Full Signatures

When we put together a signature and a compatible structure realization, i.e., a realization that at least maps all the entity paths in the signature, we have a complete static description of a structure, which we call a *full signature*. Where a structure expression has no explicit signature ascribed, the elaborator will synthesize a signature and a matching realization to construct a full signature for the structure. Actually, we always infer a full signature for a structure expression, even in a structure declaration with an ascription. Then we immediately match that inferred full signature with the ascribed signature, producing a new realization for the ascribed signature, as described in Section 3.

Multiple structure declarations can ascribe the same syntactic signature to different structures. For example, consider a second structure declared with signature S:

```
structure M2 : S =
struct
  structure A =
  struct
    type t = real
    structure B =
    struct
      type u = string
      val x = 1.0
    end
    val y = (1.0, "string")
  end
end
```

Although M and M2's realizations obviously differ in content (but not in form), their full signatures will share the same signature representation S_SEM, representing the syntactic signature S. The sharing of common signature information among all the structures matching an explicit signature is a major motivation for the factorization into signature and realization.

2.5   Functor Entities and the Entity Calculus

The complete static description of a functor is called a *full functor signature*, and it is also factored into a functor signature and a functor realization. The semantic representation of a *functor signature*, which we informally write as $(X\ (e_x):\text{SIGPARAM}) : \text{SIGBODY}$, consists of a parameter signature SIGPARAM and a functor body signature SIGBODY whose specifications may mention the bound parameter X via the associated parameter entity variable e_x. Both SIGPARAM and SIGBODY are semantic representations of signatures and thus are decorated with entity variables and use entity paths to reference volatile entities.

While the functor signature specifies the fixed shape of the parameter and result, information that is common to all calls of the functor, the *functor realization* describes how the realization of the functor body structure is computed in terms of the realization of the parameter structure. The parameter realization contains the static information that varies from call to call. This is where the signature-realization factorization clarifies the semantics of functors. The functor realization is an *entity function* of the form $\lambda e_x.strexp$ where *strexp* is a structure entity expression that evaluates to a structure realization for the functor body. These entity expressions and functions are formalized by an applied, call-by-value λ-calculus called the *entity calculus* (Fig. 3). Terms in the entity calculus express static information and are evaluated only during compilation, specifically when elaborating functor applications (see Section 3).

$$
\begin{aligned}
tycon ::=\ &\text{Formal}(tycon) \\
 |\ &\text{Def}(typeexp) \\
 |\ &\text{Data}(ConsName \text{ of } typeexp) \\
 |\ &entitypath \\
\\
strexp ::=\ &\text{STRUCTURE}\{entitydec\} \\
 |\ &fctexp(strexp) \\
 |\ &\text{FORM}\{sig\} \\
 |\ &entitypath
\end{aligned}
$$

$$
\begin{aligned}
entitydec ::=\ &\text{type } e_x = tycon \\
 |\ &\text{structure } e_x = strexp \\
 |\ &\text{functor } e_x = fctexp \\
 |\ &entitydec, entitydec \\
\\
fctexp ::=\ &\lambda e_x.strexp[entityenv] \\
 |\ &entitypath
\end{aligned}
$$

Fig. 3. A simplified entity calculus

The tycon expressions include Formals representing dummy tycons that are specified in a functor parameter. A *typeexp* is a type expression that may contain applied occurrences of tycons. A Def tycon defines a tycon as an abbreviation for a type expression. A Data tycon corresponds to an ML datatype with the given constructor name and constructor argument type. For simplicity, we are assuming here only one data constructor per datatype. Entity paths are the relativized tycon references described earlier.

Entity declarations bind entity variables to an appropriate kind of entity expression. A functor body may contain free occurrences of entities such as a tycon, structure, or functor declared in an outer functor, and these volatile entities are denoted by entity paths (see Section 2.6 for an example). Thus, the functor realization for higher-order functors requires a closure environment, and the correct form of a functor realization is an *entity function closure* of the form $\lambda e_x.strexp[entityenv]$ where *entityenv* is an *entity environment* mapping all free entity variables in *strexp* to entities. An *entityenv* has exactly the same representation as a structure realization. Section 2.6 will further explain the need for a closure environment. Structure entity expressions include a form for basic structures, which encapsulate an entity declaration for its static components, entity paths to refer to structure entities bound in the local entity environment, applications, and a special form (FORM) used in representations of functors in formal parameters, which will be explained in Section 3.

Consider the following example:

```
functor F(X: sig type t val x: t end) =
    struct
        datatype u = A of X.t
        type v = X.t * u list
        fun f(x: X.t) : u = A x
    end
```

The above functor is represented by a functor signature and a functor realization. The inferred functor signature is:

```
(X (eₓ) :  sig type t (eₜ) val x : [eₜ] end)
    : sig
            type u (eᵤ) type v (eᵥ)
            val f : [eₓ, eₜ] → [eᵤ]
    end
```

where e_X, e_t, e_u, and e_v are fresh entity variables.

The realization for the functor has to specify how realizations for the static components of the result (entities for the types u and v) are constructed given a structure realization for X, which includes a tycon entity for X.t. The functor realization for F is the entity function:

$$\lambda e_X.\text{STRUCTURE}\{\text{type } e_u = tycon_u, \text{ type } e_v = tycon_v\}$$

where $tycon_u$ and $tycon_v$ are tycon entity expressions for the datatype u and type abbreviation v:

$$tycon_u = \text{Data}(\text{A of } [e_X, e_t])$$
$$tycon_v = \text{Def}([e_X, e_t] * [e_u] \; list)$$

Here the closure environment can be empty, assuming the functor is defined at top level (it is also closed, having no references to nonlocal volatile entities). When this functor is applied to an argument structure, the argument structure is coerced by signature matching (described in Section 3) with the parameter signature yielding a structure realization for the parameter signature. This parameter realization is bound to the entity variable e_X and the body of the entity function is evaluated in the resulting entity environment.

The body specifies that a structure realization is to be constructed, whose contents will be defined by a sequence of two entity declarations. e_u will be bound to a new tycon generated from the datatype specification, with the associated entity paths referencing imported types being evaluated relative to the *evaluation entity environment*, the entity environment at that point of elaboration. Similarly, the definition of type v will be instantiated by evaluating its embedded entity paths in that same entity environment extended with the binding of e_u.

In particular, in the application F(**struct type** t = int **end**), the realization bound to e_X will be the entity environment $\{e_t \mapsto \text{int}\}$, and the evaluation entity environment for the body declarations is $\{e_X \mapsto \{e_t \mapsto \text{int}\}\}$. Evaluating $tycon_u$ in this environment yields a fresh datatype corresponding to the definition **datatype** u = A **of** int. Evaluating $tycon_v$ yields an instantiated type abbreviation definition equivalent to type v = int * (u list). The creation of the fresh datatype tycon u is an example of a *static effect* in the entity language. Other tycon creation effects are associated with the process of opaque signature matching, where fresh abstract types are introduced.

2.6   Higher-Order Functors

The preceding example involves the classic case of a first-order functor defined at top level, *i.e.*, not defined within another functor, where the closure environment of the functor realization can be empty. Here we show that higher-order functors can require a nontrivial closure environment. Consider the following example:

```
functor F(X: sig type t end) =
  struct
    datatype u = C of X.t
    functor G(Y : sig type v val x : v * u * X.t end) =
      struct
        datatype s = D of X.t * u → Y.v
      end
  end
```

We can see that all the tycons X.t, u, Y.v, and s are volatile in that their actual bindings are to be determined later, when F is applied. When we relativize the specification of datatype s with respect to these volatile tycons, we get:

$$tycon_s = \mathsf{Data}(\text{D of } [e_X, e_t] * e_u \to [e_Y, e_v])$$

Now consider an application of F, **structure** A = F(**struct type** t = int **end**). When this expression is evaluated, we will develop an entity environment that binds e_X and its extension $[e_X, e_t]$ as before, and the definition of u will give rise to a new datatype that will be bound to e_u. As before, the realization of functor G will involve a lambda expression in our entity calculus:

$$\lambda e_Y.\mathsf{STRUCTURE}\{\text{type } e_s = tycon_s\}$$

But note that this term binds only the entity variable e_Y, leaving e_X and e_u occurring free in $tycon_s$. So the lambda term is not closed. As usual, we need to close it by supplying a closure environment, namely the entity environment mentioned above that binds e_X and e_u.

Now when we apply A.G we will add a binding of e_Y to its closure environment and use this when evaluating the body of the lambda term for G. For instance, after

structure B = A.G(**struct type** = bool **val** x = (true, A.C 3, 1) **end**)

the B.s will denote the datatype Data (D **of** int * A.u → bool).

3   Elaboration

Elaboration is the translation of simple syntax trees produced by the parser into (1) a typed abstract syntax for use in subsequent compiler stages, and (2) a static environment mapping identifiers defined at top-level to their static representations. As mentioned in the introduction, we are focusing exclusively on how the static environment is produced; the construction of abstract syntax is relatively straightforward in comparison.

At the core language level, the elaborator does type checking and type inference for value declarations, and produces static bindings mapping type names to tycon representations, and variable, data constructor, and exception constructor names to their types. At the module level, the elaborator translates signature, structure, and functor expressions and declarations into the internal representations described in Section 2. The type information is recorded as new bindings added to the static environment, which is used for elaborating later compilation units (e.g., source files) that import them. An initial static environment contains predefined modules, types, and values (the SML Basis libraries).

Elaboration can be broken down into a set of subtasks. The main tasks are elaborating signature expressions, structure expressions, and functor declarations, and these involve subsidiary processes including functor application, signature matching, and signature *instantiation*. Signature expressions and structure expressions often occur as the definiens in a declaration, but they can also occur "in-lined", in an ascription in the case of signatures, or as a functor parameter or functor body in the case of structures.

Elaboration modes. It is useful to distinguish two contexts in which elaboration takes place: *functor context*, where the expression or declaration elaborated occurs within the body of a functor, and *top level*, when outside of any functor. Elaboration in a functor context is more complicated, because in addition to performing the usual type-checking and static environment building tasks, it must also "compile" declarations to the entity calculus expressions used to encode the functor static action. Thus in a functor context elaboration must operate in dual, simultaneous, modes. We use the term *direct elaboration* for the basic mode that deals with type checking and translation to static representations, while *entity compilation* refers to the parallel process of compiling static declarations into the entity calculus. Direct elaboration occurs in both contexts, while entity compilation is relevant only to the functor context. In practice, to simplify the code, we always perform both modes of elaboration and if we are in top level mode we discard the unneeded byproducts of entity compilation. The extra work involved in unnecessary entity compilation is not a significant overhead.

Functor volatile entities. A related factor associated specifically with functor mode is that static entities constructed within a functor (and the functor parameter itself) are *volatile*, as opposed to entities constructed in top level mode, which are fixed and hence *nonvolatile*. During functor elaboration, the functor volatile entities are virtual or potential, in the sense that the actual entities will be created later at functor application time. However, in the direct elaboration mode volatile entities need to be represented by dummy entities to support type checking, so they will have static representations in the "working" static environment used for direct elaboration of functor bodies. In embedded, in-line signatures, and in compiled entity calculus expressions, references to volatile entities (e.g., structures and tycons) must be "relativized" by translating them into entity paths.

The process of relativizing references to volatile entities, and the interpretation of the resulting entity paths, require that two additional parameters be provided to the elaboration process. An entity environment is threaded through to be used (1) to interpret entity paths of functor volatile entities in embedded signatures, and (2) to construct closure environments for structure realizations and functor realizations (entity functions). Elaboration of declarations will add new entity variable bindings to this entity environment. The second new ingredient is called an *entity path context*. It is an inverse environment that maps dummy volatile entities to their entity paths, and it is used for relativization of references to those dummy entities. So a complete schematic of the inputs and outputs of elaboration is shown in Fig. 4.

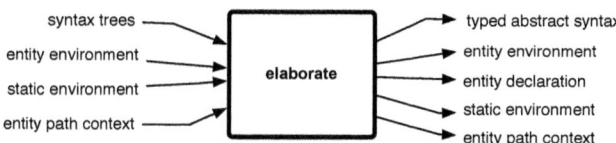

Fig. 4. Schematic for elaboration

Signature elaboration. The specifications in the body of the signature are translated into a mapping from component names to internal specs in the form of formal tycons for tycon specs, types for values, and semantic representations of signatures and functor signatures for structure and functor elements respectively. Each static element (tycon or module) is assigned a fresh entity variable. The types of value elements, data constructors, and types occurring in definitional type specs, are relativized by replacing local tycon references (which we can call *signature volatiles* to distinguish them from functor volatiles) with entity paths. If the signature is in-line in a functor context it may contain functor volatiles, which are also relativized. Any *where type* constraints are elaborated and pushed inward to the type specifications they apply to. Sharing constraints are recorded in a normalized form as pairs of symbolic paths.

Structure elaboration. There are several cases for structure expression elaboration, corresponding to the syntactic forms for such expressions (e.g., structures declared in-line: **struct** ... **end**, structure symbolic paths: A, A.B, and functor applications). A symbolic name or path for a structure is looked up in the current static environment, returning a full signature for the structure. A basic in-line structure expression **struct** *decls* **end** form is elaborated as follows:

1. elaborate the body declarations *decls*, yielding a static environment *envBody*, an entity environment *entEnv*, and an entity declaration *entityDec*;
2. derive from *envBody* a signature and matching structure realization (entity environment), and combine them to create a full signature;
3. return the full signature from step 2, a structure entity expression STRUC-TURE{*entityDec*}, and the entity environment *entEnv* from step 1.

Signature matching. When a signature is ascribed to a structure in a structure declaration, or when a functor is applied to a structure, implicitly ascribing the parameter signature to the argument, we must verify that the structure in question *matches* the signature. This is a kind of module-level type checking, but it also has a coercive effect, producing a modified structure realization that exactly conforms to the ascribed signature (similar to coercive subtyping). Signature matching involves scanning the specifications in the signature and verifying that the matching structure satisfies these specifications. There are two modes of signature matching. Opaque signature matching generates fresh tycons for signature volatile tycon specifications using signature instantiation (see below), whereas transparent signature matching uses the corresponding tycons from the matching structure.

Signature instantiation. At a couple of points during elaboration, we have only a signature on hand when what we need is a full signature. To synthesize a full signature from the signature, we need to produce a dummy structure realization for the signature. *Signature instantiation* is the process of creating a "free" structure realization for a signature. This process is nontrivial because of type sharing specifications, which require two tycon names/paths to refer to the same tycon.

This realization includes fresh formal tycons for each type component, but chosen to satisfy the signature's sharing constraints, and only those sharing constraints (i.e., no incidental sharing not forced by the specifications). The algorithm used for signature instantiation is adapted from the Patterson-Wegman linear unification algorithm [22].

When instantiating a functor specification in a signature, we must create a corresponding functor realization. This will be, as usual, an entity function, but one where the body of the lambda abstraction is the special structure entity expression form (FORM{sig}) containing only the formal functor signature. What happens when such a formal functor is applied will be explained below.

Functor application. When a functor is applied, the argument structure expression is elaborated to a full signature, and then signature matching is performed to verify that it matches the parameter signature and to coerce the argument structure realization to a realization for the parameter signature, yielding a full signature for the coerced argument. The functor realization, which is an entity calculus lambda-abstraction complete with a closure entity environment, is then applied to the argument realization using a conventional call-by-value, environment-based interpreter for the entity calculus. As usual, this entails extending the closure environment with a binding of the argument realization to the lambda-bound entity variable, and then evaluating the body structure expression with respect to this extended entity environment.

This is the standard case. But in a functor context, the functor being applied may be an element of an outer functor parameter, *i.e.* a formal functor. Suppose, for example, the elaborator encountered the following program:

```
funsig FS() = sig type t end
functor F(X:sig functor G : FS end) =
struct
    structure M = X.G()
end

functor H0() = struct type t = int end
structure FR0 = F(struct functor G = H0 end)
```

where FS is a functor signature where the parameter signature is empty and the result signature specifies a single tycon t. When elaborating the application of functor X.G in the direct mode, we do not seem to have a functor realization for X.G because that will only be supplied by an actual parameter (as in the definition of FR0). We solve this problem by synthesizing a special entity function from the functor signature FS. This entity function is, as usual, a closure of a lambda expression, but the body of this lambda expression is a special form of structure entity expression that simply wraps the body signature from FS: FORM{**sig type t end**}. When elaborating X.G() in functor F's body, we evaluate this new form of structure expression by *instantiating* **sig type t end** with respect to the evaluation environment. In this case, this will create a fresh abstract tycon as the realization of t. This allows the type checking of the body of F to proceed with no information about actual parameters other than that they match the signature of X.

The entity declaration corresponding to M in the lambda abstraction for F applies the relativized entity path for G to an empty structure entity expression:

$$\textbf{structure } e_M = [e_X, \ e_G](\text{STRUCTURE}\{\})$$

When this declaration is evaluated at the call of F defining FR0, $[e_X, e_G]$ will evaluate to the entity function for H0, and this function will define the entity binding of e_t to be int. So FR0.M.t is int. On the other hand, in the following example, the definition of functor H1 uses an opaque ascription to cause a new abstract tycon to be generated for t on each application.

```
functor H1() = struct type t = int end :> sig type t end
structure FR1 = F(struct functor G = H1 end)
```

FR1.M.t will be a new abstract tycon. Thus, while the direct mode elaboration of the body of F has to assume a conservative approximation to the functor action of the G parameter, when F is applied it uses the actual functor action associated with G in the argument. This technique is the key to supporting true higher-order functor semantics.

Functor elaboration. Functor elaboration involves several new problems. One issue is how to deal with references to the formal parameter structure in the body, both during elaboration of the body and later during application of the functor. As we have seen in the earlier example, when applying the functor, the functor parameter will be represented by an entity variable that serves as the formal parameter of the entity function.

During direct mode elaboration of the functor body, we bind the parameter name to a full signature for the parameter structure obtained by instantiating the parameter signature. This instantiation can serve as a formal representative of all possible actual arguments because it embodies the minimal required sharing among its tycon components. Any actual parameter will have to satisfy at least as much sharing.

Now having bound the formal parameter symbol to the instantiation of the parameter signature in the static environment, the body structure of the functor is elaborated. This produces a full signature and a structure entity expression for the functor body. A functor signature is created by combining the parameter signature and the signature part of the body full signature. The functor's entity function is created by wrapping a lambda abstraction around the body's structure entity expression, and closing it with respect to the entity environment in which the functor is elaborated.

4   Related Work

Although the literature on module system semantics is rich, there are few accounts of implementation techniques. As far as the authors know, this paper is one of the few besides Crégut and MacQueen [2], which reported on an earlier version of the SML/NJ implementation. In that implementation, the internal representations and algorithms were considerably more baroque and less principled. Before the implementation of the entity path and signature-realization factorization, the compiler relied on comparison of stamp creation times to index into several arrays containing the relevant static information. The former design was fragile and insufficiently abstract. This new design is a clear advancement that greatly simplifies the implementation.

Most of the literature focuses on the ML module system. Both Haskell [3] and Scheme's [7] module systems are primarily concerned about namespace management through explicit import and export syntax. Because Haskell and Scheme have no equivalent of functors in their module languages, and in the case of Scheme no type components, they are not directly comparable to ML module systems. The several proposals addressing module system semantics and design can be classified as falling under a continuum with the abstract approach on one end and the operational approach on the other. The former, a term coined by Shao [25], refers to the type-theoretic accounts in Harper-Lillibridge [8] and Leroy [13]. The latter refers to the approach embodied in MacQueen-Tofte and the Definition of Standard ML [19]. Several accounts [16, 10, 5, 24] follow the abstract approach closely. Module systems in that group generally do not have semantic representations of signatures distinct from syntactic signatures. Type equivalence and generative types are generally modeled by a simple nominal check and existential types respectively. Consequently, they do not support true higher-order functor semantics. The TILT [10], Moscow ML [24], and Caml/O-Caml [15] compilers are implementations from this line of development.

The Definition [19] does not include higher-order functors. The semantic objects in its treatment differ from ours primarily in our use of entity environments and entity expressions. The Definition has a notion of type realizations, which are maps from type names to tycons, and instantiation of both signatures and functor signatures, producing a static environment and a pair of static environments with a set of flexible names. In contrast to SML/NJ, the result of functor instantiation is only an approximation of our functor realization – there are no entity functions to express functor actions. Signatures in the Definition explicitly name the volatile tycons, but there are no analogues of entity variables associated with tycon, structure, and functor specs.

Other proposals fall somewhere in between the abstract and operational approaches. Biswas [1] and Shao [25] propose type-theoretic accounts that support limited forms of higher-order functors. Both of these module systems can represent some functor actions (which they refer to as "argument-to-result dependency") in functor signatures. Biswas utilizes higher-order variables that have about the same expressiveness as applicative functors in OCaml. A variant of Biswas's design is implemented in the Moscow ML compiler. Shao's solution uses a higher-order tycon that serves a similar role. Unlike Biswas and SML/NJ, Shao's account admits syntactic signatures that can express some functor actions in terms of higher-order type constructor expressions.

More recent variations of the ML module system such as Dreyer's RMC [4] and MixML [6] express type abstraction using an existential type discipline following Mitchell and Plotkin [20] and Russo [24]. Signature matching is non-coercive, though coercions are definable in the module language [5]. Montagu and Rémy [21] develop a more modular form of the existential type calculus by splitting open and pack into separate scoping and witness packing/unpacking constructs to address the tension between modularity and existential-encoded abstract types as pointed out by MacQueen [17]. None of these accounts handles true higher-order functor semantics.

5   Conclusion

The type information generated during elaboration of ML modules can grow quite large, and experience with early, relatively naive versions of the elaborator demonstrated that the size of static data structures could become a real resource bottleneck. The implementation described here has proved very scalable in practice: SML/NJ is self-hosting and compiles a wide range of large Standard ML programs that stress the module system [23]. We believe that factorization of modules into signatures and realizations and the resulting sharing of signature representations is a major factor in this scalability. Hash-consing of type information turned out to be necessary in SML/NJ's FLINT intermediate language, but this technique has not been required in the front end, due partly to signature sharing.

The current implementation of higher-order modules is also a marked improvement over the previously reported version in terms of simplicity and maintainability of the code. It is based on well-understood principles embodied in a formal semantic model that allows us to have confidence in the correctness of the approach. The key abstraction is the static entity calculus for representing the static-level mapping defined for functors. This idea allows us to generalize from first-order to higher-order functors with essentially no extra complexity in the implementation. In essence, we have higher-order functors for free!

References

1. Biswas, S.K.: Higher-order functors with transparent signatures. In: POPL 1995: Proceedings of the 22nd ACM SIGPLAN-SIGACT Symposium on Principles of Programming Languages, pp. 154–163. ACM, New York (1995)
2. Crégut, P., MacQueen, D.: An implementation of higher-order functors. In: ACM SIGPLAN Workshop on Standard ML and its Applications (June 1994)
3. Diatchki, I.S., Jones, M.P., Hallgren, T.: A formal specification of the Haskell 98 module system. In: Haskell 2002: Proceedings of the 2002 ACM SIGPLAN Workshop on Haskell, pp. 17–28. ACM, New York (2002)
4. Dreyer, D.: A type system for recursive modules. In: ICFP 2007: Proceedings of the, ACM SIGPLAN International Conference on Functional Programming, pp. 289–302. ACM, New York (2007)
5. Dreyer, D., Crary, K., Harper, R.: A type system for higher-order modules. In: POPL 2003: Proceedings of the 30th ACM SIGPLAN-SIGACT Symposium on Principles of Programming Languages, pp. 236–249. ACM, New York (2003)
6. Dreyer, D., Rossberg, A.: Mixin' up the ML module system. In: ICFP 2008: Proceeding of the 13th ACM SIGPLAN International Conference on Functional Programming, pp. 307–320. ACM, New York (2008)
7. Flatt, M.: Composable and compilable macros: you want it when? In: ICFP 2002: Proceedings of the 7th ACM SIGPLAN International Conference on Functional Programming, pp. 72–83. ACM, New York (2002)
8. Harper, R., Lillibridge, M.: A type-theoretic approach to higher-order modules with sharing. In: POPL 1994: Proceedings of the 21st ACM SIGPLAN-SIGACT Symposium on Principles of Programming Languages, pp. 123–137. ACM, New York (1994)
9. Harper, R., Pierce, B.C.: Design Considerations for ML-Style Module Systems. In: Advanced Topics in Types and Programming Languages. MIT Press, Cambridge (2005)

10. Harper, R., Stone, C.: An interpretation of Standard ML in type theory. Technical Report CMU–CS–97–147, CMU, Pittsburgh, PA (June 1997) (Also published as Fox Memorandum CMU–CS–FOX–97–01)
11. Kuan, G.: True Higher-Order Module Systems, Separate Compilation, and Signature Calculi. PhD thesis, Department of Computer Science, University of Chicago, 1100 East 58th Street, Chicago, IL 60637 (June 2010)
12. Kuan, G., MacQueen, D.: Engineering Higher-Order Modules in SML/NJ. Technical Report TR-2010-01, Univ. of Chicago, Dept. of Computer Science, Chicago, IL (January 2010)
13. Leroy, X.: Manifest types, modules, and separate compilation. In: POPL 1994: Proceedings of the 21st ACM SIGPLAN-SIGACT Symposium on Principles of Programming Languages, pp. 109–122. ACM, New York (1994)
14. Leroy, X.: Applicative functors and fully transparent higher-order modules. In: POPL 1995: Proceedings of the 22nd ACM SIGPLAN-SIGACT Symposium on Principles of Programming Languages, pp. 142–153. ACM, New York (1995)
15. Leroy, X.: Le système Caml Special Light: modules et compilation efficace en Caml. In: Actes des Journées Francophones des Langages Applicatifs, pp. 111–131. INRIA (January 1996)
16. Leroy, X.: A modular module system. J. Funct. Program. 10(3), 269–303 (2000)
17. MacQueen, D.B.: Using dependent types to express modular structure. In: POPL 1986: Proceedings of the 13th ACM SIGACT-SIGPLAN Symposium on Principles of Programming Languages, pp. 277–286. ACM, New York (1986)
18. MacQueen, D.B., Tofte, M.: A semantics for higher-order functors. In: Sannella, D. (ed.) ESOP 1994. LNCS, vol. 788, pp. 409–423. Springer, Heidelberg (1994)
19. Milner, R., Tofte, M., Harper, R., MacQueen, D.: The Definition of Standard ML - Revised. The MIT Press, Cambridge (May 1997)
20. Mitchell, J.C., Plotkin, G.D.: Abstract types have existential types. In: POPL 1985: Proceedings of the 12th ACM SIGACT-SIGPLAN Symposium on Principles of Programming Languages, pp. 37–51. ACM, New York (1985)
21. Montagu, B., Rémy, D.: Modeling abstract types in modules with open existential types. In: Proceedings of the 36th ACM Symposium on Principles of Programming Languages (POPL 2009), Savannah, Georgia, USA, pp. 63–74 (January 2009)
22. Paterson, M.S., Wegman, M.N.: Linear unification. In: STOC 1976: Proceedings of the 8th annual ACM Symposium on Theory of Computing, pp. 181–186. ACM, New York (1976)
23. Ramsey, N.: ML module mania: A type-safe, separately compiled, extensible interpreter. Electr. Notes Theor. Comput. Sci. 148(2), 181–209 (2006)
24. Russo, C.V.: Types for Modules. PhD thesis, Edinburgh University (1998)
25. Shao, Z.: Transparent modules with fully syntactic signatures. In: ICFP 1999: Proceedings of the 4th ACM SIGPLAN International Conference on Functional Programming, pp. 220–232. ACM, New York (1999)

Author Index

GPSR Compliance

The European Union's (EU) General Product Safety Regulation (GPSR) is a set of rules that requires consumer products to be safe and our obligations to ensure this.

If you have any concerns about our products, you can contact us on ProductSafety@springernature.com

In case Publisher is established outside the EU, the EU authorized representative is:

Springer Nature Customer Service Center GmbH
Europaplatz 3
69115 Heidelberg, Germany

Batch number: 09474011

Printed by Printforce, the Netherlands